# FOOD for FITNESS

# FOOD for FITNESS

- **Nutrition guide • Eating plans**
- **Over 200 recipes**

**Anita Bean**

A & C Black • London

First published 1998 by
A & C Black (Publishers) Ltd
35 Bedford Row, London WC1R 4JH

Reprinted 1999
Copyright © 1998 by Anita Bean

ISBN 0 7136 4794 9

A CIP catalogue record for this book
is available from the British Library.

Typeset in 11 on 12pt Palatino

**Acknowledgements**
The author would like to thank Simon Bean,
Chloe Bean and the rest of the family, as well
as many friends, for sampling hundreds of dishes
and for their constructive advice; the author would
also like to thank Liz Taylor for recipe testing.
Cover photograph courtesy of Action-Plus.

Printed and bound in Great Britain by
WBC Book Manufacturers, Bridgend

Anita Bean is also the author of *The Complete Guide to Sports Nutrition:*

*The Complete Guide to Sports Nutrition* presents an uncomplicated approach that is appropriate for all sports-active people, from the recreational exerciser to the top-level competitor. It is ideal for those who want to enhance performance and boost energy levels.

*Health and Fitness* magazine

At last, a book written by a British author which gives practical nutrition advice to all exercisers! The information in this book is relevant to EVERYONE who works out on a regular basis. It goes beyond the average 'healthy eating' recommendations that form the basis for most nutrition texts, covering the science behind the practice in a readable and interesting way.

The Exercise Association

*The Complete Guide to Sports Nutrition* is packed with practical advice for all levels of sport, from jogger to élite athlete. Anita Bean gives her information in a flowing style which is as easy to absorb as a hypotonic drink. I recommend this book for everyone involved in sporting performances, not only for its commonsense approach but also for its sudden insights and scattered gems of information.

*Scottish Journal of Physical Education*

This text represents good value for money. Not only does it answer numerous questions about diet, health and performance, it also provides extremely tempting recipes! This book is full of advice and sensible suggestions . . . is easy to read and well presented.

*Physical Education Review*

# Contents

**Introduction**     viii

## Part I **Nutrition guide**     1

*Chapter 1*

**Training diet**    1
**checklist**

*Chapter 2*

**The carbohydrate**    14
**connection**

*Chapter 3*

**Fat counter**    22

*Chapter 4*

**Vitamins and**    30
**minerals**

*Chapter 5*

**Bulking up**    36

*Chapter 6*

**Losing weight**    45

*Chapter 7*

**The vegetarian**    57
**athlete**

*Chapter 8*

**Eating on**    67
**the run**

*Chapter 9*

**Drinking**    73

*Chapter 10*

**Diets for**    78
**different sports**

*Chapter 11*

**Competition**    98
**countdown**

# Part II **Recipes** 107

*Chapter 12*
**Soups** 108

*Chapter 13*
**Salads and** 115
**dressings**

*Chapter 14*
**Rice and** 125
**other grains**

*Chapter 15*
**Beans and** 139
**lentils**

*Chapter 16*
**Pasta** 149

*Chapter 17*
**Bread** 163

*Chapter 18*
**Potatoes** 176

*Chapter 19*
**Pie crusts and** 189
**pastry substitutes**

*Chapter 20*
**Breakfasts** 192

*Chapter 21*
**One-minute meals** 202
**and lunch on the go**

*Chapter 22*
**Healthy fast food** 208

*Chapter 23*
**Snack bars and** 216
**cookies**

*Chapter 24*
**Puddings and** 222
**desserts**

*Chapter 25*
**Muffins** 234

*Chapter 26*
**Cakes** 238

**Index** 245

# Introduction

*Food for Fitness* is the practical complement to my book *The Complete Guide to Sports Nutrition* (A & C Black, 1996). It is a nutrition manual, a menu planner and a recipe book all rolled into one volume. The book shows you how to work out your calorie and nutritional requirements and develop an eating plan, to enable you to get the most out of your particular training programme or sport. It is packed with hundreds of top nutrition tips, eating strategies, snack ideas and quick tasty recipes and is an essential resource for every sportsperson, fitness enthusiast and active person.

Fitting healthy meals around a demanding training schedule is often difficult but *Food for Fitness* provides time-saving kitchen tips, easy solutions for eating on the run, ideas for quick healthy snacks, as well as an invaluable guide to the best (and worst!) fast food choices.

If you are confused about what and how much to drink when training, this book gives you the low-down on popular sports drinks, provides clear advice on preventing dehydration before, during and after exercise and gives easy recipes for home-made sports drinks.

Every sport and activity places unique nutritional demands on the athlete, and I have included step-by-step eating plans for those wishing to lose body fat or gain weight, as well as detailed plans for specific athletic activities such as long distance running, swimming, cycling and sprinting.

There's nutrition advice for vegetarian athletes and those who avoid red meat. The simple diet planner will help you put together a balanced diet without meat and there's a checklist of the best foods for meat-free eating.

Finally, there are over 200 recipes for sportspeople and those leading an active lifestyle. They are all quick and easy to prepare, and make use of simple, everyday ingredients. They conform to the latest sports nutritional guidelines, being low in fat (especially saturated fats), and high in complex carbohydrates, vitamins and minerals. Most importantly, they taste delicious and have become firm favourites among my own family and athletic friends. With sections on pasta dishes, rice- and potato-based meals, one-minute meals, breakfasts, home-made breads, healthy cakes, puddings, muffins and snack bars, there's plenty to inspire even the busiest athlete or the most reluctant cook.

**Anita Bean**

# CHAPTER
# 1

# Training diet checklist

A good training diet is an essential part of every exercise or sports training programme, and will help you achieve your training and competitive goals. The right type and quantity of food will help you maintain peak health and perform at your best.

## How to put together your training diet

One of the quickest and easiest ways to put together your training diet plan is to use the **'Balance of Good Health'** plate model. This is based on the recommendations of the Government's **Health of the Nation** white paper, published in 1992. Simply balance your food choices to match the plate model shown on page 2. This features the five food groups with the number of recommended daily portions from each one. These portion goals will help you adjust your current food intake and develop a low fat nutrient-dense eating plan that will meet your nutritional needs.

Each of the main food groups is rich in different nutrients. For example, milk and dairy products are rich in calcium; vitamin C is available from fruit and vegetables; and the bread, cereal and starchy vegetable group provides complex carbohydrates and fibre.

**A balanced choice from the plate model means:**
- one third of your intake should ideally be complex carbohydrate foods such as bread, cereal and potatoes
- one third of your food should ideally be fruit and vegetables
- one third of your food should ideally be low fat protein foods (such as lean meat, fish and pulses) and low fat dairy produce
- fatty and sugary foods should be regarded as treats or extras.

## Goal

**Minimum 5 portions.** Fruit and vegetables are rich in many vitamins and minerals, particularly beta-carotene, vitamin C and folic acid, as well as hundreds of other beneficial plant substances called phyto-chemicals (including the antioxidant nutrients).

## How to achieve your goal

- Include one portion of fresh fruit with your breakfast, e.g. sliced banana on breakfast cereal.
- Eat at least two portions of fresh fruit as snacks throughout the day.
- Add a side salad to your lunch or dinner.
- Include two portions of vegetables in your main meals either on their own or in soups, curries and sauces.
- Include extra salad vegetables in sandwiches.
- Follow your main meals with fresh fruit or a fruit-based dessert such as apple crumble, banana custard, baked apples, or fruit mixed with yoghurt, ice cream or rice pudding.

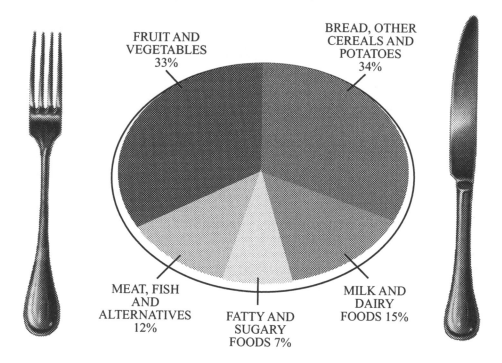

**Figure 1** *The 'Balance of Good Health' plate model*

|                | *Size of 1 portion*                              |
|----------------|--------------------------------------------------|
| **Fresh fruit** | 1 apple/pear/peach/orange/banana<br>100 g (4 oz) berries (e.g. strawberries, raspberries)<br>100 g (4 oz) pineapple/grapes<br>4 apricots/plums<br>2 kiwi fruit<br>½ mango |
| **Tinned fruit** | ½ tin (200 g) of pineapple/peaches/apricots (drained) |
| **Fruit juice** | 1 glass (100 ml/3½ fl oz) juice |
| **Vegetables** | In general, 100 g (4 oz) vegetables<br>2 carrots/courgettes<br>2 florets broccoli<br>10 Brussels sprouts<br>3 tbsp peas<br>2–3 tbsp spinach/cabbage/runner beans |
| **Salad** | 1 large tomato<br>3-in piece cucumber<br>1 bunch watercress<br>3 sticks celery<br>1 cos lettuce/½ iceberg lettuce |

---

◆ *Top tips* ◆

Each day aim to have:

- at least one orange/yellow fruit or vegetable (e.g. mango, apricots, carrot, tomato) for antioxidants and beta-carotene
- at least one red fruit or vegetable (e.g. tomatoes, watermelon) for cancer-beating lycopene
- at least one berry fruit or citrus fruit (e.g. strawberries, raspberries, oranges) for immunity-boosting bioflavanoids and vitamin C
- at least one dark green vegetable a day (e.g. broccoli, cabbage, watercress, spinach) for iron and folic acid.

## Eat more veggies!

Health experts recommend eating at least three portions of vegetables a day. Here are some easy ways of sneaking extra veggies into your diet:

◆ add a handful of frozen peas or mixed vegetables to the saucepan while cooking pasta
◆ add extra mushrooms, peppers, aubergines, courgettes or okra to ready-made curry sauces
◆ keep a container of vegetable crudités (carrots, cucumber, courgette, cauliflower) in the fridge for snacking on or for starters
◆ throw in a cupful of chopped broccoli, courgettes or frozen spinach to pasta sauces
◆ hide puréed vegetables in soups, lasagnes, stews and pies
◆ make fast foods healthier by adding extra veggies, e.g. pizza with mushrooms, peppers, tomatoes; hamburgers with tomatoes and cucumber; kebabs with extra salad; burritos with lettuce and fresh salsa.

## Liven up your veggies

A knob of butter on your vegetables can add an extra 12 g of fat and 100 kcal. Liven up your veggies with the following fresh herbs and spices instead:

◆ coriander with carrots
◆ basil with tomatoes
◆ mint with peas
◆ thyme with peppers
◆ oregano with aubergine
◆ rosemary with leeks
◆ nutmeg with spinach
◆ dill with cabbage.

## Cereals and starchy vegetables

**Goal**

**5–11 portions.**

| | |
|---|---|
| Sedentary men | = 6–8 portions |
| Sedentary women | = 5–6 portions |
| Active men | = 9–11 portions |
| Active women | = 7–10 portions |

Foods in this group provide complex carbohydrates, B vitamins, vitamin C (potatoes only) and fibre. Check your portion sizes to make sure you are eating the right amount and not underestimating.

### How to achieve your goal

- Start your day with at least 2–3 portions from this group, e.g. one large bowl of wholegrain cereal or porridge; 2–3 thick slices of wholemeal toast; a couple of English muffins.
- Be more adventurous with the type of bread you choose – try rye, Spanish, focaccia, ciabatta, seeded, pitta, muffins, bagels, sunflower, herb bread.
- Aim to have at least 2–3 portions of foods from this group with each meal – base meals around pasta, noodles, potatoes, rice, cous cous, bulgar wheat or bread.
- Use cooked grains, e.g. rice or bulgar, to fill vegetables such as aubergines, courgettes and peppers.
- Use a thin scrape of low fat spread, butter or peanut butter on bread, or nothing at all.
- Make pie crusts from mashed potatoes or bread slices (see pages 190 and 29).

---

### Get your day off to a healthy start

Instead of grabbing a croissant and a cup of hot chocolate (331 kcal/ 17.1 g fat), have an English muffin with fruit spread, a banana and a glass (140 ml) of orange juice instead (330 kcal/1.8 g fat).

---

| | *Size of 1 portion* |
|---|---|
| **Bread** | 1 slice bread<br>1 small roll/½ bap/½ bagel<br>½ large pitta/chappati |
| **Cereals/grains** | 2 heaped tbsp cooked pasta/rice/noodles<br>25 g (1 oz) uncooked weight pasta/rice/noodles |
| **Starchy vegetables** | 1 medium (175 g/6 oz) baked or boiled potato<br>3 new potatoes<br>2 tbsp cooked sweet potato/yam/plantain<br>2 tbsp sweetcorn<br>1 large parsnip |
| **Breakfast cereals** | 1 small bowl (25 g/1 oz) breakfast cereal<br>2 Weetabix<br>1 'variety pack' box cereal |
| **Crackers** | 3 crackers/crispbreads/rice cakes |

---

◆ *Top tips* ◆

- ◆ Make sure at least half of your portions are wholegrain varieties, e.g. wholemeal bread/pasta, wholegrain cereal.
- ◆ Instead of butter, top jacket potatoes with fromage frais, yoghurt, cottage cheese, half fat crème fraîche.
- ◆ Eat baked, boiled or roast potatoes with their skin left on. There is no need to peel potatoes used in soups, stews and casseroles.

## Milk and dairy products

### Goal

**2–3 portions.** The foods in this group are the best sources of calcium. They also provide protein, vitamin B$_{12}$, riboflavin and (apart from fat-free varieties) vitamins A and D. Many athletes misguidedly cut down on milk and dairy products because of their fat content, but this means missing out on other nutrients such as calcium and vitamin B$_{12}$. Switch to low fat varieties; they provide all the protein, minerals and water-soluble vitamins of full fat varieties, but with less fat and fat-soluble vitamins A and D.

### How to achieve your goal

- Include 200 ml (⅓ pint) milk per day (semi-skimmed or skimmed milk instead of full fat) for breakfast cereals, drinks or cooking.
- If you don't like milk on its own, use it in custard, sauces or rice pudding.
- Aim to have one portion of cheese (preferably low fat) per day.
- Have a pot of low fat yoghurt or fromage frais for dessert.
- Use yoghurt as a base for salad dressings – add herbs, spices or lemon juice.

| | *Size of 1 portion* |
|---|---|
| **Milk** | 200 ml (⅓ pint) full fat/semi-skimmed/skimmed milk |
| **Cheese** | 1 matchbox-sized piece (40 g/1½ oz) hard cheese (e.g. Cheddar)/soft ripened cheese (e.g. brie) 1 small pot (100 g/4 oz) cottage cheese or low fat soft cheese |
| **Yoghurt/fromage frais** | 1 small pot (150 g/5 oz) yoghurt or fromage frais |

### ◆ *Top tips* ◆

- Use mainly semi-skimmed or skimmed milk.
- Limit hard (full fat) cheese to 1–2 portions per day.
- Choose low fat varieties of yoghurt/fromage frais.
- Aim for at least half your cheese portions to be low fat varieties.
- In recipes, use a strong flavoured or mature cheese so you can cut down on the amount needed.

## Goal

**2–3 portions.** These foods supply protein, iron, B vitamins and other minerals such as zinc and magnesium. Vegetarians can get adequate protein from pulses, cereals, nuts, seeds and soya products, while wholegrains, dark green vegetables, pulses and fortified breakfast cereals supply iron.

## How to achieve your goal

- Aim to have at least half of your portions from non-meat sources.
- Use smaller amounts of meat in stews, bolognese sauce, pasta sauces, risotto, shepherds pie – substitute pulses and vegetables.
- Eat at least two portions of oily fish per week, e.g. mackerel, trout or sardines. The oils are rich in omega-3 fatty acids, important for preventing strokes and heart attacks, and, according to Norwegian researchers, their beneficial circulatory properties help boost exercise performance.
- Include at least three portions of pulses per week – make pulses the base for stews, curries, salads and casseroles.
- Limit processed meat (e.g. burgers, sausages) to once a week or less.

|  | *Size of 1 portion* |
|---|---|
| **Meat** | 2 thin slices (50–75 g/2–3 oz) red meat<br>1 small chop (50–75 g/2–3 oz)<br>3 thin slices ham |
| **Poultry** | 75 g (3 oz) chicken/turkey (weighed without bone)<br>1 small breast |
| **Fish** | 1 medium fillet (150 g/5 oz) white fish<br>1 small fillet (75 g/3 oz) oily fish<br>1 small tin (100 g/4 oz) tuna<br>75–100 g (3–4 oz) prawns |
| **Eggs** | 2 |
| **Pulses** | Half a large (420 g) tin baked beans/red kidney beans/chick peas/other beans<br>3 heaped tbsps cooked beans/lentils/peas |
| **Nuts** | Small handful (50 g/2 oz) nuts or seeds |
| **Tofu/quorn** | 100 g (4 oz) tofu/quorn |

---

◆ *Top tips* ◆

- Choose lower fat foods from this group wherever possible – very lean meat, fish, poultry (without skin), pulses, eggs (up to 6 per week), quorn and soya.
- If you eat meat, make sure it is lean and well trimmed.
- If you eat poultry, remove the skin before or after cooking.
- In restaurants, order grilled fish not fried, and reduce fat by 15 g (145 kcal).
- Cook meat, fish and poultry without added fat – dry frying, grilling, baking or poaching.

## Fats and oils

### Goal

**0–3 portions.** Most people exceed this goal and therefore need to look carefully at their diet for ways of reducing their fat intake.

### How to achieve your goal

- Use butter or fat spreads sparingly on bread, toast and sandwiches.
- Reduce saturated fats, e.g. butter, meat fat, lard, and foods made with them (e.g. pastry, biscuits, puddings).
- Don't try to cut fat out completely otherwise you will go short of essential fatty acids (necessary for making prostaglandins, cell membranes and healthy skin), and fat-soluble vitamins (fat is needed to absorb vitamins A, D and E), especially the antioxidant vitamin E.
- Get most of your fats from unsaturated sources, e.g. vegetable oils and foods made with them, oily fish, nuts or seeds.
- Aim to have 1 tbsp of oil/nuts/seeds per day.

|  | *Size of 1 portion* |
|---|---|
| **Spreading fats** | 1 tsp butter/margarine<br>2 tsps low fat spread |
| **Oils** | 1 tsp vegetable/olive oil |
| **Dressings** | 1 tsp oil-based salad dressing, e.g. French dressing/mayonnaise<br>1 tbsp salad cream |

---

### ◆ *Top tips* ◆

- Flavour salads and vegetables with herbs, lemon/lime juice, fruit or balsamic vinegar.
- Limit foods made with animal fats or hydrogenated vegetable fats as they contain larger amounts of trans fatty acids, e.g. some margarines, biscuits, cakes and bakery items. Check the label!
- Limit fried food, e.g. chips, to once a week or less.
- Limit high fat 'fast foods', e.g. hamburgers, to once a week or less.
- Cook without fat wherever possible, e.g. bake, boil, grill or steam, or use small amounts of unsaturated oils to stir fry or sauté.

# Alcohol

## Goal

Up to three units per day and 14 units per week (women); up to four units per day and 21 units per week (men).

## How to achieve your goal

- Have at least two alcohol-free days per week.
- Pace your drinking – alternate low calorie soft drinks with alcoholic drinks, or mix dry white wine and sparkling water or soda water to make your drink last longer.
- Keep a tally on your alcohol intake when you go out – set yourself a safe limit.

### Size of 1 unit

250 ml (½ pint) ordinary strength beer/lager
1 glass (125 ml/4 fl oz) wine
1 pub measure sherry/vermouth
1 pub measure spirits

---

### ◆ Top tips ◆

- Don't nibble salty snacks with your alcoholic drink – they will make you more thirsty.
- Extend your alcoholic drink (e.g. wine, spirits) with water, low calorie mixers or soda water, or alternate alcoholic and non-alcoholic drinks.
- If you think you have drunk too much, drink plenty of water/sports drink before retiring to bed – at least one pint per 2–3 units.
- Do not feel obliged to drink excessively even if your friends press you. Tell them you are training the next day or that you are driving.
- Do not drink on an empty stomach as this speeds alcohol absorption. Try to eat something first or reserve drinking for meal times. Food slows down the absorption of alcohol.
- To minimise a hangover, choose pale-coloured drinks (e.g. white wine) rather than dark drinks; avoid carbonated alcoholic drinks (e.g. gin & tonic, champagne) as the alcohol is absorbed faster.

---

### Did you know

Cutting down – but not giving up – on your alcohol intake can help you lose unwanted body fat. One glass of wine is equivalent to 95 kcal so if you reduce your intake by seven glasses of wine per week, you'll save 2660 kcal a month, that's nearly a pound of body fat!

11

## Fatty and sugary foods

Goal

Up to 1 portion.

How to achieve your goal

+ Regard fatty and sugary foods as treats rather than everyday foods.
+ Limit high fat puddings and cakes to three times per week or less.
+ Limit salty/sugary snacks to three times per week or less.

*Size of 1 portion*

1 packet crisps
1 slice cake
3 biscuits
1 large scoop ice cream
1 chocolate/confectionery bar

---

+ *Top tips* +

Substitute the following low fat snacks for high fat snacks:

+ sandwiches/rolls/pitta/bagels (filled with cottage cheese/ peanut butter/banana/salad/honey/marmite/tuna/chicken/ turkey/ham)
+ low fat yoghurt and fromage frais
+ fresh fruit (e.g. apples, bananas, nectarines, grapes)
+ English muffins/scones/crumpets/potato cakes
+ dried fruit
+ dried fruit bars/low fat 'energy' bars/cereal bars
+ nuts and dried fruit mixtures
+ rice cakes/crackers/bread sticks.

---

### Did you know?

One packet of crisps contains 11 g fat (about 2 tsps) and 160 kcal – that's 62% of calories from fat! Switching to reduced fat crisps won't make much difference – you'll save a mere 24 kcal and 3.4 g fat. Better substitutes include:

+ 1 cup (15 g) of plain popcorn (55 kcal/0.3 g fat)
+ 5 bread sticks (100 kcal/0.5 g fat)
+ 3 rice cakes (75 kcal/0.3 g fat).

**References**

(1) *The National Food Guide*, Health Education Authority in partnership with the Dept of Health and MAFF, July 1994
(2) *Nutritional Aspects of Cardiovascular Disease*, COMA, HMSO, November 1994

# The carbohydrate connection

Carbohydrates are the number one fuel for energy for virtually every activity and sport, and should supply at least 60% of your calorie intake. They are also needed to fuel the brain and other vital functions in the body. A high carbohydrate diet gives you the following benefits.

*Increases stamina*
High levels of stored carbohydrate (glycogen) in the muscles allow you to exercise longer before feeling fatigued. Low glycogen stores result in early exhaustion. While fat and protein can also provide fuel during aerobic (cardiovascular) activities, it is carbohydrate only that is burned during the earlier stage of exercise and also during anaerobic (very high-intensity, explosive) activities. Carbohydrate is therefore the best fuel for fighting fatigue.

*Increases performance*
High glycogen levels help you to maintain a higher training intensity for longer and so increase your sports performance. This is important for all types of activities. Studies prove that athletes on high carbohydrate diets (i.e. above 60% energy) achieve significantly better training times compared with those on lower carbohydrate diets.

*Good for health*
Many foods rich in carbohydrates, such as cereals, bread, rice and potatoes also contain B vitamins for a healthy nervous system and efficient energy production, fibre for healthy digestion, and iron for healthy blood. Fruit, also high in carbohydrates, is an excellent source of vitamin C for immunity and other antioxidants that fight cancer and heart disease.

## How much carbohydrate?

To work out how much carbohydrate you need each day, multiply your weight (in kg) by the corresponding figure shown in the table.

| Activity level * | g carbohydrate/kg body weight per day |
|---|---|
| Light (less than 1 hour) | 4–5 |
| Light–moderate (approx. 1 hour) | 5–6 |
| Moderate (1–2 hours) | 6–7 |
| Moderate–heavy (2–4 hours) | 7–8 |
| Heavy (more than 4 hours) | 8–10 |

* Activity levels take account of both duration and intensity of activity. The time refers to the hours of continuous activity (i.e. not including rest periods).

For example, if you weigh 60 kg and your activity level is moderate:

**Carbohydrate needs =**
60 kg x 6–7 = **360–420g per day**

To give you an idea of how much food you should eat, you could get 400 g carbohydrate from:

- 17 bananas
- 27 slices of toast
- 14 baked potatoes
- 40 biscuits
- 2 rolls, 2 slices of toast, 2 baked potatoes, 2 apples, 1 small tin (200 g/ 7 oz) of baked beans, 1 generous portion (75 g/3 oz) of pasta, 2 bananas, 2 cartons fruit yoghurt, ½ pint semi-skimmed milk and 1 fruit scone.

Use the carbohydrate counter on p. 16 to work out how much food you should eat.

## The carbohydrate counter

| Food | Portion | Carbohydrate (total) (g) | Of which sugars (g) | Of which starch (g) |
|------|---------|--------------------------|---------------------|---------------------|
| **Bread and cereals** | | | | |
| Bread | 1 slice (36 g) | 15 | 0.6 | 14 |
| Roll | 1 roll (48 g) | 23 | 0.7 | 22 |
| Pitta bread | 1 pitta (75 g) | 43 | 1.8 | 42 |
| Cracker | 1 cracker (7 g) | 4.8 | 0 | 4.8 |
| Crispbread | 1 crispbread (10 g) | 7.1 | 0.3 | 6.7 |
| Pasta | 100 g raw | 76 | 2.2 | 74 |
| Rice (white) | 100 g raw | 87 | 0 | 87 |
| Weetabix | 1 Weetabix (20 g) | 15 | 1 | 14 |
| Bran Flakes | Large bowl (60 g) | 42 | 11 | 30 |
| Muesli | Medium bowl (50 g) | 33 | 13 | 20 |
| Porridge oats | 3 tbsps (30 g) | 20 | 0.3 | 20 |
| **Potatoes/ vegetables** | | | | |
| Baked potato | Medium (160 g) | 29 | 1.1 | 28 |
| Sweetcorn | 3 tbsps (85 g) | 23 | 8.1 | 14 |
| Crisps | 1 bag (30 g) | 16 | 0 | 16 |
| Baked beans | Half a tin (200 g) | 30 | 12 | 19 |
| **Cakes/ desserts/ biscuits** | | | | |
| Sponge cake | 1 slice (60 g) | 39 | 29 | 10 |
| Digestive biscuit | 1 biscuit (15 g) | 10 | 2 | 8.2 |
| Flapjack | 1 flapjack (70 g) | 42 | 25 | 18 |
| Fruit cake | 1 slice (70 g) | 42 | 34 | 7.8 |
| Currant bun | 1 bun (60 g) | 32 | 9.1 | 23 |
| Ice cream | 2 scoops (85 g) | 17 | 14 | 3 |

| Food | Portion | Carbohydrate (total) (g) | Of which sugars (g) | Of which starch (g) |
|---|---|---|---|---|
| **Confectionery/ sugars** | | | | |
| Milk chocolate | Small bar (54 g) | 31 | 31 | 0 |
| Mars Bar | Standard bar (65 g) | 43 | 43 | 0 |
| Jam/ marmalade | 1 tbsp (15 g) | 10 | 10 | 0 |
| Cola | 1 can (340 g) | 37 | 37 | 0 |
| Sugar | 1 tsp (6 g) | 6 | 6 | 0 |
| **Dairy products** | | | | |
| Milk | 1 pint (585 g) | 29 | 29 | 0 |
| Cheddar cheese | Matchbox-size (40 g) | 0 | 0 | 0 |
| Fruit yoghurt | 1 carton (150 g) | 27 | 27 | 0 |
| **Fruit** | | | | |
| Apple/ pear/orange | 1 apple (100 g) | 12 | 12 | 0 |
| Banana | 1 large banana (100 g) | 23 | 21 | 2.3 |
| Raisins | 1 handful (30 g) | 21 | 21 | 0 |
| Orange juice | 1 glass (160 g) | 14 | 14 | 0 |

## Carbohydrate and recovery

It takes a minimum of 20 hours to fully replenish carbohydrate stores. During the first two hours after exercise, glycogen is restored at a faster rate than normal (almost one and a half times faster). You should therefore eat or drink carbohydrate as soon as possible after exercise to make sure that maximum refuelling takes place. This will speed up overall recovery.

Aim to consume 1 g carbohydrate per kg body weight within two hours of training. For example, if you weigh 60 kg you need to consume approximately 60 g of carbohydrate during this period.

The best types of carbohydrates are those which are absorbed rapidly into the body; both solid and liquid forms are equally effective. Many athletes prefer taking a drink containing carbohydrate such as diluted juice, squash or a sports drink. This has the added advantage of providing essential fluid.

| ◆ *Suitable snacks providing 60 g carbohydrate* ◆ |
| --- |
| ◆ 2 large bananas<br>◆ 3 handfuls raisins<br>◆ 4 slices bread or toast (plain)<br>◆ 2 slices bread or toast with 2 tbsps jam<br>◆ 2 fruit bars/cereal bars<br>◆ 8 rice cakes or crispbreads<br>◆ 1 litre isotonic sports drink (6% carbohydrate)<br>◆ 200 ml squash diluted with 800 ml water |

### Did you know?

Many brands of sports nutrition bars are no healthier than ordinary chocolate bars, containing similar amounts of fat and sugar. Most derive 35% of calories from fat, exactly the same as a Mars Bar, and cost around three times as much! Stick to a banana or a handful of raisins for boosting your energy before exercise.

## Digesting carbohydrates

Don't exercise on a full stomach or when your stomach is completely empty. As a general rule of thumb allow:

- 3–4 hours for a large meal to digest
- 2–3 hours for a small–medium meal to digest
- approximately one hour for a snack to digest.

---

### ◆ Suitable pre-exercise meals ◆

The pre-exercise meal should have a moderate–low glycaemic index and be relatively low in fat.

- Porridge with fruit
- Breakfast cereal with milk
- Pasta with chicken and vegetables
- Rice with beans and salad
- Low fat cheese or tuna sandwich
- Baked potato with beans or poultry

---

**The benefits of a pre-exercise meal include:**

- preventing hunger pangs and settling the stomach
- fuelling the muscles and improving performance
- preventing low blood sugar levels (hypoglycaemia).

In addition, have a high carbohydrate snack just before exercise. Studies show that consuming 25–50 g of a high glycaemic carbohydrate less than 30 minutes before training improves exercise performance. It helps to maintain blood sugar levels, prevent hypoglycaemia (low blood sugar concentration) and delay fatigue. There is no truth in the myth that pre-exercise sugar causes hypoglycaemia.

---

### ◆ Suitable pre-exercise snacks supplying 25 g carbohydrate ◆

- 1 large banana
- 400 ml isotonic sports drink (6% carbohydrate)
- 1 large handful raisins
- 1 slice bread with 1 tbsp jam
- 1 low fat cereal or fruit bar

Consume the snack 0–30 minutes before exercise.

---

## Carbohydrate during exercise

If you are exercising hard for more than 90 minutes, you can delay fatigue by consuming additional carbohydrate (in solid or liquid form) during exercise. Most studies show that 30–60 g carbohydrate per hour helps maintain blood sugar levels, delay glycogen depletion and improve endurance. Start consuming carbohydrate after about 30 minutes and continue at regular intervals until the end of your training session. If you have solid forms of carbohydrate, drink plain water rather than a sports drink.

---

◆ *Suitable snacks and drinks during exercise supplying 30 g per hour* ◆

---

- ◆ 500 ml isotonic sports drink (6% carbohydrate)
- ◆ 500 ml diluted fruit juice (1:1)
- ◆ 1 energy bar (e.g. 'Power Bar')
- ◆ 50g (2 oz) chocolate bar
- ◆ 1½ handfuls dried fruit

*\* At higher exercise intensities, consume up to 60 g carbohydrate per hour.*

---

## Eat regularly

Active people need to eat at regular intervals throughout the day to ensure efficient refuelling between hard training sessions. Eating 'little and often' also keeps up your energy levels, maintains a steady blood sugar concentration and minimises body fat storage. Leaving long gaps between meals results in plummeting energy levels, incomplete glycogen refuelling and a lower nutrient intake. Aim to eat 3–4 moderate-sized meals and top up your energy levels throughout the day with 2–3 nutritious snacks.

## Fast and slow carbs

Some carbohydrates are quickly absorbed producing a rapid rise in blood sugar. These foods give a quick energy boost. Others are absorbed more slowly, producing a smaller but more prolonged rise in blood glucose.

The ability of a food to raise blood sugar levels is measured by its **glycaemic index (GI)**.

**High glycaemic index foods** (e.g. bananas, sugar, potatoes, rice) produce a rapid rise in blood sugar. These foods are quickly digested and absorbed giving a quick energy boost, and are readily converted into energy or glycogen. Foods with a high GI are advantageous to performance immediately before, during and immediately after exercise.

**Low glycaemic index foods** (e.g. pulses, oats, most fruit) produce a slower blood sugar rise so the carbohydrate becomes available more slowly. These foods are best eaten 2–4 hours before exercise because they produce more sustained energy, and also in-between exercise sessions to promote efficient glycogen refuelling.

**Combining foods with high and low GIs** (e.g. cheese and bread) results in an intermediate GI. In general, protein and fat reduce the speed of carbohydrate absorption and therefore the GI. For example, plain bread produces a rapid blood sugar rise, desirable immediately before or after exercise; adding a layer of butter or a slice of cheese slows the blood sugar rise, desirable during the refuelling period.

## Glycaemic index of some popular foods

| Breakfast cereals | Fruit | Bakery products |
|---|---|---|
| All Bran 51 | Pineapple 66 | Pastry 59 |
| Cornflakes 80 | Apple 39 | Digestive 59 |
| Muesli 66 | Mango 51 | Shortbread 48 |
| Porridge oats 49 | Banana 62 | Sponge cake 46 |
| Shredded Wheat 67 | Orange 40 | |
| Weetabix 75 | Grapefruit 26 | **Vegetables/** |
| | Cherries 23 | **pulses** |
| **Bread/grains** | Kiwi fruit 58 | |
| | Grapes 44 | Baked potato 98 |
| White bread 69 | Peach 29 | Boiled potato 70 |
| Wholemeal bread 72 | Pear 33 | Sweet potato 48 |
| Bagel 72 | Plum 25 | Sweetcorn 59 |
| Barley 22 | Raisins 64 | Carrots 92 |
| Cous cous 65 | Dried Apricots 30 | Baked beans 40 |
| Millet 71 | | Chick peas 36 |
| Brown rice 80 | | Soya beans 15 |
| White rice 82 | **Snacks/drinks** | Lentils 29 |
| Whitepasta 50 | | Peas 51 |
| Wholemeal pasta 42 | Corn chips 72 | Red kidney beans 29 |
| Rice cakes 82 | Crisps 51 | |
| | Mars Bar 68 | **Dairy products** |
| | Peanuts 13 | |
| | Milk chocolate 34 | Milk (whole) 34 |
| | Sugar (sucrose) 59 | Milk (skimmed) 32 |
| | Glucose 100 | Yoghurt 36 |
| | Soft drink 68 | Ice cream 36 |
| | Orange juice 46 | |

CHAPTER

3

# Fat counter

A small amount of fat is essential for health, but the average person's intake is greatly in excess of this. Around 40% of the calories we eat are in the form of fat. This should be reduced to 30% or less. Fat has more than twice as many calories as carbohydrate or protein (9 kcal/g compared with 4 kcal/g) so it is easy to consume a lot of calories in only a small amount of food.

---

### ♦ Why fat makes you fat ♦

The fat you eat is readily converted into body fat. It takes far fewer calories to metabolise fat than carbohydrate or protein, so you are more likely to accumulate body fat on a high fat diet than a high carbohydrate diet containing the same number of calories.

Fat does not satisfy the appetite as well as carbohydrate or protein so it is easy to overeat fatty foods without feeling full. Numerous studies have shown that diets with a high percentage of fat result in increased fat accumulation.

---

Too much fat (especially saturated fat) increases the risk of obesity, heart disease and certain types of cancer. Also, a high fat diet is likely to be too low in carbohydrate and can therefore leave your muscles under-fuelled.

### Low fat, not no fat!

An entirely fat-free diet is not desirable either and a minimum of 15% calories from fat is recommended. This allows you to:

- get adequate essential fatty acids (e.g. linoleic acid and linolenic acid) needed for prostaglandin (hormone-like substances) manufacture, tissue growth, cell membranes and healthy skin. They are found in vegetable oils, nuts, seeds and oily fish
- obtain the fat-soluble vitamins A, D and E
- make vitamin A from beta-carotene
- absorb and transport fat-soluble vitamins in the body
- enjoy a palatable diet and include a wide range of foods without the guilt! Fat adds to the flavour and texture of many foods.

## How much fat should you eat?

Aim to get between 20 and 25% of your calories from fat

How much fat does this translate into? For example, if you consume 2500 kcal a day, 25% calories from fat equals 625 kcal. Since 1 g of fat provides 9 kcal, that gives you a daily allowance of $625 \div 9 = 69$ g of fat. The chart below shows how 25% of calories from fat translates into grams of fat depending on your calorie intake.

| Calorie intake | Fat (g) |
|---|---|
| 1500 | 42 |
| 2000 | 56 |
| 2500 | 69 |
| 3000 | 83 |
| 3500 | 97 |
| 4000 | 111 |

It is best to choose fats with the greatest health benefits – foods containing more polyunsaturated and monounsaturated fatty acids than saturated fatty acids (see pages 24–5). Keep foods high in saturated fatty acids to a minimum.

Most people need to reduce their overall fat intake and saturated fatty acids in particular. A low fat diet can be achieved by:

- minimising the addition of fat to your food – use less butter and spreads, dressings and cooking oil
- choosing reduced fat dairy products, such as low fat milks and cheeses
- avoiding high fat snack foods such as crisps, chocolate and cakes
- choosing lean cuts of meat and substituting skinless poultry, white fish or pulses for some of the meat in your diet.

## Fats in your food

| Worst choices |
|---|

*Saturated fatty acids*
These are solid fats, mostly of animal origin, and encourage the body to produce more LDL (bad) cholesterol. Associated with a higher cancer risk.

**Sources:** meat, lard, butter, dairy products (except skimmed milk), products containing palm and coconut oil (e.g. hard margarine, biscuits and processed snacks).

*Trans fatty acids*
These are polyunsaturates artificially hardened by adding extra hydrogen. They are as bad or more harmful than saturates; they increase LDL cholesterol and heart disease risk, and lower HDL (good) cholesterol.

**Sources:** hard margarine, products containing hydrogenated vegetable fats, e.g. biscuits, cakes.

| Good choices |
|---|

*Polyunsaturated fatty acids*
Polyunsaturates are liquid oils mainly from plant sources or oily fish. They are better than saturates as they lower total and LDL cholesterol levels and so reduce heart disease risk, however they also reduce HDL cholesterols.

**Sources:** vegetable, seed and nut oils, margarine and other products made from these oils, oily fish.

*Essential fatty acids*
These are a sub-group of polyunsaturates which are essential for health but cannot be made by the body. They are used for making cell membranes and hormone-like substances called prostaglandins which regulate many body processes. The two main EFAs are linoleic acid (an omega-6 fatty acid) and linolenic acid (an omega-3 fatty acid).

*Omega-6 fatty acids*
These polyunsaturated fatty acids include linoleic acid and its derivatives. They reduce LDL (bad) cholesterol, but at very high intakes may also reduce HDL (good) cholesterol. High intakes may also encourage increased free radical damage and, therefore, increase the risk of cancer. A moderate intake is recommended.

**Sources:** vegetable oils, polyunsaturated margarine, products made from these oils.

| Best choices |
|---|

*Monounsaturated fatty acids*
These are liquid at room temperature but solidify when chilled. Replacing saturates with monounsaturates reduces the risk of heart disease. They can reduce LDL (bad) cholesterol but maintain HDL (good) cholesterol, and appear to reduce free radical damage associated with certain cancers, heart disease and rheumatoid arthritis.

**Sources:** olive oil, rapeseed oil, nut oils, avocados, nuts and seeds.

*Omega-3 fatty acids*
These polyunsaturated fatty acids include linolenic acid and its derivatives. These long chain derivatives reduce the risk of thrombosis (blood clots) and, therefore, heart attacks and strokes. They also help to control inflammation and reduce the risk of inflammatory diseases such as rheumatoid arthritis.

**Sources:** oily fish, walnuts, linseeds, dark green leafy vegetables.

## Hidden fats

It's easy to cut down on visible fat such as butter, margarine, the fat on meat, the skin on poultry, cream, and the oil you cook in. However, much of the fat we eat is hidden inside foods such as biscuits, cakes, sauces, savoury snack foods and fast foods. The fat finder below will help you to recognise some of these sources and choose your foods more wisely.

## Fat finder

| Very low fat foods (<2% fat) | Fat content (g/100 g) |
|---|---|
| White bread | 1.9 |
| Rice | 1.3 |
| Pasta | 0.7 |
| Bran flakes | 1.9 |
| Apples | 0.1 |
| Bananas | 0.3 |
| Potatoes | 0.1 |
| Carrots | 0.4 |
| Broccoli | 0.8 |
| Egg white | 0 |
| White fish/tuna tinned in brine | 0.2 |
| Skimmed milk | 0.1 |
| Quark | 0.1 |
| Low calorie yoghurt | 0.2 |
| Low fat yoghurt | 0.8 |
| Baked beans | 0.6 |
| Sugar | 0 |
| Jam | 0 |
| Cola | 0 |
| **Low fat foods (2–5% fat)** | |
| Cottage cheese | 3.9 |
| Whole milk yoghurt | 3 |
| Fillet steak (extra lean) | 5 |
| Semi-skimmed milk | 2.8 |
| Chicken breast | 5 |

| Medium fat foods (5–20% fat) | Fat content (g/100 g) |
|---|:---:|
| Muesli | 6 |
| Muesli (deluxe) | 14 |
| Plain biscuits | 17 |
| Eggs | 11 |
| Beef (regular cut) | 12 |
| Bacon (lean) | 13 |
| Sausages (grilled) | 17 |
| Minced beef | 14 |
| Ice cream | 10 |
| **High fat foods (20–40% fat)** | |
| Sponge cake | 26 |
| Cheddar cheese | 34 |
| Shortbread | 26 |
| Chocolate biscuits | 24 |
| Pastry | 28 |
| Whipping cream | 39 |
| Chocolate | 31 |
| Reduced fat mayonnaise | 28 |
| **Very high fat foods (40–100% fat)** | |
| Sunflower/olive oil | 100 |
| Butter | 82 |
| Margarine | 82 |
| Mayonnaise | 76 |
| Peanuts | 53 |
| French dressing | 72 |
| Low fat spread | 41 |

Here's the fat lowdown on some popular foods and snacks.

| | | | |
|---|---|---|---|
| 1 croissant | 10 g | Confectionery bar | 12 g |
| 1 slice chocolate cake | 21 g | 1 slice of cheese (40 g) | 14 g |
| 1 packet of crisps | 10 g | Small portion of chips | 20 g |
| 1 tablespoon mayonnaise | 23 g | 2 chocolate biscuits | 9 g |
| 1 knob of butter | 8 g | 1 flapjack | 19 g |
| Quarter pounder with cheese | 26 g | 1 cereal bar | 8 g |
| Cheese and tomato pizza | 35 g | | |

### Twelve ways to cut fat in your cooking

1. Use as little oil or butter as possible when cooking. Instead of frying, use other methods which involve very little or no added fat, such as grilling, boiling, baking, microwaving, or barbecuing on an open grill plate.
2. Use a non-stick frying pan, brush lightly with oil or use an oil spray before cooking.
3. When preparing soups and casseroles, pre-cook onions or vegetables in a little passata (smooth sieved tomatoes) or vegetable stock.
4. Reduce the amount of meat needed in casseroles, bolognese sauces and stews by adding extra beans or vegetables; cooked aubergine flesh or chestnut mushrooms provide a 'meaty' texture.
5. Cook meat, poultry or fish en papillote ('in a bag'). Simply encase in either greaseproof paper or foil along with herbs or spices and chopped vegetables so the meat/fish steam-roasts within the bag.
6. Trim all the visible fat from meat and remove the skin from poultry. Choose cuts of meat with the least marbling.
7. Substitute two egg whites for one whole egg when baking cakes and puddings.
8. Use low fat Greek yoghurt, fromage blanc or quark in place of cream for making 'creamy' sauces. Unlike ordinary yoghurt, these ingredients can all be heated to high temperatures without curdling.
9. Marinate meat and chicken before cooking to improve tenderness and flavour. You will then need to add less or no fat when cooking.
10. For salads, modify the usual oil/vinegar dressings by diluting with water or extra vinegar or using less oil. Substitute mayonnaise with yoghurt or fromage frais-based dressings (see pages 121–3).
11. Make 'pastry' cases from ordinary bread slices moulded into bun tins and baked for 15–20 mins at 150° C/300° F/gas mark 2 until dried through. These are perfect for filling with spreads and dips.
12. Stir frying is an excellent way to cook foods quickly in minimal quantities of oil. Allow one tablespoon per 450 g (1 lb) of vegetables.

| High fat ingredient | Low fat alternatives |
|---|---|
| Shortcrust/puff pastry | Filo pastry; bread dough (see page 163); line pie dish/muffin tins with thin slices of bread; potato pastry (see page 189); vegetable pie crust (see page 191). |
| Margarine/butter in cakes | For each 100 g (4 oz) fat, substitute 175 g (6 oz) prunes puréed with 4 tbsps water or 175 g (6 oz) mixture of apricots, dates and prunes puréed with 4 tsps water or fruit juice. |
| Margarine/butter in white sauce | Omit fat. Blend 1 heaped tbsp cornflour with 250 ml (½ pint) milk. |
| Cream | Greek yoghurt (standard or low fat); low fat yoghurt; fromage blanc; half fat crème fraîche; quark; evaporated skimmed milk; lightly beaten soft tofu. |
| Cheddar cheese | Smaller quantity of strong flavoured cheese; for topping use half grated cheese and half breadcrumbs or oats. |
| Cream cheese | Ricotta cheese; quark (blended with a little sugar and vanilla essence in sweet dishes). |

# 4

# Vitamins and minerals

Vitamins are vital for energy production and to ensure healthy cell and muscle tissue; minerals are needed for energy production and help to build healthy bones and teeth.

Regular exercise increases the requirements for most vitamins and minerals, however most athletes can meet these needs from a balanced diet. There is usually a direct relationship between food intake and vitamins – the more you eat the more vitamins and minerals you will take in.

## Supplements

Many athletes take vitamin and mineral supplements in the belief that they will lead to better performance. In fact, the vast majority of research shows that supplements have no effect on performance if you already have an adequate intake of nutrients. While a vitamin deficiency could adversely affect your performance, an excess will not improve it. Large doses of certain vitamins and minerals can actually be harmful and interfere with the absorption of other nutrients in the diet.

Many people do however take a simple multi-vitamin and mineral supplement as an 'insurance policy' to ensure they are getting enough. If you feel your diet is lacking in a particular vitamin or mineral this could be a good idea. Remember, supplements should not replace a healthy diet; no vitamin or mineral will compensate for a high fat or low calorie/carbohydrate intake.

### Who needs them?

A simple multi-vitamin and mineral supplement may benefit those people who are at risk of nutritional deficiencies. You may need supplements if you are or are doing any of the following.

**Dieting.** Restricting your calories below 1500 kcal a day will result in deficient intakes of certain nutrients.

**Eating an erratic diet.** Certain lifestyles, e.g. travelling, shift working, can result in low intakes of many nutrients.

**Pregnant.** Requirements of several vitamins and minerals increase during pregnancy. Folic acid supplements (0.4 mg per day) are recommended prior to pregnancy and during the first 12 weeks of pregnancy in order to reduce the risk of neural tube defects such as spina bifida.

**Allergic to certain foods.** People who have to omit major food groups (dairy products, wheat products) need to consume alternative sources of certain nutrients. (Consult your doctor or dietician.)

**A vegan.** Those people who eat no animal products may have deficient intakes of calcium, iron, riboflavin and vitamin $B_{12}$.

**A heavy smoker.** Smoking has an adverse effect on athletic performance and health and depletes the body's vitamin C levels.

## Ten nutrient-rich fruit and vegetables

| Fruit | Vegetables |
|-------|------------|
| 1. Oranges | 1. Broccoli |
| 2. Mangoes | 2. Brussels sprouts |
| 3. Strawberries | 3. Peppers |
| 4. Apricots | 4. Spinach |
| 5. Raspberries | 5. Cabbage |
| 6. Blackcurrants | 6. Watercress |
| 7. Papaya | 7. Carrots |
| 8. Bananas | 8. New potatoes |
| 9. Kiwi fruit | 9. Peas |
| 10. Tomatoes | 10. Pumpkin |

### ♦ Keep the vitamins in! ♦

- Buy fresh, firm fruit and vegetables; avoid bruised, soft or wilted produce.
- Keep vegetables in a cool dark place, such as the salad compartment in the fridge.
- Don't prepare food too far in advance – vitamins are lost if cut up fruit or vegetables are left to stand.
- Keep the skin or peel on wherever possible as most vitamins are found just beneath the surface.
- Cut into large pieces rather than small; vitamins are lost from cut surfaces.
- Cook vegetables in the minimum amount of water – steaming, microwaving or stir frying retains vitamins.
- Make sure water is fast-boiling before adding vegetables.
- Cook vegetables for as little time as possible until they are tender-crisp.
- Save the cooking water for soup, stock and sauces.

## The essential vitamins and minerals guide

| Vitamin | Recommended intake (RNI) | Functions | Sources |
|---|---|---|---|
| Vitamin A | 700 ug (men) 600 ug (women) | Vision in dim light; maintains healthy skin and linings of the digestive tract, nose and throat. | Full fat dairy products; meat; offal; oily fish; margarine. |
| Beta-carotene | No official RNI 15 mg suggested | Antioxidant which protects against certain cancers; converts into vitamin A. | Fruit and vegetables, e.g. apricots, peppers, tomatoes, mangoes, broccoli. |
| Vitamin $B_1$ (Thiamin) | 1 mg (men) 0.8 mg (women) OR 0.4 mg/1000 kcal | Releases energy from carbohydrates; maintains healthy nervous system and digestive system. | Wholemeal bread and cereals; pulses; meat. |
| Vitamin $B_2$ (Riboflavin) | 1.3 mg (men) 1.1 mg (women) | Releases energy from carbohydrates; maintains healthy skin, eyes and nerves. | Milk and dairy products; meat; eggs. |
| Vitamin $B_3$ (Niacin) | 17 mg (men) 13 mg (women) OR 6.6 mg/1000 kcal | Releases energy from carbohydrates; maintains healthy skin, nerves and digestion. | Meat and offal; nuts; milk and dairy products; eggs; whole-grain cereals. |
| Vitamin $B_6$ (Pyridoxine) | 1.4 mg (men) 1.2 mg (women) | Metabolism of protein, carbohydrate, fat; red blood cell manufacture; maintains healthy immune system. | Pulses; nuts; eggs; cereals; fish; bananas. |

| Vitamin | Recommended intake (RNI) | Functions | Sources |
|---|---|---|---|
| Pantothenic acid | No official RNI | Metabolism of protein, carbohydrate, fat; maintains healthy skin, hair and immune system. | Wholegrain cereals; nuts; pulses; eggs; vegetables. |
| Folic acid | 200 ug (+ 400 ug in pregnancy) | Formation of DNA and red blood cells; reduces risk of spina bifida in developing babies. | Green leafy vegetables; yeast extract; pulses. |
| Vitamin $B_{12}$ | 1.5 ug | Formation of red blood cells; energy metabolism. | Milk and dairy products; meat; fish; fortified breakfast cereals, soya products and yeast extract. |
| Vitamin C | 40 mg | Maintains healthy connective tissue, bones, teeth, blood vessels, gums and teeth; promotes immune function; helps iron absorption. | Fruit and vegetables, e.g. raspberries, blackcurrants, kiwi, oranges, peppers, broccoli, cabbage, tomatoes. |
| Vitamin D | No official RNI (10 ug in pregnancy) | Builds strong bones; needed to absorb calcium and phosphorus. | Sunlight; oily fish; fortified margarine and breakfast cereals; eggs. |
| Vitamin E | No official RNI | Antioxidant which helps protect against heart disease; promotes normal cell growth and development. | Vegetable oils; oily fish; nuts; seeds; egg yolk; avocado. |

| Mineral | Recommended intake (RNI) | Functions | Sources |
|---|---|---|---|
| Calcium | 700 mg | Builds bone and teeth; blood clotting; nerve and muscle function. | Milk and dairy products; sardines; dark green leafy vegetables; pulses; nuts and seeds. |
| Iron | 8.7 mg (men) 14.8 mg (women) | Formation of red blood cells; oxygen transport; prevents anaemia. | Meat and offal; wholegrain cereals; fortified breakfast cereals; pulses; green leafy vegetables. |
| Zinc | 9.5 mg (men) 7 mg (women) | Healthy immune system; wound healing; healthy skin; cell growth. | Eggs; wholegrain cereals; meat; milk and dairy products. |
| Magnesium | 300 mg (men) 270 ug (women) | Healthy bones; muscle and nerve function; cell formation. | Cereals; fruit; vegetables; milk. |
| Potassium | 3.5 mg | Fluid balance; muscle and nerve function. | Fruit; vegetables; cereals. |
| Sodium | 1.6 mg | Fluid balance; muscle and nerve function. | Salt; processed meat, ready meals, sauces, soup; cheese; bread. |
| Selenium | 0.9 ug (men) 0.8 ug (women) | Antioxidant which helps protect against heart disease and cancer. | Cereals; vegetables; dairy products; meat; eggs. |

**Warning signs of a bad diet**

Do your nails split easily? Do you feel constantly tired? Is your hair dull and lifeless? These could be warning signs that you are not getting enough vitamins and other essential nutrients in your diet. It could take just a few simple dietary alterations to change the way you look and feel.

| Symptom | Possible missing nutrients | Solutions |
|---|---|---|
| Dry, thin, dull hair | Protein, folic acid, vitamin $B_{12}$, $B_6$, iron | Eat at least two green leafy vegetables per day, such as spinach and broccoli for iron and folic acid. Two portions of fish, chicken, pulses or lean meat will provide protein, iron, vitamin $B_{12}$ and $B_6$. |
| Lethargy, fatigue | B vitamins, iron, magnesium, vitamin C | Eat several small meals through-out the day. Eat four slices of wholemeal bread, 50 g (2 oz) bran-based breakfast cereal for B vitamins and iron. At least one citrus fruit or one portion of berries will boost vitamin C levels. |
| Gums bleed easily | Vitamin C | Eat more fresh fruit and vegetables. A couple of kiwi fruit, half a red pepper or eight new potatoes will give you your daily requirement. |
| Flaky, dry skin | Essential fatty acids, beta-carotene | Add one tbsp of sunflower or rapeseed oil to your diet (in dressings, stir frying etc.), or 25 g (1 oz) nuts or seeds. Eat beta-carotene-rich foods daily – a couple of carrots, a sweet potato, half a mango, or a quarter of a cantaloupe melon. |
| Brittle, fragile nails | Iron | A large (85 g) bowl of fortified breakfast cereal with a glass of orange juice will boost iron levels. Also include three servings of other iron-rich foods such as lean meat, dark green leafy vegetables, pulses and wholemeal bread. |
| Cramps | Water, potassium | Drink at least two litres of water per day. Have at least five portions of fruit or vegetables daily for potassium, e.g. one portion = one apple, one peach, 100 g (4 oz) grapes, 2 tomatoes. |

# Bulking up

Gains in strength and muscle size involve a balance of diet and training. Simply eating more food will not increase your muscle bulk unless you follow a sensible weight training programme. Similarly, spending hours in the gym will not produce the results you want unless you change your diet.

## Bulking up – the formula for success

### Step 1: training

- Obtain a professionally planned weight training programme. This should include 1–3 different exercises for each body part; 3–4 sets and 6–10 repetitions of each exercise.
- Intermediate and advanced trainers should use a split training system so each body part is trained once every 5–7 days. Get plenty of rest between workouts so your muscles are fully recovered and refuelled.
- Aim to complete each workout in about 45 minutes.
- Ensure you use strict technique – perform each repetition through the full range of movement in a controlled manner. Avoid 'cheating', e.g. swinging the weight, performing incomplete movements or using too heavy a weight for your ability.

### Step 2: increase your calorie intake

- Increase your calorie intake by 15–20%. If you normally consume 2500 kcal a day, add an extra 375–500 kcal.
- Divide your food intake into three meals and at least 2–3 nutritious snacks. Avoid leaving longer than four hours between eating.
- Get organised, prepare meals in advance and take snacks with you so you always have suitable food to hand.
- If feeling full is a problem, supplement your food intake with liquid meals (home-made milkshakes or carbohydrate/protein meal replacement supplements), reduce your fibre intake, and include more energy-dense snacks.

## Step 3: get the right balance of carbohydrate, protein and fat

- Eat enough carbohydrate (around 60% of your calorie intake). Your body will break down protein (muscle) if your carbohydrate intake is too low.
- Consume between 1.4–1.7 g protein/kg body weight per day. Include a low fat, high protein food with each meal.
- Don't go overboard on protein; excess is simply converted into glycogen or fat.
- Keep your fat intake low (20–25% of calorie intake) to prevent gains in body fat.

## Step 4: monitor your progress

- Expect to gain between ½–1 kg a month on an established training programme.
- Avoid rapid gains in weight; this usually indicates excess body fat gain.
- Keep a record of your body fat percentage, body weight and girth (vital statistics) measurements.

---

### ◆ Five tips for gaining weight ◆

1. Do not skip meals or leave long gaps between eating.
2. Eat bigger portions than usual.
3. Eat high calorie foods, not high fat foods.
4. Supplement your food intake with liquid foods, such as milk-based drinks and fruit juice.
5. Add extra carbohydrate to your meals, e.g. dried fruit, jam or fruit spread, rather than extra fats, e.g. butter.

---

### ◆ Ten energy snacks for gaining weight ◆

1. Low fat muffins (see pages 234–7).
2. Energy bars, cereal bars and fruit bars.
3. Home-made snack bars, e.g. Apricot Bars (see page 218), Fruit and Nut Bars (see page 218), and Muesli Bars (see page 216).
4. Dried fruit: raisins, sultanas, dates, apricots, peaches, figs, mango, papaya.
5. Fruit juice (preferably diluted 1:1 with water).
6. Yoghurt and fromage frais.
7. Rolls and sandwiches filled with peanut butter, cheese, chicken, cottage cheese, tuna, ham, prawns, hummous, or banana.
8. Milk and milkshakes.
9. Protein: carbohydrate supplements.
10. Nuts and raisins.

## Protein and exercise

Active people need between 1.2–1.7 g protein/kg body weight per day, approximately twice as much as sedentary people (0.75 g/kg per day). This is equivalent to approximately 15% of your energy needs.

---

**♦ *Three reasons why active people need more protein* ♦**

1. Exercise increases the breakdown of muscle proteins into amino acids (catabolism) for use as fuel.
2. To repair tissue damage and maintain muscle protein mass.
3. To facilitate new muscle tissue growth.

---

### Strength training

In general, athletes involved in strength and high-intensity activities, e.g. weight training, sprinting and bodybuilding need 1.4–1.7 g/kg per day.

### Aerobic training

Athletes involved in aerobic activities, e.g. long distance running, aerobic classes and swimming need 1.2–1.4 g/kg per day.

Studies prove that a low protein diet will result in a loss of lean body mass. In other words, if you do not eat enough protein to meet your needs, excessive muscle proteins are lost and no new tissue growth occurs. Strength and body weight are therefore reduced.

On the other hand, a high protein diet is not necessarily beneficial either. Excessive protein is converted into a fuel source rather than lean tissue, and may be used for energy or stored as glycogen or fat. Eating more protein than you need will not result in additional strength or lean mass gains.

- This eating plan provides approximately 3000 kcal per day.
- In addition, you should include a minimum of 2 litres of fluid per day plus ½–1 litre for each hour of training. Each pre- and post-workout snack should be accompanied by 150–250 ml water.
- Where one portion of fruit is indicated on the menu, check page 3 for portion sizes.

| Day 1 |
|---|
| **Breakfast**<br>4 Weetabix or Shredded Wheats<br>450 ml (¾ pint) skimmed or semi-skimmed milk<br>50 g (2 oz) dried fruit<br>1 carton low fat yoghurt<br><br>**Snack**<br>1 sandwich: 2 thick slices of bread with 40 g (1½ oz) cheese and salad<br>2 portions fresh fruit<br><br>**Lunch**<br>300 g (11 oz) jacket potato filled with 100 g (4 oz) tuna, chicken or turkey mixed with a little fromage frais<br>Large mixed salad with 1 tbsp oil/vinegar dressing<br>1 carton low fat yoghurt<br>1 portion fresh fruit<br><br>**Pre-workout snack**<br>2 bananas<br><br>**Post-workout snack**<br>400 ml glucose polymer or energy drink<br><br>**Dinner**<br>75 g (3 oz) pasta with Chicken and Mushroom Sauce (see page 156)<br>Broccoli or other green vegetables<br>Fruit Rice Pudding (see page 225) |

| Day 2 |
|---|

**Breakfast**
Milkshake: 250 ml (½ pint) semi-skimmed milk, 1 carton (150 g) low fat yoghurt, 225 g (8 oz) chopped fresh or tinned fruit (e.g. strawberries, peaches, bananas)
2 slices toast with honey

**Snack**
1 sandwich: 2 slices of bread with a little butter or low fat spread, 1 tbsp peanut butter and sliced tomatoes

**Lunch**
2 Lean Hamburgers (see page 210)
2 portions fresh fruit

**Pre-workout snack**
375 ml (⅔ pint) isotonic sports drink (home-made or commercial)

**Post-workout snack**
3 slices malt loaf

**Dinner**
175 g (6 oz) cod or haddock steak baked in foil with herbs and lemon juice
1 large (300 g/11 oz) jacket potato with 1 tbsp plain yoghurt
Peas and carrots
Baked Bananas (see page 231)
1 carton (150 g) low fat yoghurt

## Day 3

**Breakfast**
2 boiled/poached/scrambled eggs
3 slices wholemeal toast with a little butter/low fat spread

**Snack**
Milkshake: 250 ml (½ pint) skimmed milk, 2 tbsps skimmed milk powder or commercial protein powder and 1 banana

**Lunch**
Rice with Haddock and Peas (see page 131)
Side salad with 1 tbsp oil/vinegar dressing
2 portions fresh fruit

**Pre-workout snack**
2 Fruit and Nut Bars (see page 218)

**Post-workout snack**
600 ml (1 pint) isotonic sports drink (home-made or commercial)

**Dinner**
100 g (4 oz) grilled skinless chicken or turkey breast
Potato Salad (see page 187)
Tomatoes or other salad vegetable
2 portions fresh fruit
1 carton (150 g) low fat fromage frais

- This eating plan provides approximately 4000 kcal per day.
- In addition, you should include a minimum of 2 litres of fluid per day plus ½–1 litre for each hour of training. Each pre- and post-workout snack should be accompanied by 150–250 ml water.
- Where one portion of fruit is indicated on the menu, check page 3 for portion sizes.

| Day 1 |
| --- |

**Breakfast**
Power Porridge (see page 198)

**Snack**
Peanut Bagel Melt (see page 203)
1 glass (200 ml) fruit juice

**Lunch**
3 sandwiches: 6 slices of bread with a little butter/low fat spread, filled with 150 g (5 oz) chicken, ham or low fat cheese, salad vegetables and 2 tbsps reduced fat dressing

1 carton (200 g) cold rice dessert
1 portion fresh fruit

**Pre-workout snack**
400 ml glucose polymer or energy drink

**Post-workout snack**
3 Banana Muffins (see page 237)

**Dinner**
Baked Macaroni Pie (see page 158)
Broccoli or other green vegetables
Yoghurt and Fruit Pudding (see page 232)

**Snack**
50 g (2 oz) breakfast cereal
300 ml (½ pint) skimmed or semi-skimmed milk
50 g (2 oz) dried fruit

## Day 2

**Breakfast**
Omelette made with 2 eggs and 2 egg whites
2 slices grilled lean bacon or 25 g (1 oz) cheese
Tomatoes and mushrooms
2 slices toast with a little butter/low fat spread and jam

**Snack**
2 bagels with 2 tbsps jam

**Lunch**
3 pitta breads with 150 g (5 oz) chicken or tuna and salad vegetables
with 2 tbsps oil/vinegar dressing
2 bananas
1 carton (150 g) whole milk yoghurt

**Pre-workout snack**
600 ml (1 pint) isotonic sports drink (home-made or commercial)

**Post-workout snack**
3 Fruit and Nut Bars (see page 218)

**Dinner**
175 g/6 oz grilled cod or haddock steak
Perfect Potato Pie (see page 182)
Broccoli or other green vegetables
2 cartons (150 g) whole milk yoghurt

**Snack**
2 slices toast
40 g (1½ oz) cheese

## Day 3

**Breakfast**
6 Breakfast Pancakes (see page 195)

**Snack**
1 large glass (250 ml/½ pint) skimmed or semi-skimmed milk
2 rolls with a little butter/low fat spread and 50 g (2 oz) ham or cottage cheese

**Lunch**
300 g (11 oz) jacket potato with a little butter/low fat spread
Spicy Bean Topping (see page 178)
Side salad with 1 tbsp oil/vinegar dressing
2 portions fresh fruit

**Pre-workout snack**
2 energy bars

**Post-workout snack**
600 ml (1 pint) isotonic sports drink (home-made or commercial)
6 rice cakes with fruit spread or jam

**Dinner**
Chicken and Broccoli Stir Fry (see page 135)
2 slices bread with a little butter/low fat spread
2 portions fresh fruit
1 carton (150 g) fromage frais

**Snack**
Milkshake: 250 ml (½ pint) skimmed milk, 2 tbsps skimmed milk powder or commercial protein powder and 1 banana

# Losing weight

Most people would like to shed a few surplus pounds to improve their appearance, health or confidence. A low body fat level is an especially important goal for athletes if they want to be competitive, since excess fat hinders physical performance. However, it is important not to become obsessed with dieting or embark on faddy weight loss methods.

## Guidelines for safe and effective fat loss

### Lose weight slowly

Experts recommend losing weight at a rate between ½–1 kg (1–2 lb) per week. Any faster and you risk losing muscle and depleting your glycogen reserves. To lose ½ kg (1 lb) of fat you need to create an energy deficit of 3500 kcal. So, by eating 500 fewer calories per day you will lose ½ kg (1 lb) per week. Increasing your energy expenditure will increase weight loss further.

### Don't cut calories too much

When you cut your calorie intake your resting metabolic rate (RMR) (see page 46) automatically falls as your body goes into famine mode. This means you need fewer calories to maintain your weight. The more severe the calorie drop the greater the decrease in your RMR. This could be between 10–30%. The best strategy is to reduce your calorie intake by no more than 500 kcal per day and maintain or increase your activity level. Never eat less than your resting metabolic rate.

### Reduce your fat intake

Aim to consume 15–20% of your calories from fat. This is not a no-fat diet – some fat is essential (see page 22) and can actually stop you feeling hungry. Make a food diary to identify the main sources of fat in your diet. Remember fat contains more calories (9 kcal/g) than carbohydrate or protein (4 kcal/g) so it is easier to overeat fat calories. Swap high fat foods for low fat nutritious alternatives (see below); replace high fat snacks with fresh fruit and vegetables and use less fat in your cooking.

## Eat enough carbohydrate

Carbohydrates fuel all types of exercise and should continue to make up 60% of your calorie intake. If you eat too little carbohydrate you will experience fatigue, lack of energy and your training will suffer. Low carbohydrate diets can result in protein (muscle) loss.

## Choose high fibre, filling foods

High fibre carbohydrate foods fill you up, satisfy your appetite and keep hunger at bay. Base your meals and snacks on the following nutritious bulky foods:

- wholegrain breakfast cereals
- porridge
- wholemeal bread and pasta
- brown rice and other whole grains
- beans and lentils
- potatoes and starchy vegetables
- fresh fruit
- all kinds of vegetables.

## Eat little and often

Aim to eat 5–6 small meals or snacks per day at regular intervals. This will maintain energy levels, prevent hunger and avoid fat storage.

## Resting metabolic rate

Your resting metabolic rate (RMR) is the number of calories your body would burn if you did absolutely nothing but lie down for 24 hours a day. It is basically the energy used to keep your essential body functions ticking over and accounts for 60–75% of your total daily energy expenditure.

## How many calories do you need per day?

*Step 1: estimate your RMR*
Take your body weight in kilograms and then use one of the formulae below according to your age.

**18–30 years**          (weight x 14.7) + 496 = **RMR**

**31–60 years**          (weight x 8.7) + 829 = **RMR**

*Step 2: estimate the number of calories you need for daily activities*
Multiply your RMR by one of the numbers below according to your activity level.

**Sedentary** (mostly seated or standing activities) = **RMR x 1.4**

**Moderately active** (some walking during the day or active hobbies) = **RMR x 1.7**

**Very active** (physically active during the day) = **RMR x 2.0**

*Step 3: estimate the number of calories you burn during exercise*

| Sport | kcal per hour |
|---|---|
| Aerobics (high intensity) | 520 |
| Aerobics (low intensity) | 400 |
| Badminton | 370 |
| Boxing (sparring) | 865 |
| Cycling (10 miles/h) | 385 |
| Cycling (5.5 miles/h) | 250 |
| Judo | 760 |
| Rowing machine | 445 |
| Running (6 mins/mile) | 1000 |
| Running (9 mins/mile) | 750 |
| Squash | 615 |
| Swimming (fast) | 630 |
| Tennis (singles) | 415 |
| Weight training | 270–450 |

Figures are based on the calorie expenditure of an athlete weighing 65 kg. Values will be greater for heavier body weights; lower for smaller body weights.

*Step 4: final step*
Add together the figures for steps 2 and 3.

**How can you raise your calorie expenditure?**

**Increase your fat free mass.** Regular weight training will significantly raise your RMR in as little as three months. One pound of muscle burns approximately 30–50 kcal per day per pound. So adding just one pound of muscle would use up an extra 350 kcal per week purely for maintenance purposes.

**Regular aerobic workouts.** Aerobic exercise can increase your RMR for between 6 and 36 hours after exercise. The greater the intensity of the workout and the longer the duration, the greater this effect will be.

**Get more active.** Exercise will compensate for some of the reduction in lean body mass that normally occurs during dieting and will, therefore, produce a smaller drop in the RMR.

- No organised meal times
- Emotional/boredom eating
- Eating in front of the television/no social interaction
- Eating too fast
- Eating high fat foods

### Set point

Researchers believe everyone has their own pre-determined 'set point', a weight or body fat range at which the body happily settles. This cannot easily be changed and is controlled by the interaction of several genes. If body fat levels increase, the metabolic rate increases and appetite decreases. Similarly, if body fat levels dip too low, the metabolic rate slows down and the appetite increases in an attempt to stabilise the body weight around the set point. That's why it is important to choose a realistic or attainable weight loss goal. Some scientists argue that the set point can be reset over time by high intensity exercise and a low fat diet.

## Putting it all together

**Make a commitment.** Lose weight because you want to, not to please someone else. Your motivation must come from within. It helps to compile a list of reasons why you want to lose weight.

**Establish your priorities.** Before starting a weight loss programme, make sure you are not distracted by other problems, such as relationship or financial problems. These can take up a lot of mental and physical energy, setting you up for failure. If you are unhappy with other aspects of your life you are less likely to succeed with your programme.

**Set a realistic goal.** Try to achieve a comfortable weight you maintained earlier as a young adult. Don't set a goal that you have never achieved in your adult years or one which conforms to unrealistic social/fitness ideals. Set mini-targets, e.g. monthly weight loss goals.

**Learn to recognise genuine hunger.** Eat only when you are hungry, not for emotional reasons or through boredom. Do not deny hunger however, otherwise you will end up overeating later on. Learn to stop eating when you are satisfied.

- Start your day with wholegrain cereal, porridge, wholemeal toast or low fat muffins.
- Include five portions of fruit and vegetables in your daily diet – eat fresh fruit as a snack, pile salad into your sandwich or add a side salad to your main meal.
- Make grains and starchy vegetables the base of your meals – pasta, potatoes, rice, cous cous, bulgar wheat.
- Reduce saturated fats, e.g. butter, meat, and foods made with them (e.g. pastry, biscuits, puddings).
- Avoid foods made with animal fats or hydrogenated vegetable fats as they contain larger amounts of trans fatty acids, e.g. margarine, biscuits, cakes and bakery items.
- Flavour salads and vegetables with herbs, lemon/lime juice, fruit vinegar.
- Add extra vegetables to pasta and curry sauces, stews, soups, bakes, shepherds pie, lasagne and moussaka.
- Make fresh fruit the base for dessert – add yoghurt, fromage frais, custard or half fat crème fraîche.

### ◆ *Low fat snacks* ◆

- Sandwiches/rolls/pitta/bagels (filled with cottage cheese, banana, salad, honey, marmite, tuna, chicken, turkey or ham)
- Low fat yoghurt and fromage frais
- Fresh fruit (e.g. apples, bananas, nectarines, grapes)
- English muffins/scones/crumpets/potato cakes
- Dried fruit
- Dried fruit bars/low fat energy bars/cereal bars
- Rice cakes/crackers/bread sticks

## Low fat foods

**Only eat low fat versions of foods if you like the taste.** Don't expect low fat versions of foods to taste exactly the same as their high fat equivalents – they won't satisfy your taste expectations and you will end up eating the high fat version anyway. If you prefer genuine ice cream to the low fat/low calorie version, simply have a smaller portion. Accompany with your favourite fresh fruit to make a filling dessert.

**Make sure you keep the portion sizes the same.** If a low fat version contains half the fat of the ordinary food, that doesn't mean you can eat twice as much! For example, if you switch to a low fat salad dressing, don't use two tablespoons on your salad instead of one.

**Substitute high fat cooking ingredients with low fat versions.** For example, you may be better off using low fat foods such as skimmed milk and reduced fat cheese in cooking (e.g. sauces, custard, lasagne, macaroni cheese) where the taste difference is not too obvious.

**Don't use low fat foods as an excuse to indulge in high fat treats.** For example, if you eat diet yoghurt for dessert during the week, don't ruin your fat saving by indulging in creamy puddings at the weekend.

**Low fat foods cannot satisfy strong cravings!** If you crave a high fat food, allow yourself to eat a small portion once a week, rather than denying that craving and substituting low fat versions. For example, if you have a strong desire for a piece of chocolate, set aside one day a week to eat a small amount of your favourite brand. If you eat a reduced fat substitute, that may not satisfy your craving so you may end up bingeing on the real thing anyway.

**Make low fat foods more filling.** For example, low fat calorie counted meals are not usually very filling owing to their small portion size and low fat content. Fill the hunger gap by adding extra vegetables and bread and follow with fresh fruit.

## How to control your appetite naturally

- Keep a food diary – identify situations and emotions that make you overeat.
- Ignore what the clock says – eat only when hungry, not just because it is one o'clock.
- Plan to eat at intervals of 2–4 hours rather than at specific times.
- Be more flexible with meal times – don't make rigid rules.
- Don't deny genuine hunger in an effort to hang on until meal times.
- If you find yourself wanting to eat out of boredom, plan enjoyable activities to fill in the gaps.
- Don't bury your emotions in food – deal with the problem in another way.
- Learn to leave food on the plate if you are full.
- Eat slowly – it takes 20 minutes for 'full-up' signals to reach the brain. Wait before eating second helpings.
- Ask: would I still want to eat this food if it wasn't there?

## Exercise to burn fat

Exercise is the other half of the equation in weight loss. The best way to manage your weight permanently is to combine a programme of regular exercise with a balanced low fat diet.

## Aerobics

### *How much?*

The Health Education Authority and American College of Sports Medicine recommend 15–60 minutes of aerobic exercise 3–5 times per week. This need not necessarily occur in one continuous session but could be broken up into shorter sessions. For example, instead of spending 45 minutes on the stepping machine, you can take a 10-minute walk in the morning, a 20-minute swim at lunch time and 15 minutes' gardening in the evening.

### *High or low intensity?*

Although fat provides a lower percentage of calories to be burned during high-intensity aerobic exercise, you can still burn more fat over the same period of time because you use more calories per minute. Studies have shown that a shorter period of high-intensity exercise (e.g. 40 mins) burns about the same amount of fat as a longer period of low-intensity exercise (e.g. 60 mins).

However, beginners should start with low-intensity activities as these are better suited to lower levels of fitness.

## Strength training

Strength training can help you lose fat faster because of its positive effect on your body composition and metabolic rate. As well as developing muscular strength, it helps develop and maintain lean body mass. The importance of lean mass (mainly muscle) is that it burns a significant number of calories just to exist – approximately 50 kcal per day per pound – far more calories than fat. So if you increase your muscle mass by seven pounds, for example, you increase the number of calories your body burns throughout the day by 350 kcal.

## Body image

Some athletes constantly strive to attain a very low weight or a different shape. They set themselves an unrealistic goal and believe that weight loss will help to solve their problems. Such individuals are usually highly self-disciplined perfectionists and very competitive. Unfortunately weight loss is not the solution. The problem is often one of a low self-esteem and a distorted body image. This can develop into a vicious circle of undereating, overeating and guilt.

## Have you got a body image problem?

- I constantly worry about my body shape or weight.
- I don't feel in control of my body shape or my eating habits.
- I often decline invitations to meals and social occasions involving food in case I might have to eat something fattening.
- When offered food or drink I often refuse it because I am worried about my weight.
- I feel extremely guilty after eating a high calorie or high fat food.
- I avoid certain foods even though I want to eat them.
- My family/friends complain that I am too fussy about eating.
- I only buy 'diet' foods.
- I constantly scrutinise food labels to check the calorie/fat content.
- I think about food all the time.
- I try to eat the same foods every day to control myself.
- I try to eat less at meal times than I'd really like to.
- I set myself a calorie goal each day then feel guilty when I overstep it.
- I try not to eat when I am hungry.
- I have not attended social occasions, e.g. parties, because I feel bad about my weight or shape.

## How to improve your body image

- Learn to accept and like your body shape – it is unique to you – and try to emphasise your good points.
- Tell yourself that reducing your weight will not solve deep rooted problems or an emotional crisis.
- Practise seeing yourself in front of the mirror in a positive way.
- Stick to a low fat healthy diet in general but don't become obsessed by it.
- Eat whenever you are hungry – don't deny genuine hunger otherwise you will overeat later on and feel guilty.
- If you have overeaten, do not starve yourself later to punish yourself. Eat normally at your next meal.
- Make a list of your 'forbidden' foods. Make a point of eating a small amount of one of these each day for a week (e.g. one biscuit). You will find you won't gain weight and you won't feel guilty.
- Do not ban any foods – no food is suddenly going to make your weight balloon.
- Think of all food as a source of nutrients that will make our body healthier, not as a source of calories.
- Don't set yourself calorie goals. Learn to eat to your appetite.
- Enjoy eating with others – it is one of life's great pleasures.

- The following eating plan is based on 1500 kcal per day.
- In addition to the foods listed, you should also include a minimum of 2 litres (4 pints) of fluid plus 1 litre (2 pints) for each hour of training. Each pre- and post-workout snack should be accompanied by 150–250 ml water.
- Where one portion of fruit is indicated, check page 3 for portion sizes.

| Day 1 |
|---|
| **Breakfast**<br>1 medium bowl (50 g/2 oz) wholegrain breakfast cereal<br>200 ml (⅓ pint) skimmed or semi-skimmed milk<br>1 portion fresh fruit<br><br>**Snack**<br>4 rice cakes<br>1 banana<br><br>**Lunch**<br>'Cream' of Tomato Soup (see page 109)<br>1 wholemeal roll with low fat spread<br>Vegetable crudités (e.g. peppers, carrots, celery)<br>1 portion fresh fruit<br><br>**Pre-workout snack**<br>50 g (2 oz) raisins<br><br>**Post-workout snack**<br>1 Raisin Muffin (see page 234)<br><br>**Dinner**<br>1 Fish Burger (see page 209)<br>Large green salad with 1 tbsp Italian Dressing (see page 122)<br>Yoghurt and Fruit Pudding (see page 232) |

| Day 2 |
|---|
| **Breakfast**<br>2 slices wholemeal toast with low fat spread and Marmite<br>1 portion fresh fruit<br><br>**Snack**<br>2 portions fresh fruit |

**Lunch**
2 slices wholemeal toast
Half a large tin (210 g) baked beans
1 carton (150 g) very low fat fromage frais
1 portion fresh fruit

**Pre-workout snack**
1 Oaty Fruit Bar (see page 217)

**Post-workout snack**
4 rice cakes

**Dinner**
Quick Supper Salad (see page 116)
1 medium jacket potato (225 g/8 oz) with a little yoghurt or fromage frais
1 portion fresh fruit, chopped and mixed with 1 carton (150 g) low
calorie yoghurt

## Day 3

**Breakfast**
1 carton (150 g) low calorie yoghurt
1 portion fresh fruit
1 slice wholemeal toast with low fat spread and Marmite

**Snack**
1 Muesli Bar (see page 216)
1 portion fresh fruit

**Lunch**
1 wholemeal bap with 50 g (2 oz) chicken and salad
Side salad with 1 tbsp reduced fat dressing
2 portions fresh fruit

**Pre-workout snack**
1 banana

**Post-workout snack**
1 Oatmeal Muffin (see page 236)

**Dinner**
Quick Vegetable Curry (see page 133)
75 g (3 oz) rice (uncooked weight)
1 carton (150 g) low fat plain yoghurt with 100 g (4 oz) chopped fruit

- ◆ The following eating plan is based on 1750 kcal per day.
- ◆ In addition to the foods listed, you should also include a minimum of 2 litres (4 pints) fluid plus 1 litre (2 pints) for each hour of training. Each pre- and post-workout snack should be accompanied by 150–250 ml water.
- ◆ Where one portion of fruit is indicated, check page 3 for portion sizes.

| Day 1 |
|---|

**Breakfast**
1 glass (150 ml/5 fl oz) fruit juice
1 wholemeal English muffin with low fat spread and a little honey
1 glass (150 ml/5 fl oz) skimmed or semi-skimmed milk

**Snack**
2 portions fresh fruit

**Lunch**
Brown Rice and Bean Salad (see page 118)
Vegetable crudités (e.g. peppers, carrots, celery)
1 portion fresh fruit
1 carton (150 g) low calorie yoghurt

**Pre-workout snack**
1 large banana

**Post-workout snack**
1 slice of Banana Cake (see page 238)

**Dinner**
Vegetable Gratin with Potatoes (see page 186)
Hot Winter Fruit Salad or Cool Summer Fruit Salad (see page 226)

| Day 2 |
|---|

**Breakfast**
2 slices wholemeal toast with low fat spread and a little honey or fruit spread
1 portion fresh fruit
1 carton (150 g) low calorie yoghurt

**Snack**
1 portion fresh fruit
1 Raisin Scone (see page 219)

**Lunch**
Turkey Pockets (see page 204)
Large green salad with 1 tbsp Italian Dressing (see page 122)
1 portion fresh fruit

**Pre-workout snack**
300 ml isotonic sports drink (home-made or commercial)

**Post-workout snack**
50 g (2 oz) dried fruit

**Dinner**
Mexican Bean Bake (see page 142)
1 medium jacket potato (225 g/8 oz) with a little yoghurt or fromage frais
1 portion fresh fruit
150 ml (¼ pint) low fat custard

| Day 3 |
| --- |

**Breakfast**
1 medium bowl (50 g/2 oz) wholegrain breakfast cereal
200 ml (⅓ pint) skimmed or semi-skimmed milk
1 portion fresh fruit

**Snack**
1 carton (150 g) low calorie yoghurt
1 thick slice toast with low fat spread and Marmite

**Lunch**
1 wholemeal pitta with salad and 60 g (2 oz) sliced turkey, chicken or ham
Side salad with 1 tbsp reduced fat dressing
2 portions fresh fruit

**Pre-workout snack**
1 cereal bar

**Post-workout snack**
3 Oatmeal Cookies (see page 220)

**Dinner**
75 g (3 oz) pasta
A–Z Vegetable Sauce (see page 152)
50 g (2 oz) low fat soft cheese or fromage frais
1 carton (150 g) low fat plain yoghurt with 100 g (4 oz) chopped fruit

# The vegetarian athlete

A couple of decades ago, the traditional 'meat and two veg' was regarded as the mainstay of an athlete's diet. Now more and more athletes are shunning meat in favour of a different style of eating. Meat-free diets range from a strict vegan diet to a more relaxed pescatarian diet (includes fish). These can be equally – if not more – healthy for active people, owing partly to the high carbohydrate/low fat content and partly to the higher content of fresh fruit and vegetables.

Current thinking is that a meat-free diet can provide athletes with all the essential nutrients needed by the body. But before embarking on a new style of eating, whether for health or ethical reasons, you need to know the pitfalls as well as the benefits.

## Vegan diet (excludes meat, poultry, fish, dairy products and eggs)

**Benefits.** Vegans tend to be leaner and lighter than the rest of the population and obesity is less common. This is mainly due to their lower calorie and fat intake. Vegans eat more unsaturated fatty acids and less saturated fatty acids. The strong emphasis on fruit, pulses and vegetables means you get plenty of fibre, which protects against bowel cancer, and phytochemicals, plant substances with cancer-fighting properties.

**Pitfalls.** Vegans may have low intakes of protein, calcium, iron, vitamin $B_{12}$, vitamin D, and iodine. Dairy products are a major source of calcium so make sure you eat alternative calcium sources (see below). Vegans are also at risk of pernicious anaemia unless they include vitamin $B_{12}$ found in fortified foods such as soya milk, tofu, breakfast cereals, yeast extract, vegetable stocks, soya burger mixes, or a supplement.

Recommended supplements: vitamin $B_{12}$ (in a multivitamin or B complex); calcium (with vitamin D or in a multivitamin/mineral).

- 50 g (2 oz) tofu
- 100 g (4 oz) hummous
- 2 tbsps sunflower or sesame seeds
- 350 g (12 oz) cooked beans
- 7 slices white bread
- 5 figs
- 10 tbsps spinach or spring cabbage
- 4 oranges

## Vegetarian diet (excludes meat and fish)

**Benefits.** Vegetarians are 40% less likely to develop cancer (especially of the breast, colon and prostate), and 30% less likely to suffer from heart disease. This is partly due to their healthier lifestyle and partly due to their diet which is lower in saturated fats and high in fibre, fruit and vegetables. The result is lower levels of blood cholesterol (especially the LDL (bad) cholesterol) and higher intakes of cancer-protective antioxidants.

**Pitfalls.** Omitting meat may result in lower intakes of iron and zinc and increased risk of iron-deficiency anaemia. The absorption of these minerals is reduced by plant substances such as fibre, phytates and oxalic acid. However, there is evidence that the body adapts over time by increasing the efficiency of iron and zinc absorption so in reality the risk of iron-deficiency anaemia is small for long term vegetarians. Eating vitamin-C rich foods also greatly increases iron absorption and may counteract any negative effects of phytates. Zinc can be obtained from wholemeal bread, nuts, seeds and eggs.
Both vegetarians and vegans may go short of omega-3 fatty acids found in oily fish. Non-fish sources include soya bean and rapeseed oil, linseeds and walnuts.

◆ *Food portions providing 3 mg iron* ◆
*(⅕ female daily needs; ⅓ male daily needs)*

- 2 tbsps (15 g) bran flakes
- Half a tin (240 g) baked beans
- 4 slices wholemeal bread
- 12 prunes
- 45 g (1½ oz) cashew nuts
- Medium portion (150 g) broccoli

## Pescatarian diet (excludes meat and poultry; includes fish)

**Benefits.** Pescatarian diets are usually low in fat so, again, there's a lower risk of obesity and heart disease. Omega-3 fatty acids (provided oily fish varieties are eaten regularly) will be in good supply and this helps protect against strokes, thrombosis and heart attacks.

**Pitfalls.** Like vegetarians, the main nutrient likely to be in short supply is iron so you need to eat iron-rich plant foods (see page 58).
Omega-3 fatty acids may pose a problem if you stick only to white fish; include oily fish such as mackerel, sardines or herring in your diet twice a week to get your recommended intake of these fatty acids.
Choose fresh or frozen fish wherever possible as the B vitamin content is higher than that found in tinned fish. Fish tinned in brine is high in sodium – rinse thoroughly to extract as much sodium as possible.

## Demi-vegetarian diet (excludes meat; includes poultry and fish)

**Benefits.** Typically lower in fat compared with diets containing meat, which will have a beneficial effect on blood cholesterol levels. It is easier to get all the vitamins and minerals from a demi-vegetarian diet than a vegetarian diet as it doesn't require a drastic change in eating habits.

**Pitfalls.** You may go short on iron if you eat only the light meat of poultry rather than the dark meat, e.g. a leg portion, which is relatively rich in iron. There is practically no iron in the light meat (breast) so eat both types of poultry meat to boost iron intake.
Chicken and turkey contain a good deal of fat in and beneath the skin, so ensure that you skin chicken or turkey portions before cooking. Instead of adding oil, sauté in a pan with apples and herbs, or potatoes and garlic, then add a little stock or wine. When roasting a whole bird, marinate in lemon juice and spices or soy sauce/sherry/ginger and use this to baste the bird during cooking. Discard the skin before eating as it is quite fatty.

## Protein

Protein is found in a wide variety of plant foods, including cereals, pulses, nuts, seeds and soya products, as well as dairy products and eggs. Vegetarians eating a variety of these foods each day will be consuming a mixture of proteins that complement each other. Any shortfall of amino acids in one protein source can be compensated for by greater amounts in another source, thus increasing the overall biological value (or usefulness) of the proteins. For example, cereals are low in lysine and rich in methionine. These are complemented by pulses which are rich in lysine and low in methionine. So, beans on toast or lentils with rice would make excellent meals.

The idea that protein complementation needs to occur within a single meal is no longer valid. It is now known that the body keeps a short term store of essential amino acids and can maintain a positive protein balance provided an adequate intake of amino acids is consumed over the course of a day.

### Is it a healthier diet?

Scientific studies of vegetarians have found that, in general, they live longer and are healthier than people who eat meat. They suffer much less from illnesses such as cancer, heart disease, high blood pressure and other common health problems. The 12-year Oxford Health Study (1994) of more than 6000 vegetarians and 5000 meat-eaters found that vegetarians had a 30% lower risk of heart disease, a 40% lower risk of cancer (especially breast and colon), and were 20% less likely to die of any specific cause. They also had a lower risk of bowel disorders, diabetes and osteoporosis.

---

**♦ *Top tips for going vegetarian* ♦**

- ♦ Cut back on meat gradually and introduce more pulses, e.g. beans, lentils, chick peas, in your diet.
- ♦ Include more grains and cereals, e.g. bread, barley, oats, buckwheat, cous cous.
- ♦ Choose low fat versions of dairy products.
- ♦ Try adding different types of nuts and seeds to food, e.g. vegetables and almond stir fry; vegetable/bean curry with cashews; sunflower or sesame seeds in home-made cakes; peanut burgers.
- ♦ Buy some good vegetarian cookery books.
- ♦ Don't always eat cheese/eggs in place of meat.
- ♦ If you are not used to a high fibre diet, use a mixture of wholemeal/white cereal products to start with. Increase fibre-rich foods gradually.

---

Plan your vegetarian diet around the following four main food groups to ensure you get the right balance of amino acids and all the nutrients needed for good health.

| Fruit and vegetables | Legumes and vegetarian protein foods |
|---|---|
| **5 or more servings per day**<br><br>Vegetables and fruit are packed with vitamin C, beta carotene, iron, calcium and fibre. Try to eat at least one serving of a dark green leafy vegetable (e.g. broccoli, spinach) and one serving of yellow/orange vegetables or fruit (e.g. carrots, tomatoes) each day.<br><br>**Serving size** = 1 apple/pear/orange; 100 g (4 oz) any fruit or vegetables; 3 heaped tbsps of cooked vegetables; 2 carrots. | **2–3 servings per day (4–5 if dairy products are excluded)**<br><br>Beans, lentils and peas are good sources of protein, fibre, iron, calcium, zinc and B vitamins. This group also includes eggs, nuts, seeds, soya milk (fortified), soya mince, tofu, tempeh, all of which supply protein, vitamins and minerals.<br><br>**Serving size** = 100 g (4 oz) cooked pulses, tofu, soya mince; 2 eggs; 25 g (1 oz) nuts or seeds. |
| **Cereals and starchy vegetables** | **Milk and dairy products** |
| **5–11 servings per day depending on activity level**<br><br>This group includes bread, rice pasta, breakfast cereals and potatoes. They are rich in complex carbohydrates as well as B vitamins and certain minerals.<br><br>**Serving size** = 1 slice of bread; 25 g (1 oz) uncooked grains or breakfast cereal; 75 g (3 oz) potato. | **2–3 servings per day**<br><br>This group includes milk, yoghurt and cheese. Choose the low fat versions wherever possible. They supply calcium, protein and B vitamins.<br><br>**Serving size** = 200 ml (⅓ pint) milk; 1 carton yoghurt/fromage frais; 40 g (1½ oz) hard cheese; 100 g (4 oz) cottage cheese. |

## Getting all the nutrients you need on a vegetarian diet

| Nutrient | Vegetarian sources |
|---|---|
| Protein | Milk, cheese, yoghurt, eggs, beans, lentils, peas, nuts, seeds, soya products (e.g. soya milk, TVP, tofu, tempeh), quorn. |
| Iron | Wholemeal bread, whole grains, nuts, pulses, green vegetables (e.g. broccoli, iron, watercress), fortified soya products, fortified breakfast cereals, seeds, dried fruit. |
| Vitamin $B_{12}$ | Dairy products, eggs, fortified foods (e.g. soya products, breakfast cereals, yeast extract), soya burger mixes. |
| Calcium | Dairy products, sunflower and sesame seeds, spinach, broccoli, almonds, brazils, fortified soya products (e.g. tofu, figs). |
| Zinc | Whole grains, wholemeal bread, pulses, nuts, seeds, eggs. |
| Iodine | Seaweed, iodised salt. |

## ◆ Vegetarian athlete's eating plan ◆

- ◆ The following six-day menu provides approximately 2500 kcal per day. Decrease or increase the quantities according to your individual calorie requirements (see page 46).
- ◆ In addition to the foods listed, you should also include a minimum of 2 litres (4 pints) of fluid plus 1 litre (2 pints) for each hour of training. Each pre- and post-workout snack should be accompanied by 150–250 ml water.
- ◆ Where one portion of fruit is indicated, check page 3 for portion sizes.

| Day 1 |
|---|
| **Breakfast**<br>1 large bowl (75 g/3 oz) wholegrain breakfast cereal<br>200 ml (⅓ pint) skimmed or semi-skimmed milk<br>1 portion fresh fruit<br><br>**Snack**<br>1 Date and Walnut Bar (see page 217)<br>1 portion fresh fruit<br><br>**Lunch**<br>Athlete's Cold Pasta Salad with red kidney beans (see page 115)<br>1 portion fresh fruit<br>1 carton (150 g) low fat yoghurt<br><br>**Pre-workout snack**<br>50 g (2 oz) raisins or dates |

**Post-workout snack**
2 Oatmeal Muffins (see page 236)

**Dinner**
300 g (11 oz) jacket potato
100 g (4 oz) fromage frais or cottage cheese
Large green salad with 1 tbsp Italian Dressing (see page 122)
2 Oatmeal and Raisin Scotch Pancakes (see page 232)
1 portion fresh fruit

## Day 2

**Breakfast**
Raisin Toast (see page 193)
1 glass (200 ml) fruit juice

**Snack**
25 g (1 oz) nuts (e.g. cashews, almonds)
25 g (1 oz) raisins

**Lunch**
2 thick slices wholemeal toast with butter/low fat spread
Half a large tin (210 g) baked beans
Side salad
1 carton (150 g) low fat fromage frais
1 portion fresh fruit

**Pre-workout snack**
1 large banana

**Post-workout snack**
4 rice cakes with 4 heaped tsps fruit spread

**Dinner**
Spicy Bean Enchiladas (see page 139)
1 medium (225 g/8 oz) jacket potato with a little butter/low fat spread
Broccoli or carrots
Low Fat Tiramisu (see page 230)

## Day 3

**Breakfast**
1 egg (boiled/poached/scrambled)
2 thick slices wholemeal toast with butter/low fat spread and Marmite
1 portion fresh fruit

**Snack**
1 wholemeal English muffin with fruit spread or honey
1 portion fresh fruit

**Lunch**
Millet Pilaff with Nuts and Raisins (see page 138)
Side salad with 1 tbsp reduced fat dressing
2 portions fresh fruit

**Pre-workout snack**
1 fruit bar

**Post-workout snack**
1 banana sandwich (2 slices wholemeal bread and 1 sliced banana)

**Dinner**
Bean and Tomato Casserole (see page 141)
75 g (3 oz) rice (uncooked weight)
Broccoli or other green vegetables
1 carton (150 g) low fat plain yoghurt with 1 tbsp granola-type cereal

---

## Day 4

**Breakfast**
3 Breakfast Muffins (see page 194)
1 portion fresh fruit

**Snack**
1 carton (150 g) low fat yoghurt
1 portion fresh fruit

**Lunch**
Greek Filled Pitta (see page 205)
2 portions fresh fruit

**Pre-workout snack**
1 energy bar

**Post-workout snack**
2 Banana Muffins (see page 237)

**Dinner**
Store-cupboard Bean Bake (see page 140)
75 g (3 oz) pasta (uncooked weight)
Mixed salad with 1 tbsp oil/vinegar dressing
100 g (4 oz) tinned apricots
150 ml (¼ pint) low fat custard

## Day 5

**Breakfast**
75 g (3 oz) muesli (no added sugar)
150 ml (¼ pint) skimmed or semi-skimmed milk
1 carton (150 g) low fat yoghurt

**Snack**
2 slices Banana Bread (see page 171) or Blueberry Bread (see page 172)

**Lunch**
2 sandwiches: 4 slices wholemeal bread with low fat soft cheese, dates
and chopped walnuts
Vegetable crudités (e.g. carrots, celery, red peppers)
2 portions fresh fruit

**Pre-workout snack**
2 slices toast with fruit spread or jam

**Post-workout snack**
1 banana
4 rice cakes

**Dinner**
75 g (3 oz) pasta
Vegetarian Chilli Sauce (see page 153)
Large side salad with 1 tbsp Italian dressing (see page 122)

## Day 6

**Breakfast**
2 Breakfast Pancakes (see page 195)
1 glass (200 ml) fruit juice

**Snack**
1 wholemeal roll filled with 50 g (2 oz) cottage cheese

**Lunch**
2 Muffin Pizzas (see page 207)
Large side salad with 1 tbsp oil/vinegar dressing

**Pre-workout snack**
2 Fruit Buns (see page 175)

**Post-workout snack**
4 low fat crackers
1 portion fresh fruit

**Dinner**
Dahl (see page 141)
75 g (3 oz) rice (uncooked weight)
Broccoli or other green vegetables
Hot Winter Fruit Salad or Cool Summer Fruit Salad (see page 226)

| Day 7 |
|---|

**Breakfast**
Pineapple Bagel (see page 193)
1 portion fresh fruit

**Snack**
2 portions fresh fruit

**Lunch**
Lentil and Vegetable Soup (see page 112)
2 wholemeal rolls with butter/low fat spread
2 portions fresh fruit

**Pre-workout snack**
50 g (2 oz) dried fruit

**Post-workout snack**
2 Apricot Bars (see page 218)

**Dinner**
Vegetable Cous Cous (see page 136)
Crunchy Apple Crumble (see page 224)

# Eating on the run

It's often difficult to squeeze healthy meals into a busy schedule. However, skipped meals, irregular meal times and hurried fatty snacks will leave you low in energy, glycogen and important vitamins and minerals. The following practical advice will help you develop healthy eating strategies that fit in with your hectic lifestyle.

## Strategies for eating on the run

**Organisation.** Take your food with you so you won't end up skipping meals or grabbing the nearest high fat snack when you are ravenous.
**Planning.** Plan your day in advance so you always make time to eat no matter how busy your schedule is.
**Identifying eating opportunities.** Make a list of times and places where you could eat, e.g. in the changing room; sports club; killing time between appointments; driving or travelling; working at your desk.
**Preparing ahead.** Prepare meals in advance by cooking larger quantities one day and keeping the remainder in the fridge or freezer.
**Shopping wisely.** Routinely shop with a planned shopping list; this will save you a good deal of time and ensure you have enough food to last you for a week. Avoid frequent small shopping trips which cost you more time.
**Stocking up.** Keep healthy staple foods in your kitchen cupboard so you always have a good choice of healthy food to hand.

## Eating healthily on the run

- Include at least one portion of fruit and vegetables at each meal.
- If you must have chips and fried food for lunch, balance it out with a side salad and follow it with fresh fruit.
- Get into the breakfast habit every day – no more skipped meals! Eat a big bowl of wholegrain cereal topped with fresh or dried fruit and milk.
- Eat bigger portions of carbohydrate foods, e.g. pasta, bread or potatoes, at meal times and reduce the fats and rich sauces.
- Choose healthier snacks like apples, satsumas, bananas or toast with marmite.
- Choose speedy meals which contain less fat and more carbohydrates and vegetables, e.g. home-made vegetable soup (make a big pot in advance) and rolls, jacket potatoes with tuna or cottage cheese.

- Add a big crunchy salad (ready prepared if you like) to your lunch time sandwiches; also add a little low fat dressing if you prefer.
- Drink at least 2 litres (4 pints) of fluid per day (allow an extra 1 litre (2 pints) for each hour of sport you play), e.g. water, diluted fruit juice, diluted squash or isotonic sports drinks.

## Super sandwiches

Sandwiches make a high carbohydrate healthy meal for eating on the run. Beware of ready prepared sandwiches from supermarkets and snack bars as they can contain extra butter and mayonnaise. A typical prawn mayonnaise sandwich contains more than 22 g fat!

For a really healthy sandwich it is best to make your own. Cut thick slices of bread and fill them with one of the low fat fillings suggested below.

- Wholemeal bread with low fat soft cheese, dates and chopped walnuts.
- French baguette with tuna, tomato, watercress and low fat salad dressing.
- Malted grain bread with turkey or chicken and low calorie coleslaw.
- Ciabatta with reduced fat mozzarella, beef tomatoes, olives and low calorie salad dressing.
- Bap with chicken, dried apricots, celery and tarragon.
- Foccacia bread (cut into wedges) with roasted peppers, aubergine and onion.
- Pitta bread with crumbled feta, beansprouts, baby spinach and cucumber.
- Rye bread with cottage cheese and chopped dates.
- Wheat tortilla wrapped around sliced chicken, salad and taco relish.
- Rolls with ham, lettuce, grated carrot and low fat salad dressing.
- Olive bread with hummous and salad leaves.
- Raisin bread with banana, sultanas and cinnamon.
- Soda bread with mature grated Cheddar, tomato and lettuce.
- Bagel with low fat soft cheese, salmon and tomato.

### ◆ Sandwich fact file ◆

- Wholemeal bread contains twice as much fibre as white bread (6.5 g per 100 g compared with 2.8 g per 100 g).
- A thin spreading of butter equals about 5 g butter (4.1 g fat) per slice; a medium spreading is 7 g (5.7 g) and thickly spread it is 12 g (9.8 g).
- For a substantial meal, make a sandwich using three slices of bread.
- Mayonnaise contains 22 g fat per spoonful. Use fromage frais or low calorie salad dressing instead.
- If preparing sandwiches in advance, wrap and store in the fridge or an insulated cool bag.

## Fast food guide

| High fat choices | kcal per portion | Healthier choices | kcal per portion |
|---|---|---|---|
| **Burger King** | | | |
| BK Double Whopper | 870 | BK Flamer | 315 |
| BK Double Whopper with cheese | 1010 | BK Hamburger | 290 |
| BK Beanburger | 535 | Turkey Flamer with cranberry sauce | 300 |
| **McDonald's** | | | |
| Quarterpounder with cheese | 520 | Hamburger | 245 |
| Chicken McNuggets (20) | 885 | Filet-o-Fish | 350 |
| Large fries | 535 | Scrambled eggs and muffin | 280 |
| Big Breakfast | 630 | Pasta salad with egg | 355 |
| **Kentucky Fried Chicken** | | | |
| Hot Wings | 410 | Barbecue beans (large) | 225 |
| Zinger Burger | 445 | Corn on the cob | 245 |
| **Fish and Chip Shop** | | | |
| Plaice in batter | 650 | Mushy peas | 100 |
| Chips (large) | 860 | Scampi in breadcrumbs | 240 |
| **Chinese Takeaway** | | | |
| Peking Duck with accompaniments | 750 | Chicken Chop Suey | 425 |
| Sweet & Sour Pork | 860 | Prawn Chop Suey | 300 |
| Chicken Chow Mein with noodles | 715 | Mixed Vegetable Chop Suey | 375 |
| **Indian Takeaway** | | | |
| Chicken Korma | 870 | Chicken Tikka | 340 |
| Lamb Biriani | 905 | Tandoori Chicken | 200 |
| Roghan Josh | 695 | Vegetable Curry | 315 |
| Chicken Dhansak | 725 | Chapati | 140 |
| **Pizza Express** | | | |
| American | 930 | Marinara | 700 |
| Four Seasons | 890 | Mushroom | 705 |
| Mozzarella and tomato salad with dough balls | 920 | Fresh fruit salad | 80 |

## Store-cupboard stand-bys

Keep a basic stock of the following non-perishable foods in your store-cupboard so you've always got something healthy on stand-by for a quick meal.

**Tins**
Tomatoes
Baked beans
Various beans (e.g. red
  kidney, butter beans)
Soup
Fish (e.g. tuna, sardines)
Rice pudding (low fat)
Custard (low fat)
Fruit in juice
  (e.g. pineapple, peaches)

**Packets**
Pasta
Rice
Other grains (e.g.
  cous cous, bulgar
  wheat, millet)
Breakfast cereal
Porridge oats
Dried fruit (e.g.
  raisins, apricots,
  dates)

**Jars**
Pasta sauce
Curry sauce
Low fat
  cooking sauce
Salsa
Passata
Honey, fruit
  spread, jam
Dried herbs

## Time-saving kitchen strategies

Develop healthy habits and you will dramatically reduce the time spent in the kitchen.

- Get all the ingredients together before you begin cooking.
- Cook as many ingredients as possible together in one saucepan by working backwards with the cooking times, e.g. add the chopped vegetables to the rice saucepan 10 minutes before the end of the rice cooking time; add tinned beans or tuna 5 minutes before the end.
- Make one huge bowl of mixed salad instead of several separate bowls of individual ingredients.
- Stir pasta sauces into the drained pasta and continue heating in the saucepan rather than heating the sauce in a separate pan.
- Make use of cooking times, e.g. toss a salad or stir fry some vegetables while the potatoes are cooking in the microwave.
- Make one-pot meals.
- Make larger quantities than you need and save the remainder in the fridge or freezer.
- Use baking dishes or cooking dishes that double up as serving dishes.
- Make use of ready-made pasta, Indian or Chinese sauces.
- Organise your time efficiently, e.g. pop a couple of potatoes in the oven before you go for a workout; they will be ready by the time you return.

**For travelling**

The following snacks can be taken with you and eaten when travelling to competitions, in-between business appointments, in fact anytime you are on the move. They can all be prepared the day before and wrapped and packed into your kit bag or travelling case.

- Sandwiches and rolls
- English muffins
- Fresh fruit
- Vegetable sticks, e.g. carrots, celery, peppers
- Home-made bread and cake (see pages 163–75 and 238–44)
- Mini boxes of breakfast cereals
- Fruit bars
- Home-made bars (see pages 216–21)
- Home-made muffins (see pages 234–7)
- Malt loaf
- Raisin bread
- Fig rolls and low fat biscuits
- Low fat yoghurt, cottage cheese and fromage frais
- Sliced chicken or turkey breast
- Mini pancakes; oat pancakes
- Potato cakes or scones

**For your desk drawer**

Keep a supply of healthy non-perishable snacks in your desk drawer or briefcase so you can refuel while at work.

- Low fat crackers
- Breadsticks
- Rice cakes
- Cereal bars
- Dried fruit (apples, apricots, dates etc.)
- Long life fruit juice
- Tinned fruit (ring pull tins)
- Baby food jars
- Oatcakes
- Plain popcorn

| Snack | Healthier swap | Calorie-saving | Fat-saving |
|---|---|---|---|
| Crisps (1 packet, 30 g) | Plain popcorn (2 cups, 25 g) | 55 kcal | 10 g |
| Tortilla chips (1 packet, 40 g) | Breadsticks (7) | 69 kcal | 9 g |
| Digestive biscuits (2) | Rice cakes (2) | 86 kcal | 6 g |
| Chocolate biscuits (2) | Oatcakes (2) | 55 kcal | 2.6 g |
| Chocolate bar | Fruit bar | 150 kcal | 13 g |
| Doughnut | Currant bun | 90 kcal | 11 g |
| Sweets (25 g) | Raisins (25 g) | 30 kcal | 0 g |
| Dairy ice cream (2 scoops, 125 g) | Low fat yoghurt (150 g) | 50 kcal | 8.5 g |
| Slice of cake (85 g) | Banana | 200 kcal | 13 g |

## Travelling overseas

When travelling overseas it is essential to plan your food intake. Local foods may turn out to be unsuitable for athletes or, in many cases, simply unavailable. One of the dangers of overseas travel is consuming contaminated food or drink and suffering from gastroenteritis (traveller's diarrhoea). Follow the guidelines below to ensure that you remain healthy while abroad.

- Research the types of foods likely to be available at your destination. Check the provision of local shops, your hotel/accommodation facility and the sports venue before you travel.
- Take a supply of non-perishable foods such as boxes of breakfast cereal, energy bars, fruit bars, jars of baby food, rice cakes and crackers.
- Stick to plain and familiar foods. Do not experiment with unusual or spicy local delicacies.
- Drink only bottled water/drinks; avoid ice in drinks.
- Avoid unpasteurised milk and dairy products.
- Peel fruit and vegetables; avoid salads which may have been washed in tap water.
- Avoid dishes which have been reheated unless they are piping hot.
- Avoid food sold from street vendors.
- Avoid meat dishes as far as possible as there is a greater chance of contamination.
- Avoid alcohol and caffeine before competing as they are diuretics.

# Drinking

Exercise increases the production of heat from your body; sweating helps to keep you cool and stops you overheating. But fluid losses during exercise can be high (1–2 litres per hour in warm conditions) and it is easy to become dehydrated. If dehydration does set in, body temperature rises, performance suffers and heat stress results. Just a 2% reduction in body weight through dehydration causes a 10–20% loss of performance, early fatigue and circulatory stress. Higher losses cause nausea, dizziness, vomiting and, ultimately, heat stroke.

## Early warning symptoms of heat stress

- ◆ Dizziness
- ◆ Fatigue
- ◆ Headache
- ◆ Feeling excessively hot
- ◆ Nausea
- ◆ Little or no sweating
- ◆ Cool skin
- ◆ Disorientation
- ◆ Confusion

## Preventing dehydration

### Pre-exercise

Ensure you are fully hydrated before exercise – top up with around 200–250 ml (⅓–½ pint) of fluid 15–20 minutes beforehand. You can check for dehydration by noting the frequency, colour and volume of your urine. Aim for:

- ◆ light coloured urine
- ◆ high volume
- ◆ high frequency.

### During exercise

During exercise, regular drinking will help replace fluid and prevent dehydration. It is best to drink frequent small amounts than too much too quickly. By this stage your body may already be dehydrated. Fluid empties more slowly from the stomach when you are dehydrated so this can make you feel nauseous and even cause vomiting, delaying fluid absorption even further! Aim to:

◆ consume 150–250 ml (¼–½ pint) water or isotonic drink every 10–20 minutes
◆ start drinking early; do not wait until you are thirsty
◆ consume 25–50 g (1–2 oz) carbohydrate per hour during strenuous exercise lasting more than 90 minutes.

### Post-exercise

It is important to replace fluid as rapidly as possible after exercise. Drink freely but do not stop once your thirst has been satisfied; you could still be dehydrated.

### How much fluid?

Fluid loss depends on how hard and long you have been exercising, the surrounding temperature and humidity, and also on your individual body chemistry. To get an idea of your fluid requirements, weigh yourself before and after exercise. The amount of weight lost corresponds to the amount of water lost as sweat – 1 kg is equivalent to 1 litre of water. For example, a weight loss of 1½ kg means you have lost 1½ litres of fluid. Aim to replace this amount plus more during and after exercise, allowing 1½ litres for each 1 litre of lost fluid, since urination increases after exercise. Your body weight should be fully restored within 3–4 hours of exercise.

### What to drink?

Water is a good fluid replacer, and if you are exercising for less than one hour at a low or moderate intensity, drinking plain (or flavoured unsweetened) water is fine. For longer or particularly strenuous workouts, fluid replacement sports drinks have a number of advantages.

*Benefits of a fluid replacement sports drink*

- Rapid replacement of fluid. The carbohydrate (sugars) and sodium speed water absorption in the small intestine.
- Maintains blood volume and decreases urine output (due to sugar and sodium content). This is especially important during prolonged events, e.g. marathon, ultra-distance, cycle touring.
- Provides additional fuel. The sugars (glucose, fructose, sucrose) and glucose polymers in the drink provide readily available fuel which helps offset glycogen depletion and delays fatigue. Aim to consume 30–60 g per hour in events lasting more than 90 minutes. You can achieve this by drinking 1 litre of a drink containing 30–60 g carbohydrate.
- Pleasant taste. The drink must be palatable to encourage people to drink enough to replace fluid.

*What to look for on the label of an isotonic sports drink*

**Check: types of carbohydrate**
- Mostly glucose (dextrose) and sucrose; small amounts of glucose polymers or fructose are acceptable.
- Avoid high-fructose drinks.

**Check: carbohydrate content**
4–8 g/100 ml (isotonic).

**Check: sodium content**
40–110 mg/100 ml

| Hypotonic | • A hypotonic drink is more dilute than body fluids, therefore it contains a lower concentration of particles (sugars and electrolytes) per 100 ml.<br>• Typical carbohydrate content: < 4 g/100 ml.<br>• Examples: water, low calorie or 'diet' drinks, very dilute squash, low calorie sports drinks, e.g. Lucozade, Low Calorie Sport, Isostar Light. |
|---|---|
| Isotonic | • An isotonic drink contains the same concentration of particles (sugars and electrolytes) as body fluids and is absorbed in the small intestine faster than plain water.<br>• Typical carbohydrate content: 4–8 g/100 ml.<br>• Examples: diluted squash (1:4), diluted fruit juice (1:1), commercial isotonic sports drinks, e.g. Isostar, Gatorade, Lucozade Sport. |
| Energy drinks | • Energy drinks have a relatively high carbohydrate concentration (greater than that of body fluids), and usually contain no sodium. They are emptied more slowly from the stomach and absorbed more slowly than plain water.<br>• Typical carbohydrate concentration: 8–20 g/100 ml. |
| Glucose polymers/malto-dextrins | • Glucose polymers are a common ingredient in sports drinks. They are made from chemically-treated corn-starch which breaks down to produce short chains of glucose molecules (4–20 units). They are closer to simple carbohydrates (sugars) than complex carbohydrates.<br>• The main advantage of adding them to sports drinks is that they increase the carbohydrate content of the drink (by 4–20 times depending on chain length) without affecting its osmolality ('concentration') and speed of absorption. In other words, they provide more carbohydrate per 100 ml than glucose or sucrose at the same 'concentration'. This is particularly useful for refuelling during strenuous events lasting for more than 90 minutes. Also, glucose polymers are not sweet tasting so a manufacturer can achieve a palatable drink with a high carbohydrate content by using a mixture of simple sugars and glucose polymers. |

- If you are exercising for 30 minutes or less, water is a good fluid replacer.
- If you are exercising at a moderate intensity for up to 90 minutes, drink water or a hypotonic or isotonic drink.
- If you are exercising at a high intensity for up to 90 minutes, drink an isotonic sports drink.
- If you are exercising at a moderate or high intensity for longer than 90 minutes, drink an isotonic drink based on glucose polymers to provide extra fuel.

**Ten ways to keep cool**

1. Drink a minimum of two litres of fluid per day: water, diluted fruit juice and soft drinks, fruit or herb teas, weak tea.
2. Consume at least 150–250 ml (¼–½ pint) fluid for every 20–30 minutes of exercise.
3. Children and teenagers lose fluid more readily than adults and dehydration can set in earlier.
4. Increase your fluid intake 24 hours prior to competition.
5. Drink more fluid during hot or humid weather.
6. Gradually acclimatise yourself to new weather conditions (allow up to two weeks).
7. Wear loose fitting natural fibre clothing during training that allows you to sweat freely and allows moisture to evaporate.
8. Practise your fluid replacement strategy during training, don't leave it until competition.
9. Remember your body cannot adapt to dehydration.
10. Experiment to find which type of sports drink suits you best.

## Home-made sports drinks

**HYPOTONIC**
- 20–40 g sucrose
  1 litre water
  1–1.5 g salt
  flavouring

- 100 ml squash
  900 ml water
  1–1.5 g salt

- 250 ml fruit juice
  750 ml water
  1–1.5 g salt

**ISOTONIC**
- 40–80 g sucrose
  1 litre water
  1–1.5g salt
  flavouring

- 200 ml squash
  800 ml water
  1–1.5 g salt

- 500 ml fruit juice
  500 ml water
  1–1.5 g salt

# Diets for different sports

The general principles of sports nutrition apply to all sports, but each activity places specific nutritional and energy demands on the body. If you are serious about your sport, you can fine tune your diet to match your individual training programme.

- Each eating plan includes three meals and 2–3 snacks each day. This pattern of eating leads to more efficient glycogen refuelling after exercise and minimises fat deposition.
- In addition to the foods in the menus, you should include a minimum of 2 litres (4 pints) of fluid per day plus ½–1 litre (1–2 pints) for each hour of training. Each pre- and post-workout snack should be accompanied by 150–250 ml water.
- Where one portion of fruit is indicated on the menu, check page 3 for portion sizes.
- All of the menus and recipes serve one person. Simply multiply the amounts by the number of portions if you wish to serve more people.

## Long distance running

*Optimal diet*

| | |
|---|---|
| Carbohydrate | 60–70% |
| Fat | 20–30% |
| Protein | 10–15% |

**Tip 1**
Maintain a low body fat level as excessive weight will reduce your speed and performance. For élite male runners, the optimal body fat range is 5–12%; for élite female runners, the optimal range is 10–18%.

**Tip 2**
Do not restrict your intake of carbohydrates otherwise you will fatigue early and your endurance will be reduced. Balance your energy intake with your energy output.

**Tip 3**
Keep up your iron intake. Depleted iron stores and iron-deficiency anaemia are particularly common among female runners so include foods detailed on page 58.

| Day 1 |
| --- |

**Breakfast**
1 large bowl (75 g/3 oz) wholegrain breakfast cereal
200 ml (⅓ pint) skimmed or semi-skimmed milk
1 banana
1 glass (200 ml/7 fl oz) fruit juice

**Snack**
2 slices of Cornmeal Bread (see page 165) or wholemeal bread with honey
1 portion fresh fruit

**Lunch**
Brown Rice and Bean Salad (see page 118)
2 wholemeal rolls with butter/low fat spread
2 portions fresh fruit
1 carton (150 g) low fat yoghurt

**Pre-workout snack**
75 g (3 oz) raisins or dates

**Post-workout snack**
2 Apricot Bars (see page 218)

**Dinner**
Potato Tacos (see page 182)
1 thick slice crusty bread
Broccoli or other leafy green vegetables
2 portions fresh fruit
1 carton (150 g) low fat fromage frais

| Day 2 |
| --- |

**Breakfast**
3 Breakfast Pancakes (see page 195)
1 large glass (250 ml) fruit juice

**Snack**
2 cereal or fruit bars

**Lunch**
1 large (300 g/11 oz) jacket potato with a little low fat spread
100 g (4 oz) cottage cheese or low fat soft cheese
Large mixed salad with 1 tbsp oil/vinegar dressing
1 thick slice bread with butter/low fat spread
2 portions fresh fruit
1 carton (150 g) low fat yoghurt

**Pre-workout snack**
400 ml isotonic sports drink (home-made or commercial)

**Post-workout snack**
2 Raisin Muffins (see page 234)

**Dinner**
Minestrone Soup (see page 110)
2 Corn Muffins (see page 237)
1 tin (400 g) rice pudding
1 tbsp fruit spread or jam

| Day 3 |
| --- |

**Breakfast**
4 slices wholemeal toast
1 egg (scrambled/boiled/poached)
2 portions fresh fruit

**Snack**
Banana Hot Dog (see page 203)

**Lunch**
Ciabatta sandwich: 6 slices Ciabatta bread with reduced fat
mozzarella, beef tomatoes, olives and low calorie salad dressing
2 portions fresh fruit
1 carton (150 g) low fat fromage frais

**Pre-workout snack**
1 energy bar

**Post-workout snack**
1 Banana sandwich: 2 slices of bread with 1 sliced banana

**Dinner**
Athlete's Hot Pasta with Vegetables (see page 150)
Apricot and Date Bread Pudding (see page 228)

## Sprinting

*Optimal diet*

| | |
| --- | --- |
| Carbohydrate | 60% |
| Fat | 20–25% |
| Protein | 15–20% |

**Tip 1**
If you are an experienced or élite sprinter, consider taking creatine supplements. A loading dose of 20 g per day (4 x 5 g) for 5 days can boost muscle phosphocreatine levels. This enables you to maintain your maximal power output longer and recover faster between multiple sprints.

**Tip 2**
You have higher protein needs compared with endurance runners (1.4–1.7 g/kg per day). Include at least three portions of high protein foods in your daily diet. If you have a very high calorie expenditure (more than 3000 kcal) you may consider supplementing your diet with a protein-based drink, such as a home-made milkshake or a commercial protein/carbohydrate powder.

## ◆ Sprinter's eating plan ◆

This eating plan provides approximately 3000 kcal per day. Increase or decrease the quantities according to your individual requirements (see above).

| Day 1 |
|---|
| **Breakfast**<br>Power Porridge (see page 198)<br><br>**Snack**<br>2 slices Banana Bread (see page 171)<br><br>**Lunch**<br>2 Grilled Chicken Burgers (see page 209)<br>2 portions fresh fruit<br><br>**Pre-workout snack**<br>1 banana<br>1 fruit bar<br><br>**Post-workout snack**<br>2 Banana Muffins (see page 237)<br><br>**Dinner**<br>Mighty Mash I (see page 179)<br>175 g (6 oz) grilled cod or haddock with herbs<br>Carrots, broccoli or other vegetables<br>2 portions fresh fruit<br>1 carton (150 g) low fat fromage frais |

| Day 2 |
|---|

**Breakfast**
2 eggs (boiled/scrambled/poached)
4 slices toast with butter/low fat spread
1 large glass (250 ml) fruit juice

**Snack**
Milkshake: 600 ml (1 pint) skimmed or semi-skimmed milk, 1 banana and 2 tbsps skimmed milk powder or protein powder

**Lunch**
1 large (300 g/11 oz) jacket potato
75 g (3 oz) prawns or chicken mixed with 1 tbsp low calorie salad dressing
Large mixed salad with 1 tbsp oil/vinegar dressing
2 portions fresh fruit
1 carton (150 g) low fat yoghurt

**Pre-workout snack**
400 ml isotonic sports drink (home-made or commercial)

**Post-workout snack**
3 oatmeal cookies (see page 220)
1 glass (250 ml) skimmed or semi-skimmed milk

**Dinner**
Chicken Paella (see page 126)
Green beans, courgettes, or other vegetables
Baked Bananas (see page 231)
1 carton (150 g) plain low fat yoghurt

| Day 3 |
|---|

**Breakfast**
4 Weetabix or Shredded Wheats
300 ml (½ pint) skimmed or semi-skimmed milk
25 g (1 oz) dried fruit

**Snack**
Bagel Melt (see page 203)

**Lunch**
Rice and Sweetcorn Salad (see page 116)
100 g (4 oz) cooked chicken or turkey breast
2 portions fresh fruit
1 carton (150 g) low fat fromage frais

> **Pre-workout Snack**
> 50 g (2 oz) dried fruit
>
> **Post-workout Snack**
> 2 Date and Walnut Bars (see page 217)
>
> **Dinner**
> 75 g (3 oz) pasta (uncooked weight)
> Vegetarian Bolognese (see page 151)
> Crunchy Apple Crumble (see page 224)
> 1 carton (150 g) low fat yoghurt

## Combat sports

*Optimal diet*

| | |
|---|---|
| Carbohydrate | 55–65% |
| Fat | 15–20% |
| Protein | 15–25% |

**Tip 1**

Keep your off-season weight fairly close to your competitive weight. The difference should be no more than about 6 kg (13 lb). If you continually have difficulty making weight for competition, consider moving up to the next weight category.

**Tip 2**

Plan your pre-competition strategy, allowing sufficient time to lose weight safely and slowly (½–1 kg per week). Make weight by losing fat, not fluid and glycogen. Dehydration and starvation both have an adverse effect on your performance and health.

### ◆ Combat athlete's eating plan ◆

This eating plan provides approximately 3000 kcal per day. Increase or decrease the quantities according to your individual requirements (see above).

### Day 1

**Breakfast**
75 g (3 oz) porridge oats
450 ml (¾ pint) skimmed or semi-skimmed milk
1 banana

**Snack**
1 wholemeal sandwich: 2 slices bread with a little butter/low fat spread and 50 g (2 oz) lean ham or low fat soft cheese

**Lunch**
2 Turkey Pockets (see page 204)
2 portions fresh fruit

**Pre-workout snack**
400 ml isotonic sports drink (home-made or commercial)

**Post-workout snack**
2 Muesli Bars (see page 216)

**Dinner**
Pork and Vegetable Stir Fry (see page 129)
2 portions fresh fruit
1 glass (200 ml) semi-skimmed or skimmed milk

## Day 2

**Breakfast**
1 large bowl (100 g/4 oz) wholegrain breakfast cereal
300 ml (½ pint) skimmed or semi-skimmed milk
1 portion fresh fruit

**Snack**
2 large slices toast with fruit spread or honey

**Lunch**
Athlete's Cold Pasta Salad (see page 115)
1 thick slice bread with butter/low fat spread
75 g (3 oz) cooked chicken breast or cottage cheese
2 bananas

**Pre-workout snack**
50 g (2 oz) dried fruit

**Post-workout snack**
1 litre (2 pints) isotonic sports drink

**Dinner**
Curried Chicken and Rice (see page 130)
1 tin (400 g) low fat rice pudding
225 g (8 oz) fresh or tinned fruit

| Day 3 |
|---|

**Breakfast**
Raisin Toast (see page 193)
1 large glass (225 ml/8 fl oz) fruit juice

**Snack**
2 English muffins with honey

**Lunch**
1 large (300 g/11 oz) jacket potato
100 g (4 oz) tinned tuna in brine (drained) mixed with 1 tbsp low fat soft
cheese and 1 tbsp reduced fat mayonnaise
Tomatoes
1 portion fresh fruit
1 carton (150 g) low fat yoghurt

**Pre-workout snack**
2 bananas

**Post-workout snack**
2 Raisin Muffins (see page 234)

**Dinner**
100 g (4 oz) pasta
Turkey Bolognese (see page 152)
Side salad with 1 tbsp French Dressing
2 portions fresh fruit

## Weight training and bodybuilding

*Optimal diet*
Carbohydrate     60%
Fat              15–20%
Protein          20–25%

### Tip 1
Bodybuilders need slightly more protein per kg body weight compared
with most other sports (1.4–1.7g/kg per day). Include at least one high
biological value protein and one low biological value protein at each
meal. If your energy expenditure is greater than 3000 kcal, consider supplementing your diet with a protein-based drink, such as a home-made
milkshake or a commercial protein/carbohydrate drink.

### Tip 2
To build muscle at the optimum rate, you should increase your calories
by 15% over your maintenance requirements. In practice, this means
consuming an additional 300–500 kcal per day from a mixture of high
carbohydrate and high protein foods.

## Tip 3
The majority of supplements marketed for bodybuilders are unnecessary and lacking in scientific evidence – there is no proof that 'natural steroid replacers', 'testosterone boosters' and other herbal supplements have any effect. Creatine may be beneficial for advanced trainers and protein/carbohydrate drinks may benefit those with very high calorie and nutritional needs.

### ◆ Bodybuilder's eating plan ◆

This eating plan provides approximately 3000 kcal per day. Increase or decrease the quantities according to your individual requirements (see above).

| Day 1 |
|---|
| **Breakfast**<br>4 Weetabix or Shredded Wheat<br>300 ml (½ pint) skimmed or semi-skimmed milk<br>1 banana<br>1 carton (150 g) low fat yoghurt or fromage frais<br><br>**Snack**<br>1 large wholemeal roll with a little butter/low fat spread and<br>50 g (2 oz) cottage cheese or tuna<br>1 portion fresh fruit<br><br>**Lunch**<br>2 wholemeal pitta breads with 100 g (4 oz) cooked chopped turkey or chicken or 2 sliced boiled eggs, tomatoes and cucumber with 1 tbsp low calorie dressing<br>1 carton (150 g) low fat yoghurt<br>1 portion fresh fruit<br><br>**Pre-workout snack**<br>50 g (2 oz) dried fruit<br>200 ml fruit juice (diluted with water)<br><br>**Post-workout snack**<br>1 glass (200 ml) semi-skimmed or skimmed milk<br>2 slices Banana Bread (see page 171)<br><br>**Dinner**<br>Tuna and Pasta Bake (see page 158)<br>Broccoli or other green vegetables<br>Banana<br>200 ml (⅓ pint) low fat custard |

## Day 2

**Breakfast**
300 ml (½ pint) natural yoghurt mixed with 2 pieces or 225 g
(8 oz) chopped fruit (e.g. strawberries, nectarines, melon)
2 slices toast with honey

**Snack**
4 oatcakes
25 g (1 oz) sliced cheese

**Lunch**
Omelette made from 2 eggs and 2 egg whites. Fill with 75 g (3 oz)
chopped lean ham, sliced tomatoes and sliced mushrooms, and fresh or
dried herbs; 2 wholemeal rolls with a little butter/low fat spread
2 portions fresh fruit

**Pre-workout snack**
400 ml (⅔ pint) isotonic sports drink (home-made or commercial)

**Post-workout snack**
3 slices malt loaf

**Dinner**
Foil Baked Chicken (175 g/6 oz) skinless chicken breast baked in foil
with herbs and lemon juice
1 large (300 g/11 oz) jacket potato with 1 tbsp plain yoghurt
Vegetable Salad (see page 124)
Power Milkshake: 300 ml (½ pint) skimmed milk, 2 tbsps skimmed milk
powder or commercial protein powder, 1 carton (150 g) low calorie fruit
yoghurt and 1 banana

## Day 3

**Breakfast**
1 glass (150 ml/5 fl oz) fruit juice
2 boiled/poached/scrambled eggs
3 slices wholemeal toast and low fat spread.

**Snack**
2 fruit or low fat cereal bars
1 glass (200 ml) skimmed or semi-skimmed milk

**Lunch**
Curried Chicken Baguette (see page 206)
2 portions fresh fruit

**Pre-workout snack**
2 Fruit and Nut Bars (see page 218)

**Post-workout snack**
6 rice cakes
1 banana

**Dinner**
Quick Tacos (see page 202)
1 jacket potato (225 g/8 oz) with a little butter/low fat spread
Side salad
2 portions fresh fruit
1 carton (150 g) low fat fromage frais

## Long distance cycling

*Optimal diet*
Carbohydrate    60–70%
Fat             20–25%
Protein         10–15%

**Tip 1**
For rides lasting longer than 90 minutes, consume between 30–60 g carbohydrate per hour. This will help delay fatigue and improve your endurance. This can be provided by 500 ml isotonic drink (6 g carbohydrate/100 ml) or 2 bananas or 1 energy bar or 50 g (2 oz) raisins.

**Tip 2**
Keep well hydrated as fluid loss during long strenuous rides can be over 1 litre per hour. Drink 125–250 ml water or a sports drink immediately before your ride and 125–150ml every 10–20 minutes.
This eating plan provides approximately 3000 kcal per day. Increase or decrease the quantities according to your individual requirements (see above).

### ◆ Long distance cyclist's eating plan ◆

| Day 1 |
|---|
| **Breakfast**<br>1 large bowl (100 g/4 oz) bran flakes/wheat flakes /fruit & fibre/muesli<br>300 ml (½ pint) skimmed or semi-skimmed milk<br>1 chopped banana<br>50 g (2 oz) raisins<br><br>**Snack**<br>2 portions fresh fruit<br>2 slices toast with butter/low fat spread |

**Lunch**
1 large jacket potato (300 g/11 oz) topped with half a large tin (210 g) baked beans
Mixed vegetable salad (see page 124) with 1 tbsp oil/vinegar dressing
1 portion fresh fruit
1 carton (150 g) low fat yoghurt

**Pre-workout snack**
600 ml (1 pint) isotonic sports drink (home-made or commercial)

**Post-workout snack**
1 Oaty Fruit Bar (see page 217)

**Dinner**
75 g (3 oz) pasta (uncooked weight)
Quick Tuna and Sweetcorn Sauce (see page 154)
1 tbsp grated cheese
Fruit Rice Pudding (see page 225)

| Day 2 |
|:---:|

**Breakfast**
4 thick slices wholemeal toast with a scraping of low fat spread and 4 heaped tsps fruit spread or honey
1 glass (175 ml/6 fl oz) fruit juice

**Snack**
2 Oatmeal Cookies (see page 220)

**Lunch**
Rice and Sweetcorn Salad (see page 116)
2 portions fresh fruit

**Pre-workout snack**
2 bananas

**Post-workout snack**
Sandwich: 2 slices wholemeal bread with Marmite

**Dinner**
Quick Vegetable and Cheese Pizza (see page 214) made from 1 ready-made pizza base (approx. 150–175 g/5–6 oz), 3 tbsps pasta sauce, finely sliced onion, red and green peppers, sliced mushrooms, dried herbs, 50 g (2 oz) grated Cheddar cheese or mozzarella. Bake in a hot oven, according to instructions on the packet
1 tin (225 g/8 oz) pineapple in juice
1 carton (150 g) low fat yoghurt

| Day 3 |
|---|

**Breakfast**
75 g (3 oz) porridge oats
450 ml (¾ pint) skimmed or semi-skimmed milk
25 g (1 oz) dates or sultanas

**Snack**
1 toasted bagel
1 portion fresh fruit

**Lunch**
2 sandwiches: 4 slices wholemeal bread with a little butter/low fat spread and 100 g (4 oz) tuna, tomato, watercress and 2 tbsps low fat salad dressing
2 cartons (300 g) low fat yoghurt

**Pre-workout snack**
4 rice cakes spread with 4 tsps fruit spread
2 glasses water

**Post-workout snack**
1 Muesli Bar (see page 216)
1 banana

**Dinner**
Vegetable Paella (see page 126)
Tomato salad
Banana Bread Pudding (see page 227)

## Football, rugby, hockey and other team sports

*Optimal diet*
Carbohydrate      60–65%
Fat               20–25%
Protein           10–15%

**Tip 1**
Increase your carbohydrate intake during the last 24–48 hours before the day of a match. This will ensure adequate glycogen stores, improve your performance, and reduce the chances of injury.

**Tip 2**
Make use of the half-time break, wherever possible, to consume plenty of fluid and a high glycaemic index snack. Aim to drink at least 250–300 ml water or an isotonic sports drink after each half of the match.

This eating plan provides approximately 3000 kcal per day. Increase or decrease the quantities according to your individual requirements (see above).

| Day 1 |
|---|

**Breakfast**
3 Weetabix or Shredded Wheat
200 ml (⅓ pint) skimmed or semi-skimmed milk
1 chopped banana

**Snack**
1 portion fresh fruit
1 wholemeal roll with 50 g (2 oz) chicken, ham or cheese

**Lunch**
4 slices toast
1 tin (420 g) baked beans
Side salad with 1 tbsp reduced fat dressing
1 portion fresh fruit
1 carton (150 g) low fat yoghurt

**Pre-workout snack**
600 ml (1 pint) isotonic sports drink (home-made or commercial)

**Post-workout snack**
2 bananas
1 roll or English muffin

**Dinner**
Spicy Rice (see page 127)
1 boneless chicken or turkey portion (100 g/4 oz)
2 Raisin Muffins (see page 234)

| Day 2 |
|---|

**Breakfast**
Dried Fruit Muesli (see page 194)
300 ml (½ pint) skimmed or semi-skimmed milk
1 glass (175 ml/6 fl oz) fruit juice

**Snack**
1 bagel (any variety)
1 portion fresh fruit

**Lunch**
75 g (3 oz) pasta (uncooked weight)
Tomato and Tuna Sauce  (see page 153)
2 thick slices bread with butter/low fat spread
2 portions fresh fruit

**Pre-workout snack**
75 g (3 oz) raisins or dates

**Post-workout snack**
2 Oaty Fruit Bars (see page 217)

**Dinner**
Chilli Con Carne (see page 147) or Mixed Bean Chilli (see page 144)
Large mixed salad with 1 tbsp reduced fat dressing
1 carton (150 g) low fat yoghurt
1 banana

---

## Day 3

**Breakfast**
75 g (3 oz) porridge oats
450 ml (¾ pint) skimmed or semi-skimmed milk
1 banana

**Snack**
2 slices toast with butter/low fat spread and Marmite
2 portions fresh fruit

**Lunch**
One-minute Burrito (see page 143)
Tomatoes, cucumber
2 cartons (300 g) low fat yoghurt

**Pre-workout snack**
2 cereal bars (low fat)

**Post-workout snack**
4 rice cakes
1 banana

**Dinner**
Chicken and Mushrooms with Pasta (see page 161)
1 wholemeal roll with butter/low fat spread
Crunchy Apple Crumble (see page 224)

*Optimal diet*

| | |
|---|---|
| Carbohydrate | 55–65% |
| Fat | 20–30% |
| Protein | 10–15% |

## Tip 1

Forget the myth that swimmers need extra body fat. Unless you are a very long distance swimmer (e.g. cross-Channel), a lower body fat percentage will improve your performance. Women should be below 25% and men should be below 15%.

## Tip 2

Swimming often enhances the appetite immediately following exercise. Refuel on high carbohydrate foods such as toast, sandwiches, jacket potatoes, bananas or breakfast cereal; avoid fatty foods (frequently on offer at swimming venues). Aim to consume 1 g carbohydrate/kg body weight within two hours of training.

### ◆ Swimmer's eating plan ◆

This eating plan provides approximately 3000 kcal per day. Increase or decrease the quantities according to your individual requirements (see above).

| Day 1 |
|---|
| **Breakfast**<br>75 g (3 oz) wheat or bran flakes<br>200 ml (⅓ pint) skimmed or semi-skimmed milk<br>25 g (1 oz) raisins<br><br>**Snack**<br>2 portions fresh fruit<br>2 slices toast with butter/low fat spread<br><br>**Lunch**<br>1 large jacket potato (300 g/11 oz) topped with half a large tin (210 g) baked beans<br>Mixed vegetable salad (see page 124) with 1 tbsp oil/vinegar dressing<br>1 portion fresh fruit<br>1 carton (150 g) low fat yoghurt<br><br>**Pre-workout snack**<br>600 ml (1 pint) isotonic sports drink (home-made or commercial) |

**Post-workout snack**
2 Oaty Fruit Bars (see page 217)

**Dinner**
75 g (3 oz) pasta (uncooked weight)
Quick Tuna and Sweetcorn Sauce (see page 154)
50 g (2 oz) grated cheese
Fruit Rice Pudding (see page 225)

## Day 2

**Breakfast**
4 thick slices wholemeal toast with a scraping of low fat spread and 4
heaped tsps fruit spread or honey
1 glass (175 ml/6 fl oz) fruit juice

**Snack**
2 Oatmeal Cookies (see page 220)

**Lunch**
Rice and Sweetcorn Salad (see page 116)
2 portions fresh fruit

**Pre-workout snack**
2 bananas
2 glasses water

**Post-workout snack**
Sandwich: 2 slices wholemeal bread with Marmite

**Dinner**
Quick Vegetable and Cheese Pizza (see page 214) made from 1 ready-
made pizza base (approx. 150–175 g/5–6 oz), 3 tbsps pasta sauce, finely
sliced onion, red and green peppers, sliced mushrooms, dried herbs, 50 g
(2 oz) grated Cheddar cheese or mozzarella. Bake in a hot oven, according to instructions on the packet
1 tin (225 g/8 oz) pineapple in juice
1 carton (150 g) low fat yoghurt

## Day 3

**Breakfast**
1 large bowl (100 g/4 oz) muesli
300 ml (½ pint) skimmed or semi-skimmed milk
1 chopped banana
50 g (2 oz) raisins

**Snack**
1 toasted bagel
1 portion fresh fruit

**Lunch**
2 sandwiches: 4 slices wholemeal bread with a little butter/low fat spread and 100 g (4 oz) tuna, tomato, watercress and 2 tbsps low fat salad dressing
2 cartons (300 g) low fat yoghurt

**Pre-workout snack**
4 rice cakes spread with 4 tsps fruit spread
2 glasses water

**Post-workout snack**
1 Muesli Bar (see page 216)
1 banana

**Dinner**
Mexican Rice (see page 132)
1 portion fresh fruit

## Aerobics

*Optimal diet*

| | |
|---|---|
| Carbohydrate | 60–65% |
| Fat | 20–25% |
| Protein | 10–20% |

### Tip 1

Plan your diet carefully so you eat at regular intervals (every 2–3 hours) and avoid leaving long gaps between meals. Take a supply of low fat snacks with you if you have to eat on the run, e.g. sandwiches, rolls, cereal and fruit bars, oatcakes, fresh fruit, popcorn, breadsticks, low fat yoghurt. If you teach or participate in back-to-back classes, have at least 500 ml of an isotonic drink in-between to maintain blood sugar levels and prevent dehydration.

### Tip 2

If your eating habits tend to be erratic, consider taking a multi-vitamin and mineral supplement to safeguard against deficient intakes.

### ◆ Aerobics eating plan ◆

This eating plan provides approximately 2500 kcal per day. Increase or decrease the quantities according to your individual requirements (see above).

| Day 1 |
|---|

**Breakfast**
1 medium bowl (50 g/2 oz) wholegrain breakfast cereal
150 ml (¼ pint) skimmed or semi-skimmed milk
1 chopped banana

**Snack**
2 portions fresh fruit

**Lunch**
A–Z Vegetable Soup (see page 110)
2 wholemeal rolls with a little butter/low fat spread
75 g (3 oz) cottage cheese or tuna
1 portion fresh fruit
1 carton (150 g) low fat yoghurt

**Pre-workout snack**
4 rice cakes with fruit spread

**Post-workout snack**
2 Fruit and Nut Bars (see page 218)

**Dinner**
75 g (3 oz) pasta (uncooked weight)
Tomato and Herb Sauce (see page 154)
Fruit Rice Pudding (see page 225)

| Day 2 |
|---|

**Breakfast**
3 thick slices wholemeal toast with a scraping of low fat spread and 2 heaped tsps fruit spread or honey
1 glass (175 ml/6 fl oz) fruit juice

**Snack**
1 Oatmeal Muffin (see page 236)
1 portion fresh fruit

**Lunch**
Bean Feast (see page 119)
2 thick slices bread with butter/low fat spread
2 portions fresh fruit

**Pre-workout snack**
1 banana

**Post-workout snack**
Pineapple Bagel (see page 193)

**Dinner**
Stir Fried Rice with Vegetables (see page 130)
1 tin (225 g/8 oz) pineapple in juice
1 carton (150 g) low fat yoghurt

---

### Day 3

**Breakfast**
Granola (see page 197)
200 ml (⅓ pint) skimmed or semi-skimmed milk
1 portion fresh fruit

**Snack**
1 slice of Banana Cake (see page 238)
1 portion fresh fruit

**Lunch**
2 sandwiches: 4 slices wholemeal bread with a little butter/low fat spread and 100 g (4 oz) tuna, tomato, watercress and 2 tbsps low fat salad dressing
1 carton (150 g) low fat fromage frais

**Pre-workout snack**
1 thick slice bread with honey or jam

**Post-workout snack**
1 Muesli Bar (see page 216)
1 banana

**Dinner**
Chicken Enchiladas or Spicy Bean Enchiladas (see pages 139–40)
1 medium (225 g/8 oz) jacket potato with yoghurt
Side salad with 1 tbsp oil/vinegar dressing
Hot Winter Fruit Salad or Cool Summer Fruit Salad (see page 226)

# 11

# Competition countdown

Your diet during the week before your competition will have a big effect on your performance, and could provide that edge to help you win. Your nutritional preparation will depend on the type of sport you participate in and the duration of the event. The following guide will help you perform at your best.

## Pre-competition

### The week before

You should aim to fully replenish your glycogen stores during the final week and keep well hydrated. Those competing in endurance events lasting longer than 90 minutes may benefit from carbohydrate loading which involves increasing glycogen levels higher than normal (see below). For shorter events, optimal glycogen levels can be achieved by tapering your training and consuming a high carbohydrate diet (60–70% energy) during the week. In practice, this means gradually increasing the amount of carbohydrate and reducing the amount of fat in your diet.

---

### Carbohydrate loading

Carbohydrate loading is useful for high-intensity endurance events lasting longer than 90 minutes. It is a technique used to increase glycogen above normal levels. The classical regime involves a three-day depletion phase (low carbohydrate diet/intense training) followed by a three-day loading phase (high carbohydrate diet/tapered training). However, this is often associated with side effects such as tiredness and irritability, so a modified regime, omitting the depletion phase, is now recommended. This simply involves tapered training and a high carbohydrate diet and can produce similar results.

---

- Practise your competition strategy in training.
- Gradually reduce the amount of training to decrease the use of muscle glycogen. Rest on the day prior to competition.
- Eat extra carbohydrate during the three days prior to competition. Aim to eat 7–10 g/kg body weight per day.
- Avoid high fat foods as they may lead to unwanted fat gain.
- If bloating or feeling overfull is a problem, reduce your fibre intake, choosing more refined cereals and simple carbohydrates, e.g. white bread instead of brown, fruit juice instead of fresh fruit, adding more sugar, jam or preserves to your meals.
- Sports drinks, glucose polymer drinks and liquid meals can help boost your carbohydrate intake without adding bulk.

## The day before

The day before the event you should rest or do minimal exercise. Eat a substantial high carbohydrate dinner to top up muscle glycogen stores. Stick to simple foods, such as pasta, potatoes and rice and keep the fat content of the meal to a minimum. Avoid alcohol as it is a diuretic.

## The pre-competition meal

Eat your pre-competition meal 2–4 hours before you are due to compete. The aims are to:

- ◆ top up liver glycogen levels
- ◆ maintain blood sugar levels
- ◆ stave off hunger
- ◆ maintain hydration.

If you are competing in the morning, eat a light high carbohydrate breakfast or snack. For afternoon events, eat a more substantial high carbohydrate breakfast followed by a light lunch. For evening events, eat a substantial high carbohydrate breakfast and lunch followed by a light snack approximately two hours prior to the event. Some athletes benefit from eating a snack containing approximately 25–50 g carbohydrate less than one hour before the event.

- Stick to familiar and easily digestible foods.
- Foods should be high in carbohydrate, low in fat and moderate in protein.
- Avoid salty or spicy foods; avoid added salt.
- Foods should be low or moderate in fibre.
- Don't overeat – eat a comfortable amount of food.
- Choose a liquid meal or sports drink if you cannot tolerate solid food.
- Drink fluids liberally – 250–500 ml two hours prior to competition.

## Suitable pre-competition meals

**Pre-competition breakfast**

One bowl of breakfast cereal (e.g. Cornflakes, Weetabix)
Low fat milk
Toast with jam or honey
Fresh fruit
Water

Toast, English muffins, pancakes or bagels with honey
Fruit juice and water

**Pre-competition lunch**

Pasta with tomato sauce
Bread or roll
Fruit juice
Water

Jacket potato (large) with low fat filling
Salad (no dressing)
Fresh fruit
Water

**Pre-competition snack**

Sandwich with low fat filling
Fruit or cereal snack bar

Low fat rice pudding
Fresh or tinned fruit

## Don't forget to drink!

Make sure you are well hydrated before the event. Your urine should be pale in colour and practically odourless. Consume 250–500 ml fluid two hours before the event followed by 125–250 ml immediately before the event. Choose water or an isotonic sports drink.

## During competition

Additional carbohydrate (30–60 g per hour) can benefit performance during high-intensity events lasting more than 90 minutes. You may be able to carry solid food or drinks with you (e.g. while cycling) or arrange pick up points. Suitable choices include:

- energy bars
- home-made snack bars
- sports drinks
- bananas

- dried fruit
- glucose tablets
- sweets/sugar confectionery.

## Between events/heats

If you compete in several events or heats during the day (e.g. track and field events, swimming heats, tennis tournaments, judo, gymnastics), small light snacks will help top up glycogen and blood sugar levels during your rest periods. Aim to eat little and often and avoid long gaps. Take a good supply of snacks and drinks with you, such as:

- sandwiches
- bread, bagels, buns
- fresh fruit
- low fat yoghurt, rice pudding, fromage frais
- home-made muffins (see pages 234–7)
- home-made snack bars and cookies (see pages 216–21)
- home-made cakes (see pages 238–44)
- rice cakes
- energy bars and fruit bars
- low fat crackers and biscuits (e.g. fig rolls)
- diluted squash or fruit juice
- sports drinks (home-made or commercial)
- water.

## Post-competition

To speed your recovery, refuel and rehydrate as soon as possible after your event. A light snack containing 1 g carbohydrate/kg eaten during the two-hour post-exercise period will promote muscle glycogen refuelling. Check the carbohydrate counter (see page 16) for suitable food portions. Choose high GI carbohydrates such as bananas, sandwiches and energy bars or, alternatively, a sports drink containing 4–8 g carbohydrate/100 ml. Drink at least 500 ml water or sports drink immediately after the event and continue drinking at regular intervals.

Your post-event meal should be high in carbohydrate and contain moderate amounts of fat and protein. Avoid rich and spicy foods as these may cause a stomach upset and delay refuelling.

---

**♦ *Suitable post-event meals* ♦**

- Thick crust pizza with vegetable topping.
- Jacket potato filled with beans, fish, chicken or cheese.
- Rice dishes such as risotto, rice salad.
- Pasta dishes (avoid creamy sauces).
- Low fat or vegetable lasagne (see page 161).
- Mega salads (see pages 115–20).

---

- The following six-day menu is based on the carbohydrate needs of an athlete weighing 70 kg. Days 1–3 provide approximately 7 g carbohydrate/kg; days 4–6 provide approximately 8–10 g carbohydrate/kg. Simply decrease or increase slightly the quantities according to your actual body weight.
- In addition to the foods listed, you should also include a minimum of 2 litres (4 pints) of fluid plus 1 litre (2 pints) for each hour of training. Each pre- and post-workout snack should be accompanied with 150–250 ml of water.
- Where one portion of fruit is indicated, check page 3 for portion sizes.

| Day 1 |
| --- |

**Breakfast**
1 large bowl (75 g/3 oz) wholegrain breakfast cereal
200 ml (⅓ pint) skimmed or semi-skimmed milk
50 g (2 oz) dried fruit
1 glass (200 ml/7 fl oz) fruit juice

**Snack**
2 slices bread with butter/low fat spread and Marmite
1 portion fresh fruit

**Lunch**
Potato and Leek Soup (see page 109)
1 wholemeal roll with butter/low fat spread
50 g (2oz) cottage cheese or ham
2 portions fresh fruit
1 carton (150 g/5 oz) low fat yoghurt

**Pre-workout snack**
50 g (2 oz) raisins or dates

**Post-workout snack**
2 Muesli Bars (see page 216)

**Dinner**
300 g (11 oz) jacket potato
100 g (4 oz) fromage frais or cottage cheese
Broccoli or other green vegetables
1 portion fresh fruit

**Snack**
2 slices toast with butter/low fat spread
1 glass (200 ml/7 fl oz) skimmed or semi-skimmed milk

## Day 2

**Breakfast**
3 Breakfast Pancakes (see page 195)
1 glass (200 ml/7 fl oz) skimmed or semi-skimmed milk

**Snack**
1 Date and Walnut Bar (see page 217)
1 banana

**Lunch**
2 sandwiches: 4 thick slices of bread with 75 g (3 oz) turkey or chicken
and 2 tbsps low calorie coleslaw
2 portions fresh fruit
1 carton (150 g/5 oz) low fat yoghurt

**Pre-workout snack**
400 ml (14 fl oz) isotonic sports drink (home-made or commercial)

**Post-workout snack**
2 Raisin Muffins (see page 234)

**Dinner**
100 g (4 oz) pasta (uncooked weight)
Quick Tuna and Sweetcorn Sauce (see page 154)
1 tbsp grated cheese
Fruit Rice Pudding (see page 225)

**Snack**
2 Fruit and Nut Bars (see page 218)

## Day 3

**Breakfast**
3 slices wholemeal toast with low fat spread
2 eggs (scrambled/boiled/poached)
1 glass (200 ml/7 fl oz) fruit juice

**Snack**
1 banana sandwich: 2 slices of bread with 1 sliced banana and a little
honey

**Lunch**
300 g (11 oz) jacket potato
100 g (4 oz) sweetcorn with peppers
2 spoonfuls plain yoghurt
2 portions fresh fruit
1 carton (150 g/5 oz) low fat fromage frais

**Pre-workout snack**
1 energy bar

**Post-workout snack**
2 Raisin Muffins (see page 234)

**Dinner**
Athlete's Hot Pasta with Vegetables (see page 150)
2 slices bread with butter/low fat spread
Hot Winter Fruit Salad or Cool Summer Salad (see page 226)

**Snack**
1 medium bowl (50 g/2 oz) breakfast cereal (any variety)
150 ml (¼ pint) skimmed or semi-skimmed milk

## Day 4

**Breakfast**
1 large bowl (100 g/4 oz) breakfast cereal (any variety)
250 ml (½ pint) skimmed or semi-skimmed milk
1 chopped banana
50 g (2 oz) raisins

**Snack**
1 large roll filled with 1 sliced banana and a little honey
250 ml (½ pint) isotonic sports drink

**Lunch**
2 Banana Hot Dogs (see page 203)
½ tin (200 g) low fat rice pudding
2 tbsps fruit spread or jam

**Pre-workout snack**
1 banana
25 g (1 oz) raisins

**Post-workout snack**
2 Oaty Fruit Bars (see page 217)

**Dinner**
Hawaiian Rice (see page 128)
150 ml (¼ pint) skimmed or semi-skimmed milk

**Snack**
4 rice cakes or low fat crackers
2 tbsps fruit spread or jam

## Day 5

**Breakfast**
4 thick slices toast with 8 heaped tsps fruit spread or honey
1 glass (175 ml/6 fl oz) fruit juice
1 banana

**Snack**
2 Oatmeal Cookies (see page 220)

**Lunch**
Rice and Sweetcorn Salad (see page 116)
2 thick slices bread
2 portions fresh fruit

**Pre-workout snack**
2 bananas

**Post-workout snack**
Sandwich: 2 slices of bread and 4 tbsps jam or fruit spread
1 glass (200 ml/7 fl oz) fruit juice

**Dinner**
Pizza with extra vegetable toppings (2 portions – see page 212)
Banana Bread Pudding (see page 227)
1 glass (200 ml/7 fl oz) fruit juice

## Day 6

**Breakfast**
4 Breakfast Muffins (see page 194) or 3 English muffins
4 tbsps fruit spread or honey
2 bananas

**Snack**
1 toasted bagel with 1 tbsp fruit spread or honey
1 portion fresh fruit

**Lunch**
Athlete's Cold Pasta Salad (see page 115)
2 thick slices bread
1 portion fresh fruit
1 carton (150 g/5 oz) low fat yoghurt

**Pre-workout snack**
4 rice cakes spread with 4 tsps fruit spread

**Post-workout snack**
2 Muesli Bars (see page 216)
1 banana

**Dinner**
Vegetable Paella (see page 126)
2 slices bread
2 portions tinned fruit (e.g. peaches, pineapple, apricots)

**Snack**
1 medium bowl (50 g/2 oz) breakfast cereal
150 ml (¼ pint) skimmed or semi-skimmed milk

| Day 7 (competition day) |
| --- |

**Breakfast**
1 large bowl (75 g/3 oz) breakfast cereal
200 ml (⅓ pint) skimmed milk
1 banana
50 g (2 oz) raisins

**Pre-race snack (optional)**
1 banana or 250 ml (½ pint) isotonic sports drink

**Race snacks (if appropriate – see page 100)**
Energy bars
250–600 ml (½–1 pint) isotonic sports drinks (quantity depends on duration of event)
25–75 g (1–3 oz) dried fruit

**Post-race snack**
3 Fruit Cookies (see page 220)
250–600 ml (½–1 pint) isotonic sports drink

# Part II  Recipes

## Notes on the recipes

All the following recipes have been developed in line with the nutritional recommendations for athletes. They are high in carbohydrate, low in fat and provide a good variety of vitamins and minerals. They have been specifically designed to be quick and easy to prepare, making use of basic, nutritious ingredients and simple preparation methods. Menu plans, which include the recipes, are given throughout the previous chapters.

### Nutritional analysis

The nutritional analysis provides a breakdown of the calorie, protein, fat, carbohydrate and non-starch polysaccharide (fibre) content per serving. The nutrient values are derived from McCance & Widdowson's *Composition of Foods* (HMSO) and, where appropriate, manufacturer's own data. Figures have been rounded to the nearest whole number.

### Portion sizes

Most of the recipes make four generous-sized servings. Athletes with particularly high calorie and nutritional requirements may increase the quantities accordingly or eat two portions. You may halve or double the quantities if you wish to serve fewer or more people; alternatively, freeze any remaining portions so you always have a ready-made quantity on stand-by.

### Optional ingredients and variations

In many cases you have the choice of sticking to the basic recipe or adding additional ingredients. There are suggestions for substitutions and variations so you are able to adapt any particular recipe to your individual preferences. Experiment as you go along and feel free to add any of your own favourite ingredients.

CHAPTER

# 12

# Soups

Many people think of soup as a starter, but with the right ingredients it can be transformed into a substantial main meal. Add simple foods such as potatoes, grains, vegetables and beans and you have a nutritionally complete meal. It is also a superb way to use up any leftovers. Boil some stock or open a tin of ready-made soup, then simply add whatever meat or vegetable ingredients you have handy. Even preparing a soup from fresh ingredients takes less than 10 minutes. There is no need to serve anything else except some fresh, crusty (preferably wholemeal) bread.

## Soup savvy

Make a large quantity of soup – enough for more than one meal.

(1) Fry an onion in a little olive oil. Then add any of the following ingredients.

- Root vegetable soup: any combination of chopped carrots, swede, turnips, parsnips.
- Chicken soup: chopped chicken, sweetcorn, herbs and milk.
- Minestrone: tinned tomatoes, chopped carrots, frozen peas, baked beans and dried pasta shells.
- Vegetable soup: any chopped fresh or leftover vegetables or frozen vegetables, e.g. peas, carrots, cauliflower, green beans.
- Potato soup: sliced potato and paprika.
- Lentil soup: red lentils and any variety of vegetables.

(2) Add liquid and bring to the boil. Choose from the following:

- 1 tbsp vegetable stock concentrate dissolved in 600 ml (1 pt) water
- 1 vegetable/chicken/beef stock cube dissolved in 600 ml (1 pt) water
- a mixture of milk and water
- 1 tin of ready-made soup (dilute with extra water if necessary)
- 1 packet of soup made up with water.

(3) Cover the saucepan and simmer until the vegetables or meat are cooked.

(4) Get ready to serve.

- For a smooth soup, liquidise the soup in a blender.
- For a thick soup, blend half the soup in a blender and return to the pan.
- For a chunky soup, serve straight from the saucepan.

## Potato and Leek Soup

*Makes 4 servings*

### Ingredients

3 medium potatoes, scrubbed
and chopped into chunks
3 large leeks, chopped
1 large carrot, chopped
1 vegetable stock cube
450 ml (¾ pt) water
600 ml (1 pt) skimmed milk
Handful of chopped fresh herbs,
e.g. parsley, basil, thyme (optional)

### Method

(1) Place all of the ingredients except the milk in a large saucepan. Bring to the boil and simmer for approximately 20 minutes, or until the vegetables are soft.
(2) Remove from the heat, add the milk and liquidise (use a blender, food processor or a hand blender).
(3) Return to the saucepan, add some freshly ground black pepper and any fresh herbs. Heat through until just hot.

### Nutritional analysis

| Per serving | | % energy |
|---|---|---|
| Energy | 152 kcal | |
| Protein | 8.4 g | 22% |
| Fat | 0.7 g | 4% |
| Carbohydrate | 30 g | 74% |
| Fibre | 3.1 g | |

## 'Cream' of Tomato Soup

Although no cream is used in this recipe, a thick, creamy consistency is achieved by using potato and skimmed milk.

*Makes 4 servings*

### Ingredients

1 tbsp butter or oil
1 onion, chopped
1 large potato, chopped
2 garlic cloves, crushed
¼ tsp each of dried basil, thyme
and dill
Salt and freshly ground
black pepper
600 ml (1 pt) passata (smooth
sieved tomatoes)
1 tsp sugar
350 ml (12 fl oz) skimmed milk

### Method

(1) Heat the butter or oil in a large saucepan. Cook the onion, potato, garlic and herbs for 5 minutes.
(2) Add the seasoning, passata and sugar. Simmer for approximately 20 minutes, or until the potatoes are soft. Liquidise the soup.
(3) Add the milk and heat through until just hot.

### Nutritional analysis

| Per serving | | % energy |
|---|---|---|
| Energy | 110 kcal | |
| Protein | 5.3 g | 20 % |
| Fat | 2.4 g | 20% |
| Carbohydrate | 18 g | 60% |
| Fibre | 1.8 g | |

## A–Z Vegetable Soup

*Makes 4 servings*

### Ingredients

1 onion, chopped
1 garlic clove, crushed
1 l (1¾ pts) vegetable stock (or
water plus 2 vegetable stock cubes)
750 g (1½ lb) vegetables of your
choice (see below)
Freshly ground black pepper
1 tsp dried mixed herbs

### Method

(1) Place the onion, garlic and a little stock in a
large saucepan and cook for 5 minutes.
(2) Add the remaining stock, vegetables, seasoning and herbs. Bring to the boil and simmer for
approximately 20 minutes, or until the vegetables
are soft.
(3) Decide on your preferred consistency of soup
(see page 108) and liquidise accordingly.

A–Z Vegetables: chopped potato, sliced courgettes, sliced carrots, diced pumpkin,
chopped green beans, frozen peas, broccoli florets, cauliflower florets.

### Nutritional analysis

| *Per serving* | | *% energy* |
|---|---|---|
| Energy | 71 kcal | |
| Protein | 3.5 g | 20% |
| Fat | 0.8 g | 10% |
| Carbohydrate | 13 g | 70% |
| Fibre | 3.6 g | |

## Minestrone Soup

*Makes 4 servings*

### Ingredients

1 onion, chopped
2 garlic cloves, crushed
1 l (2 pts) vegetable stock
2 carrots, chopped
225 g (8 oz) other vegetables of
choice, e.g. courgettes, peas, green
beans
2 tsps dried basil
1 tin (400 g) haricot beans
100 g (4 oz) small pasta shapes
600 ml (1 pt) passata (smooth
sieved tomatoes) or tinned
chopped tomatoes

### Method

(1) Boil the onions and garlic in a little of the
vegetable stock for 5 minutes.
(2) Add the vegetables, herbs and remaining stock
and simmer for 10 minutes.
(3) Add the beans, pasta and passata and continue
to cook for a further 10 minutes.

### Nutritional analysis

| *Per serving* | | *% energy* |
|---|---|---|
| Energy | 225 kcal | |
| Protein | 12 g | 21% |
| Fat | 1.5 g | 6% |
| Carbohydrate | 44 g | 73% |
| Fibre | 9.2 g | |

## Broccoli and Bean Soup

This sounds like an unusual combination, but it works really well. The mild-flavoured fla-geolet beans and potato give the soup a creamy texture, while broccoli is one of the most nutritious vegetables, full of vitamin C, iron, folic acid and cancer-fighting phytochemicals.

*Makes 4 servings*

### Ingredients

4 spring onions, sliced
1 garlic clove, crushed
2 tsps mild curry powder
1½ l (3 pts) vegetable stock
1 medium potato, chopped
450 g (1 lb) broccoli florets
1 tin (420 g) flageolet beans, drained

### Method

(1) Place the onions, garlic and curry powder in a saucepan with 150 ml of the stock. Bring to the boil and simmer for about 5 minutes.
(2) Add the remaining stock, the potato and broccoli and simmer for 15–20 minutes.
(3) Add the beans, then purée the soup (in small batches if necessary).

### Nutritional analysis

| Per serving | | % energy |
|---|---|---|
| Energy | 228 kcal | |
| Protein | 12 g | 20% |
| Fat | 1.4 g | 6% |
| Carbohydrate | 45 g | 74% |
| Fibre | 8 g | |

## Pea and Potato Soup

This simple soup makes a nutritionally complete meal – it is rich in protein, fibre, vita-min C and complex carbohydrate.

*Makes 4 servings*

### Ingredients

1 onion, chopped
2 large potatoes, cubed
1 tbsp oil
1½ l (3 pts) vegetable stock
450 g (1 lb) frozen peas
Handful of fresh herbs, e.g. mint and parsley
Freshly ground black pepper

### Method

(1) Sauté the onion and potato in the oil for 5 minutes.
(2) Add the stock and bring to the boil. Simmer for 5 minutes.
(3) Add the peas and continue cooking for a further 5 minutes.
(4) Stir in the fresh herbs and season with pepper to taste.

### Nutritional analysis

| Per serving | | % energy |
|---|---|---|
| Energy | 141 kcal | |
| Protein | 10 g | 29% |
| Fat | 1.7 g | 11% |
| Carbohydrate | 23 g | 60% |
| Fibre | 9.2 g | |

## Lentil and Vegetable Soup

*Makes 4 servings*

### Ingredients

225 g (8 oz) red lentils
1½ l (3 pts) vegetable stock
2 carrots, sliced
1 onion, chopped
2 potatoes, diced
Salt and freshly ground
black pepper
Swede/turnips/parsnips/
courgettes/cauliflower/
celery/leek (optional)

### Method

(1) Place the lentils in a large saucepan with the vegetable stock and boil for 10 minutes. Alternatively, cook in a pressure cooker for 3 minutes then release the steam.
(2) Add the vegetables, bring back to the boil and simmer for a further 15–20 minutes until the vegetables and lentils are soft (or cook in the pressure cooker for a further 3 minutes).
(3) Season with salt and pepper.

### Nutritional analysis

| *Per serving* | | *% energy* |
|---|---|---|
| Energy | 195 kcal | |
| Protein | 14 g | 28% |
| Fat | 0.9 g | 4% |
| Carbohydrate | 35 g | 68% |
| Fibre | 3.7 g | |

## Corn Chowder

*Makes 4 servings*

### Ingredients

1 onion, chopped
2 tsps oil
2 potatoes, diced
600 ml (1 pt) water or stock
600 ml (1 pt) skimmed milk
1 large tin (420 g) cream-style corn
Salt and freshly ground
black pepper

### Method

(1) Sauté the onion in the oil for 5 minutes.
(2) Add the potatoes and the water or stock. Bring to the boil and cook for 10 minutes.
(3) Add the remaining ingredients and simmer for a further 10 minutes, stirring occasionally. Season with salt and pepper to taste.

### Nutritional analysis

| *Per serving* | | *% energy* |
|---|---|---|
| Energy | 257 kcal | |
| Protein | 9.8 g | 15% |
| Fat | 3.6 g | 13% |
| Carbohydrate | 50 g | 72% |
| Fibre | 2.7 g | |

## Pasta and Bean Soup

This hearty, high carbohydrate soup is also rich in protein, vitamins and potassium, and is very low in fat.

*Makes 4 servings*

### Ingredients

1 large onion, chopped
2 celery stalks, chopped
1 tsp paprika
1 tin (400 g) chopped tomatoes
1 l (2 pts) vegetable stock
100 g (4 oz) pasta shapes
1 tin (420 g) cannelini or haricot beans, drained
Salt and freshly ground black pepper
1–2 chopped carrots/100 g (4 oz) chopped cabbage (optional)

### Method

(1) Place the onion, celery, paprika, tomatoes and stock in a large saucepan. Bring to the boil and simmer for 10 minutes until the vegetables are soft.
(2) Add the pasta and beans and cook for a further 7–10 minutes. Add any additional vegetables at this stage.
(3) Season to taste with salt and pepper.

### Nutritional analysis

| Per serving | | % energy |
|---|---|---|
| Energy | 218 kcal | |
| Protein | 11 g | 20% |
| Fat | 1.2 g | 5% |
| Carbohydrate | 44 g | 75% |
| Fibre | 7.5 g | |

## Cauliflower Cheese Soup

*Makes 4 servings*

### Ingredients

1 onion, chopped
1 head of cauliflower, cut into florets
600 ml (1 pt) vegetable stock
600 ml (1 pt) skimmed milk
Salt and freshly ground black pepper
50 g (2 oz) mature Cheddar cheese, grated
2 tbsps grated parmesan (optional)

### Method

(1) Place the onion, cauliflower and vegetable stock in a saucepan. Bring to the boil and simmer for about 15 minutes until the vegetables are soft.
(2) Purée the soup in a blender or food processor until smooth.
(3) Return to the saucepan with the milk. Season to taste and heat until just boiling.
(4) Stir in the cheese until it melts.
(5) Sprinkle with parmesan to serve (if applicable).

### Nutritional analysis

| Per serving | | % energy |
|---|---|---|
| Energy | 151 kcal | |
| Protein | 13 g | 33% |
| Fat | 6.2 g | 37% |
| Carbohydrate | 12 g | 30% |
| Fibre | 2 g | |

## Baked Bean and Vegetable Soup

*Makes 4 servings*

### Ingredients

1 tbsp oil
1 onion, chopped
1 celery stick, chopped
2 carrots, sliced
1 clove garlic, crushed
1 turnip, chopped
1 tin (420 g) baked beans
75 g (3 oz) frozen green beans or peas
600 ml (1 pt) vegetable stock
2 tbsps parsley, chopped

### Method

(1) Heat the oil in a large saucepan, add the onion and fry until softened.
(2) Add the celery, carrots, garlic and turnip. Cover and cook for 5 minutes.
(3) Add the baked beans, green beans and stock. Cover and simmer for 10 minutes until the vegetables are tender.
(4) Stir in the parsley. Serve with crusty white bread, French bread or ciabatta bread.

### Nutritional analysis

| *Per serving* | | *% energy* |
|---|---|---|
| Energy | 142 kcal | |
| Protein | 6.1 g | 17% |
| Fat | 3.7 g | 23% |
| Carbohydrate | 23 g | 60% |
| Fibre | 6.9 g | |

## Chicken and Mushroom Soup

*Makes 4 servings*

### Ingredients

1 l (2 pts) chicken stock
175 g (6 oz) lean cooked chicken, skinned and chopped
100 g (4 oz) mushrooms, sliced
100 g (4 oz) small pasta shapes
½ tsp dried mixed herbs
Freshly ground black pepper

### Method

(1) Put the stock in a large saucepan. Bring to the boil.
(2) Add the mushrooms, chicken and pasta. Stir well and add the herbs. Cover the pan and simmer for about 5 minutes.
(3) Season with the black pepper and serve with baps or rolls.

### Nutritional analysis

| *Per serving* | | *% energy* |
|---|---|---|
| Energy | 184 kcal | |
| Protein | 17 g | 38% |
| Fat | 2.9 g | 14% |
| Carbohydrate | 24 g | 48% |
| Fibre | 1.3 g | |

114

# 13

# Salads and dressings

Simple salads seem slightly jaded when you've got a hearty appetite and high carbohydrate needs to fulfill. These mega salads, however, have been made into substantial main meals by teaming up the vegetables with high carbohydrate foods such as pasta, rice, grains or pulses.

◆ Prepare a larger quantity of salad than necessary and keep the remainder in the fridge for up to three days.
◆ Take individual portions in a plastic box for portable meals.
◆ Combine with one of the dressings on pages 121–3 just before serving.

## Athlete's Cold Pasta Salad

This basic recipe can be infinitely varied according to the vegetables you have available. Cold, leftover, cooked vegetables, e.g. carrots, broccoli and peas, are also suitable.

*Makes 4 servings*

**Ingredients**

350 g (12 oz) pasta shapes of your choice
4 large tomatoes, chopped
Vegetables of your choice, e.g. spring onions, peppers, broccoli, celery, radishes
One of the following: 225 g (8 oz) chopped cooked turkey or chicken; 225 g (8 oz) tinned tuna or flaked cooked white fish; 400 g (14 oz) tin red kidney beans
4 tbsps dressing of your choice (optional)

**Method**

(1) Cook the pasta according to the directions on the packet. Drain and rinse with cold water.
(2) Combine the drained pasta with the tomatoes, vegetables and your choice of protein food.
(3) Combine with the dressing, if applicable.

**Nutritional analysis**

| *Per serving* | | *% energy* |
|---|---|---|
| Energy | 411 kcal | |
| Protein | 27 g | 26% |
| Fat | 3.6 g | 8% |
| Carbohydrate | 73 g | 66% |
| Fibre | 7.1 g | |

## Rice and Sweetcorn Salad

*Makes 4 servings*

### Ingredients

350 g (12 oz) rice
4 spring onions, chopped
2 red peppers, chopped
100 g (4 oz)  sultanas
50 g (2 oz)  split almonds, roughly
chopped
225 g (8 oz) sweetcorn

### Method

(1) Cook the rice according to the directions on the packet. Drain if necessary, rinse in cold water, and drain again.
(2) Place in a large bowl and combine with the remaining ingredients.

### Nutritional analysis

| Per serving | | % energy |
|---|---|---|
| Energy | 612 kcal | |
| Protein | 13 g | 9% |
| Fat | 13 g | 19% |
| Carbohydrate | 119 g | 72% |
| Fibre | 4.4 g | |

## Quick Supper Salad

*Makes 4 servings*

### Ingredients

1 tin (420 g) pinto beans (or any other variety)
100 g (4 oz) beansprouts
2 beef tomatoes, chopped
2 sticks celery, sliced
2 tbsps chopped fresh parsley
400 g (14 oz) tinned tuna/2 tbsps
sunflower seeds (optional)

### Method

(1) Drain and rinse the beans. Combine with the vegetables and parsley.
(2) Scatter the tuna or sunflower seeds over the top if applicable. Serve with crusty bread.

### Nutritional analysis

| Per serving | | % energy |
|---|---|---|
| Energy | 99 kcal | |
| Protein | 6.8 g | 27% |
| Fat | 0.9 g | 8% |
| Carbohydrate | 17 g | 65% |
| Fibre | 6.2 g | |

# New Potato Salad

*Makes 4 servings*

## Ingredients

900 g (2 lb) new potatoes, washed
4 spring onions, chopped
Handful of fresh herbs: mint, dill,
parsley
2 tbsps natural yoghurt
2 tbsps salad cream or reduced fat
mayonnaise
225 g (8 oz) baby spinach
leaves/100 g (4 oz) chopped
cooked ham/4 chopped hard
boiled eggs (all optional)

## Method

(1) Cook the potatoes in boiling water until tender. Drain, and halve any large potatoes.
(2) Combine the onions, herbs, yoghurt and salad cream or mayonnaise in a large bowl.
(3) Mix with the potatoes. Add any optional ingredients.

## Nutritional analysis

| Per serving | | % energy |
| --- | --- | --- |
| Energy | 199 kcal | |
| Protein | 4.4 g | 9% |
| Fat | 2.6 g | 12% |
| Carbohydrate | 42 g | 79% |
| Fibre | 2.6 g | |

# Spicy Bulgar Wheat Salad

*Makes 4 servings*

## Ingredients

225 g (8 oz) bulgar wheat
1.2 l (2 pts) boiling water
1 tbsp olive oil
2 tbsps lemon juice
4 spring onions, chopped
2 tsps curry powder
4 tomatoes, chopped
1 tsp each of fresh chopped mint
and parsley
Salt and freshly ground
black pepper
50 g (2 oz) raisins/50 g (2 oz)
cashew nuts/4 chopped hard
boiled eggs/100 g (4 oz) chopped
cooked chicken (all optional)

## Method

(1) Place the bulgar wheat in a large bowl and pour on the boiling water. Leave for 30 minutes, then drain.
(2) Mix together the olive oil, lemon juice and curry powder. Combine with the bulgar wheat.
(3) Add the remaining ingredients and mix together.

## Nutritional analysis

| Per serving | | % energy |
| --- | --- | --- |
| Energy | 246 kcal | |
| Protein | 6.4 g | 10% |
| Fat | 4.2 g | 15% |
| Carbohydrate | 47 g | 75% |
| Fibre | 1.5 g | |

## Brown Rice and Bean Salad

*Makes 4 servings*

### Ingredients

175 g (6 oz) brown rice
1 tin (420 g) red kidney beans
1 red pepper, chopped
2 celery sticks, chopped
4 spring onions, chopped
3 tbsps parsley, chopped
Salt and freshly ground
black pepper
Dash of soya sauce
50 g (2 oz) cashew nuts or
walnuts/100 g (4 oz) flaked tinned
tuna/chopped tomatoes/cooked
peas (all optional)

### Method

(1) Cook the rice in boiling water for 30–40 minutes until tender. Drain and rinse in cold water.
(2) Put the rice in a bowl and combine with the remaining ingredients.

### Nutritional analysis

| Per serving | | % energy |
|---|---|---|
| Energy | 249 kcal | |
| Protein | 8.9 g | 14% |
| Fat | 2 g | 7% |
| Carbohydrate | 52 g | 79% |
| Fibre | 6.7 g | |

## Three Grain Salad

*Makes 4 servings*

### Ingredients

100 g (4 oz) brown rice
100 g (4 oz) pearl barley
50 g (2 oz) cous cous
225 g (8 oz) sweetcorn
4 tomatoes, chopped
Red or green pepper/spring
onions/courgettes/carrot (all
optional)

### Method

(1) Cover the rice in plenty of boiling water and cook for 10 minutes. Add the barley and continue to cook for a further 20 minutes. Finally, add the cous cous and cook for another 5 minutes. Add more water if necessary. Drain and rinse briefly in cold water.
(2) Mix the grains together in a bowl and combine with the sweetcorn, tomatoes and any optional ingredients.

### Nutritional analysis

| Per serving | | % energy |
|---|---|---|
| Energy | 375 kcal | |
| Protein | 8.5 g | 9% |
| Fat | 2.6 g | 6% |
| Carbohydrate | 85 g | 85% |
| Fibre | 2.2 g | |

## Bean Feast

*Makes 4 servings*

### Ingredients

225 g (8 oz) green beans, cut into
5 cm (2 in) lengths
2 tins (2 x 420 g) mixed beans
1 tbsp olive oil
2 tbsps white wine vinegar
100 g (4 oz) baby spinach leaves

### Method

(1) Boil or steam the green beans for approximately 4 minutes or until just tender. Refresh in cold water and drain.
(2) Mix together the green beans, tinned beans, olive oil and vinegar.
(3) Place the spinach leaves in the bottom of the serving bowl and pile the bean mixture on top.

### Nutritional analysis

| *Per serving* | | *% energy* |
|---|---|---|
| Energy | 200 kcal | |
| Protein | 12 g | 25% |
| Fat | 5.3 g | 24% |
| Carbohydrate | 28 g | 51% |
| Fibre | 10 g | |

## Bean and Tuna Salad

*Makes 4 servings*

### Ingredients

2 tins (2 x 420 g) cannelini or butter beans, drained
2 celery sticks, chopped
200 g (7 oz) tinned tuna
100 g (4 oz) green beans, cooked
2 tbsps red wine vinegar
1 tbsp olive oil
Handful of fresh herbs: chives, parsley

### Method

(1) Combine the beans, celery, tuna and green beans in a bowl.
(2) Mix together the vinegar, oil and herbs and combine with the salad.

### Nutritional analysis

| *Per serving* | | *% energy* |
|---|---|---|
| Energy | 195 kcal | |
| Protein | 20 g | 40% |
| Fat | 4.2 g | 20% |
| Carbohydrate | 21 g | 40% |
| Fibre | 7.8 g | |

# Oriental Chicken Noodle Salad

*Makes 4 servings*

## Ingredients

3 tbsps soy sauce
2 garlic cloves, crushed
1 tbsp oil (preferably sesame)
300 g (11 oz) chicken fillet, cut
into strips
350 g (12 oz) noodles
400 g (14 oz) mange tout
225 g (8 oz) beansprouts
200 g (7 oz) Chinese leaves,
chopped
225 g (8 oz) carrots, grated
Lemon juice

## Method

(1) Combine the soy sauce, garlic cloves and oil in a bowl. Add the chicken, stir to coat, and leave to marinate in the fridge for 1 hour or longer.
(2) Cook the noodles according to the directions on the packet. Drain.
(3) In a large bowl, combine the noodles, mange tout, beansprouts, carrots and Chinese leaves.
(4) Dry fry the chicken in a non-stick pan until cooked through. Toss in the salad and season with the lemon juice.

## Nutritional analysis

| Per serving | | % energy |
|---|---|---|
| Energy | 539 kcal | |
| Protein | 32 g | 24% |
| Fat | 12 g | 20% |
| Carbohydrate | 81 g | 56% |
| Fibre | 6.7 g | |

## Dress up a salad

A tasty dressing transforms a salad or plate of vegetables into something special. Unfortunately, traditional salad dressings are based around oil or mayonnaise and are therefore loaded with fat, e.g. 1 tbsp of mayonnaise contains 12 g fat and 100 kcal; 1 tbsp of French dressing contains 9 g fat and 80 kcal. Here are some low fat alternatives:

- a drizzle of balsamic vinegar or flavoured vinegar, e.g. raspberry, rosemary, basil, garlic
- a squeeze of lime or lemon juice
- low fat fromage frais mixed with a little mint sauce
- plain yoghurt mixed with lemon juice
- fromage frais with a little wholegrain mustard
- equal quantities of pesto and yoghurt
- low fat salad dressing or mayonnaise mixed with curry powder.

## Garlic and Herb Dressing

### Ingredients

50 ml (2 fl oz) red wine vinegar
2 tbsps orange juice
1 tbsp extra virgin olive oil
1 crushed garlic clove
1 tbsp chopped fresh parsley
1 tbsp chopped fresh tarragon

### Method

(1) Place the ingredients in a screw-top jar and shake well to combine.

*Serving suggestions:* as a dressing for lettuce and other green salads; on coleslaw, with avocado; with steamed green vegetables such as broccoli and green beans.

### Nutritional analysis

| *Per serving (¼ recipe)* | | *% energy* |
|---|---|---|
| Energy | 30 kcal | |
| Protein | 0.2 g | 3% |
| Fat | 2.8 g | 85% |
| Carbohydrate | 0.8 g | 12% |
| Fibre | 0.1 g | |

# Italian Dressing

## Ingredients

50 ml (2 fl oz) balsamic vinegar
2 tbsps water
2 tsps olive oil
2 tsps capers
1 tbsp chopped fresh oregano or
1 tsp dried
Pinch of salt

## Method

(1) Place the ingredients in a screw-top jar and shake well to combine.

*Serving suggestions:* as a dressing for leafy salads, tomatoes, raw or roasted peppers; with steamed asparagus; on cold pasta salads.

## Nutritional analysis

| *Per serving (¼ recipe)* | | *% energy* |
|---|---|---|
| Energy | 22 kcal | |
| Protein | 0.2 g | 3% |
| Fat | 2.1 g | 86% |
| Carbohydrate | 0.7 g | 11% |
| Fibre | 0 g | |

# Tangy Yoghurt Dressing

## Ingredients

2 fl oz plain yoghurt
2 tbsps orange juice
1 tbsp honey
2 tsps Dijon mustard
¼ tsp ground ginger

## Method

(1) Thoroughly combine all the ingredients together in a bowl.

*Serving suggestions:* as a dressing for potato salad or coleslaw; as a dip for raw vegetable crudités.

## Nutritional analysis

| *Per serving (¼ recipe)* | | *% energy* |
|---|---|---|
| Energy | 22 kcal | |
| Protein | 0.8 g | 15% |
| Fat | 0.1 g | 5% |
| Carbohydrate | 4.7 g | 80% |
| Fibre | 0 g | |

# Cucumber and Lime Dressing

**Ingredients**

200 g (7 fl oz) low fat plain yoghurt
1 tsp white wine vinegar
1 tsp lime juice
1 tsp lime zest
1 small cucumber, seeded and
finely chopped

**Method**

(1) Thoroughly combine all the ingredients
together in a bowl.

*Serving suggestions:* as a dressing for potato salad, coleslaw or pasta salad; as a dip for raw vegetable crudités.

**Nutritional analysis**

| *Per serving (¼ recipe)* | | *% energy* |
|---|---|---|
| Energy | 31 kcal | |
| Protein | 2.8 g | 36% |
| Fat | 0.4 g | 13% |
| Carbohydrate | 4.2 g | 51% |
| Fibre | 0.2 g | |

# Spicy Dressing

**Ingredients**

2 tbsps reduced fat mayonnaise
2 tbsps plain low fat yoghurt
Few drops of chilli sauce
(or to taste)
Chopped fresh coriander (optional)

**Method**

(1) Thoroughly combine all the ingredients
together in a bowl.

*Serving suggestions:* as a dressing for chunky vegetable salads; to accompany your favourite sandwich fillings.

**Nutritional analysis**

| *Per serving (¼ recipe)* | | *% energy* |
|---|---|---|
| Energy | 52 kcal | |
| Protein | 0.9 g | 7% |
| Fat | 4.3 g | 76% |
| Carbohydrate | 2.4 g | 17% |
| Fibre | 0 g | |

# Twenty quick and easy vegetable salads

Vegetable salads are simple to make, need no cooking, and are bursting with vitamins, minerals, and antioxidant nutrients. Adjust the quantities of the ingredients according to what you have available and to your own preferences. Toss in one of the dressings listed above and serve with some bread or baked potatoes.

1. Baby spinach, watercress, fresh herbs and radicchio.
2. Lambs lettuce, rocket and endive.
3. Cucumber, tomatoes, olives, spring onions, cubed feta cheese.
4. Lightly cooked broccoli florets, mange tout, mixed lettuce leaves, flaked tuna and strips of red and yellow peppers.
5. Grated carrot, cucumber, raisins and walnuts.
6. Bean sprouts, red pepper, celery, parsley, spring onions, chives.
7. Mixed salad leaves, avocado, steamed green beans, chopped walnuts.
8. Shredded cabbage, desiccated coconut, chopped pineapple and grapes.
9. Chicory, orange segments and dates.
10. Cooked pasta, tomato, peppers, red kidney beans.
11. Cooked rice, sweetcorn, cucumber, mushrooms and flaked tuna.
12. Mixed tinned beans (e.g. red kidney beans, borlotti, chick peas), celery and fresh herbs.
13. Tomatoes, spring onions, cucumber, fresh mint and parsley.
14. Fennel, watercress, orange segments and fresh parsley.
15. Avocado, orange segments, chicory, pine nuts.
16. Curly endive, watercress, avocado and sesame seeds.
17. Courgettes, celery, green pepper, spring onions and grapes.
18. Beansprouts, grated carrot, shredded coconut, dates.
19. Cauliflower, watercress, sesame seeds.
20. Sautéed aubergine slices, plain yoghurt, garlic, fresh parsley.

# Rice and other grains

Rice is a staple of the Asian, Far Eastern and Mediterranean diet, which are among the healthiest in the world. It is high in carbohydrates, and brown rice contains small amounts of B vitamins and fibre (white rice contains very little), making it an ideal fuel for athletes. The following recipes should inspire you to make rice a regular part of your diet too.

## Ten ways to make rice more interesting

1. Add a handful of raisins or currants to the rice half way through cooking.
2. Cook the rice in chicken or vegetable stock instead of water.
3. Stir a handful of chopped fresh herbs (e.g. parsley, basil, dill, oregano) into the cooked rice.
4. Add the grated rind and juice of a lime, lemon or orange to cooked rice.
5. Cook the rice with a tablespoon of curry powder or turmeric.
6. Add some frozen mixed vegetables or peas during the last five minutes of cooking.
7. Add some soya sauce to the cooked rice.
8. Cook the rice with a little paprika and chilli powder.
9. Stir a little French dressing (low fat if you prefer) into cold cooked rice.
10. Add a handful of toasted chopped nuts (e.g. almonds, peanuts) or seeds (e.g. sunflower, pumpkin).

## Cooking rice

Allow about 75 g (3 oz)/half a cup of rice per average portion. There are two basic ways to cook rice:

### 1. The absorption method

A measured quantity of rice is cooked with a measured quantity of cold water in a covered saucepan until all of the liquid has been absorbed. Do not stir until the end of the cooking time, then fluff up the rice with a fork. The quantity of water and cooking time depends on the variety of rice.

**Easy cook rice:**
1 part rice to 2 parts water.
Cooking time 18–20 minutes.

**Basmati rice:**
1 part rice to 1½ parts water.
Cooking time 12 minutes.

**Brown rice:**
1 part rice to 2 parts water.
Cooking time 35–45 minutes.

**Risotto or arborio rice:**
1 part rice to 3 parts water.
Cooking time 20–25 minutes.

### 2. The boiling method

Add enough boiling water to the rice to cover it by at least 2½ cm (1 in). Cover and simmer until tender, adding extra water if necessary to keep the rice very moist. At the end of cooking drain the surplus water.

## Chicken Paella

*Makes 4 servings*

### Ingredients

2 chicken breast fillets, skinned and cut into strips
1 tsp oil
350 g (12 oz) white rice
Pinch of turmeric
1½ l (2½ pts) chicken stock
8 large uncooked prawns
175 g (6 oz) frozen peas

### Method

(1) Heat the oil in a heavy-based saucepan. Stir fry the chicken for 1 minute, just enough to crisp the outside.
(2) Add the rice, turmeric and stock, bring to the boil and simmer for 12 minutes until most of the liquid has been absorbed.
(3) Add the prawns and peas and continue to cook for a further 3–5 minutes

### Nutritional analysis

| *Per serving* | | *% energy* |
|---|---|---|
| Energy | 460 kcal | |
| Protein | 25 g | 22% |
| Fat | 6.8 g | 13% |
| Carbohydrate | 79 g | 65% |
| Fibre | 2.6 g | |

## Vegetable Paella

This is a vegetarian version of the classic Spanish paella which uses vegetables instead of the fish. The peas add protein to the dish.

*Makes 4 servings*

### Ingredients

2 tbsps oil
1 onion, chopped
2 garlic cloves, crushed
4 celery sticks, chopped
1 red, yellow and green pepper, sliced
1 tsp paprika
350 g (12 oz) rice
1 tin (400 g) chopped tomatoes
900 ml (1½ pts) vegetable stock (or water plus 2 vegetable stock cubes)
225 g (8 oz) frozen peas
Salt and pepper to taste
2 tbsp chopped parsley/50 g (2 oz) black olives (optional)

### Method

(1) Heat the oil in a large pan and sauté the onion, garlic, celery and peppers for 5 minutes.
(2) Add the paprika and rice and stir for another 2–3 minutes.
(3) Add the tomatoes and stock, bring to the boil then simmer for 15–20 minutes, until the liquid has been absorbed.
(4) Add the peas, season to taste, and heat through for a few more minutes.
(5) Stir in the optional ingredients.

### Nutritional analysis

| *Per serving* | | *% energy* |
|---|---|---|
| Energy | 483 kcal | |
| Protein | 12 g | 10% |
| Fat | 10 g | 19% |
| Carbohydrate | 92 g | 71% |
| Fibre | 7 g | |

## Spicy Rice

*Makes 4 servings*

### Ingredients

350 g (12 oz) white rice
2 l (3½ pts) water or stock
2 tsps medium curry powder
225 g (8 oz) mixed frozen
vegetables (e.g. peas, carrots,
cauliflower)
50 g (2 oz) currants

### Method

(1) Place the rice, water and curry powder in a large saucepan. Bring to the boil and simmer for 12 minutes, or until the rice is tender and most of the liquid has been absorbed.
(2) Add the frozen vegetables and cook for a further 3 minutes.
(3) Stir in the currants and heat through before serving.

### Nutritional analysis

| Per serving | | % energy |
|---|---|---|
| Energy | 399 kcal | |
| Protein | 8.6 g | 9% |
| Fat | 3.5 g | 8% |
| Carbohydrate | 89 g | 83% |
| Fibre | 0.6 g | |

## Chicken and Pepper Risotto

*Makes 4 servings*

### Ingredients

2 l (3½ pts) chicken or vegetable
stock
350 g (12 oz) white rice
2 peppers, preferably one red, one
yellow, cut into thin strips
100 g (4 oz) cooked chicken,
chopped
25 g (1 oz) parmesan, grated
Handful of fresh chives or parsley,
if available

### Method

(1) Place the stock, rice and peppers in a large saucepan.
(2) Bring to the boil and simmer for 12–15 minutes, until the rice is tender and the liquid has been absorbed.
(3) Add the chicken and half the parmesan. Heat through for a few minutes.
(4) Serve topped with remaining parmesan and herbs.

### Nutritional analysis

| Per serving | | % energy |
|---|---|---|
| Energy | 438 kcal | |
| Protein | 19 g | 17% |
| Fat | 7 g | 14% |
| Carbohydrate | 80 g | 69% |
| Fibre | 1.7 g | |

## Hawaiian Rice

*Makes 4 servings*

### Ingredients

2 l (3½ pts) vegetable stock
350 g (12 oz) white rice
1 onion, chopped
½ tsp turmeric
225 g (8 oz) tinned chopped
pineapple, drained
50 g (2 oz) currants

### Method

(1) Place the stock, rice, onion and turmeric in a large saucepan.
(2) Bring to the boil and simmer for 12–15 minutes, until the rice is tender and the liquid has been absorbed.
(3) Add the pineapple and currants. Heat through before serving.

### Nutritional analysis

| Per serving | | % energy |
|---|---|---|
| Energy | 407 kcal | |
| Protein | 7.1 g | 7% |
| Fat | 3.2 g | 7% |
| Carbohydrate | 93 g | 86% |
| Fibre | 1.1 g | |

## Chinese Fried Rice

This healthy adaptation of the classic Chinese version is lower in fat. Add any vegetables or protein foods you have handy to make this a one-dish meal.

*Makes 4 servings*

### Ingredients

350 g (12 oz) rice
1 tbsp oil
1 onion, chopped
1 red pepper, chopped
2 eggs
2 tbsps soya sauce
Mushrooms, peas, green beans, peppers, sweetcorn (optional vegetables)
Prawns, chicken, tofu, almonds (optional protein foods)

### Method

(1) Cook the rice in approximately twice its volume of water.
(2) Meanwhile, heat the oil in a wok and fry the onion and pepper for 2–3 minutes. Add any additional vegetables and protein foods and fry for a further 2 minutes (or until the meat is cooked). Push the vegetables to the sides of the wok.
(3) Beat the eggs in a dish then pour into the wok and scramble them until just set.
(4) Stir in the cooked rice and soya sauce and combine all the ingredients together.

### Nutritional analysis

| Per serving | | % energy |
|---|---|---|
| Energy | 425 kcal | |
| Protein | 11 g | 11% |
| Fat | 9.3 g | 20% |
| Carbohydrate | 79 g | 69% |
| Fibre | 1.2 g | |

## Thai Chicken and Rice

*Makes 4 servings*

### Ingredients

2 tsps oil
4 spring onions (or 1 small onion), chopped
2 boneless breasts of chicken, chopped
100 g (4 oz) mushrooms, sliced
1 small jar (280 g) Thai Stir Fry sauce
2 l (3½ pts) water
350 g (12 oz) white rice
1 red pepper, chopped/50 g (2 oz) water chestnuts, sliced/100 g (4 oz) mange tout/100 g (4 oz) courgettes, sliced (all optional)

### Method

(1) Heat the oil in a wok.
(2) Sauté the onions for 2 minutes then add the chicken and sauté for a further 3 minutes. Then add the mushrooms and any optional vegetables, stirring constantly until they are tender crisp.
(3) Stir in the Thai sauce.
(4) Meanwhile, cook the rice in the water for approximately 15 minutes.
(5) Combine the cooked rice and Thai chicken.

### Nutritional analysis

| Per serving | | % energy |
|---|---|---|
| Energy | 484 kcal | |
| Protein | 18 g | 15% |
| Fat | 7.1 g | 13% |
| Carbohydrate | 93 g | 72% |
| Fibre | 0.8 g | |

## Pork and Vegetable Stir Fry

*Makes 4 servings*

### Ingredients

1 tsp oil
350 g (12 oz) lean trimmed pork fillet
1 red pepper, sliced
225 g (8 oz) broccoli florets
100 g (4 oz) green beans
1 small jar (280 g) stir fry sauce, e.g. sweet and sour, Thai stir fry, yellow bean
450 g (1 lb) noodles, cooked according to directions on the packet

### Method

(1) Heat the oil in a wok.
(2) Add the pork and stir fry for 4–5 minutes until brown and tender.
(3) Add the vegetables to the wok and continue to stir fry for 2–3 minutes. The vegetables should still be crisp.
(4) Add the jar of sauce and cook for 1 minute to heat through.
(5) Spoon the pork and vegetable mixture over the hot noodles.

### Nutritional analysis

| Per serving | | % energy |
|---|---|---|
| Energy | 593 kcal | |
| Protein | 28 g | 19% |
| Fat | 12 g | 19% |
| Carbohydrate | 99 g | 62% |
| Fibre | 5.9 g | |

## Stir Fried Rice with Vegetables

*Makes 4 servings*

### Ingredients

1 tbsp oil
1 small onion or 4 spring onions,
chopped
450 g (1 lb) vegetables: mange tout,
broccoli florets, mushrooms, red,
green or yellow peppers, water
chestnuts, aubergine
50 g (12 oz) rice (uncooked
weight), cooked according to
directions on the packet
2 tbsps light soy sauce

### Method

(1) Heat the oil in a wok. Add the onions and
other vegetables and stir fry for 4–5
minutes depending on their size.
(2) Add the rice and mix together, separating the
grains.
(3) Add the soy sauce and heat through.

### Nutritional analysis

| Per serving | | % energy |
|---|---|---|
| Energy | 406 kcal | |
| Protein | 10 g | 10% |
| Fat | 6.6 g | 15% |
| Carbohydrate | 82 g | 75% |
| Fibre | 3 g | |

## Curried Chicken and Rice

Make this dish as substantial as you like by adding extra vegetables. Adjust the amount
of curry paste according to your taste!

*Makes 4 servings*

### Ingredients

1 tbsp butter or oil
450 g (1 lb) boneless chicken, cut
into strips
1 onion, chopped
2 tbsps mild curry paste
350 g (12 oz) rice
600 ml (1 pt) stock or water
1 tin (400 g) tinned tomatoes
350 g (12 oz) vegetables of your
choice (e.g. cauliflower, peas,
carrots)
50 g (2 oz) sultanas

### Method

(1) Heat the butter or oil in a large heavy-
bottomed pan and cook the chicken strips for
5 minutes until brown. Put aside on a plate.
(2) Add the onion and cook for a few minutes.
(3) Add the curry paste, rice, stock, tomatoes and
vegetables, stir, then bring to the boil. Simmer for
15 minutes.
(4) Return the chicken to the pan, add the sultanas
and warm through.

### Nutritional analysis

| Per serving | | % energy |
|---|---|---|
| Energy | 588 kcal | |
| Protein | 36 g | 25% |
| Fat | 10 g | 15% |
| Carbohydrate | 95 g | 60% |
| Fibre | 4.5 g | |

## Beans 'n' Rice

This is a vegetarian adaptation of a traditional West Indian dish. The combination of beans and rice increases the overall protein value of the dish.

*Makes 4 servings*

### Ingredients

1 tbsp oil
1 onion, chopped
1 green chilli, seeded and finely chopped
350 g (12 oz) rice
900 ml (1½ pts) vegetable stock (or water plus 2 vegetable stock cubes)
2 large tomatoes, sliced
1 tin (420 g) beans *
50 g (2 oz) creamed coconut
2 tbsps fresh chopped coriander or parsley

### Method

(1) Heat the oil in a pan and fry the onion for about 5 minutes. Add the chilli and rice and fry for a further 2 minutes.
(2) Add the stock and tomato, bring to the boil and simmer for 10 minutes.
(3) Add the beans and a little extra water if the mixture looks dry. Cover and cook for a further 5 minutes until the rice is cooked.
(4) Stir in the coconut until it is melted and then stir in the coriander or parsley.

* Either red kidney beans, aduki, cannelini, haricot or black beans.

### Nutritional analysis

| *Per serving* | | *% energy* |
|---|---|---|
| Energy | 500 kcal | |
| Protein | 13 g | 10% |
| Fat | 12 g | 21% |
| Carbohydrate | 92 g | 69% |
| Fibre | 5.6 g | |

## Rice with Haddock and Peas

*Makes 4 servings*

### Ingredients

350 g (12 oz) easy cook rice
600 ml (1 pt) vegetable stock (or water plus 2 vegetable stock cubes)
1 bay leaf
350 g (12 oz) frozen haddock fillet, thawed
200 g (7 oz) frozen peas
Salt and freshly ground black pepper

### Method

(1) Place the rice in a large pan with the stock and bay leaf and bring to the boil. Cover and simmer for 15 minutes.
(2) Add the haddock and peas and continue cooking for a further 5 minutes until the liquid has been absorbed and the fish flakes easily. Roughly break up the fish and stir the rice mixture to distribute evenly.
(3) Serve with watercress or a green salad.

### Nutritional analysis

| *Per serving* | | *% energy* |
|---|---|---|
| Energy | 441 kcal | |
| Protein | 26 g | 24% |
| Fat | 4.1 g | 8% |
| Carbohydrate | 80 g | 6.8% |
| Fibre | 2.9 g | |

## Mexican Rice

### Ingredients

2 tbsps oil
1 large onion, chopped
1 green chilli, deseeded and
chopped
2 celery stalks, chopped
2–3 garlic cloves, crushed
2 tsps ground cumin
1 red and 1 green pepper, chopped
½ tin (200 g) chopped tomatoes
350 g (12 oz) brown rice
600 ml (1 pt) water
1 tin (400 g) sweetcorn, drained
Salt and freshly ground
black pepper
75 g (3 oz) raisins/1 tin (400 g) red
kidney beans (optional)

### Method

(1) Heat the oil in a large saucepan and sauté the onion, chilli, celery and garlic over a gentle heat until the onion is softened.
(2) Stir in the cumin, pepper and tomatoes and cook for a further 2 minutes.
(3) Add the rice and water. Bring to the boil, cover and simmer for about 35 minutes until the rice is cooked and liquid absorbed.
(4) Stir in the sweetcorn and any optional ingredients, season to taste and heat through. Serve with wholemilk plain yoghurt and chopped fresh coriander.

### Nutritional analysis

| *Per serving* | | *% energy* |
|---|---|---|
| Energy | 522 kcal | |
| Protein | 10 g | 8% |
| Fat | 9.7 g | 17% |
| Carbohydrate | 105 g | 75% |
| Fibre | 5.4 g | |

## Thai-Style Green Fish Curry

*Makes 4 servings*

### Ingredients

1 tbsp oil
1 onion, thinly sliced
40 g (1½ oz) Thai green curry paste
300 ml (½ pt) coconut milk
450 g (1 lb) firm white fish, e.g. cod or monkfish, cut into chunks
350 g (12 oz) rice
Grated zest of 1 lime

### Method

(1) Heat the oil in a wok and fry the onion for a few minutes.
(2) Stir in the curry paste, then add the coconut milk. Simmer for about 10 minutes.
(3) Add the fish and cook, stirring, for a few minutes.
(4) Cook the rice and serve topped with the fish curry and garnished with the lime zest.

### Nutritional analysis

| Per serving | | % energy |
|---|---|---|
| Energy | 463 kcal | |
| Protein | 26 g | 22% |
| Fat | 6.8 g | 13% |
| Carbohydrate | 80 g | 65% |
| Fibre | 0.6 g | |

## Quick Vegetable Curry

A bit of a cheat's curry, but many of the ready-prepared curry sauces are low in fat and taste almost as good as home-made. Vary the curry with different combinations of vegetables.

*Makes 4 servings*

### Ingredients

1 tbsp oil
1 onion, sliced
1 small jar or tin (approx. 300 g) low fat curry sauce, e.g. Dopiaza, Balti, Jalfreizi
700 g (1½ lb) any chopped vegetables, e.g. carrots, turnips, swede, potato, green beans

### Method

(1) Heat the oil in a large pan. Add the onion and cook over a high heat for 5 minutes.
(2) Add the sauce and the prepared vegetables, stirring well.
(3) Cover and cook for about 15 minutes until the vegetables are just tender.
(4) Serve with cooked rice or ready-bought chappatis and plain thick yoghurt.

### Nutritional analysis

| Per serving | | % energy |
|---|---|---|
| Energy | 480 kcal | |
| Protein | 8.7 g | 7% |
| Fat | 11 g | 20% |
| Carbohydrate | 93 g | 73% |
| Fibre | 5.4 g | |

# Tofu and Mushroom Stir Fry

*Makes 4 servings*

## Ingredients

Marinade:
2 tbsps soy sauce
2 tbsps dry sherry
1 tbsp vinegar

Stir fry:
350 g (12 oz) tofu, cubed
1 tbsp oil
2 garlic cloves, crushed
2-cm piece fresh ginger, chopped
1 red pepper, chopped
4 spring onions, chopped
225 g (8 oz) mushrooms, sliced
100 g (4 oz) beansprouts
1 tsp cornflour
350 g (12 oz) Chinese noodles

## Method

(1) Mix the marinade ingredients together, add the tofu, turn a few times and leave for 30 minutes or longer.
(2) Heat the oil in a wok and stir fry the garlic and ginger for 1 minute. Add the red pepper, onions, mushrooms and beansprouts and stir fry for 2 minutes.
(3) Drain the tofu. Blend the marinade with the cornflour, pour over the vegetables and stir quickly until the sauce has thickened. Transfer onto a serving dish.
(4) Stir fry the tofu in the wok for 1 minute, turning frequently, and arrange on the vegetables.
(5) Cook the noodles according to directions on the packet and serve with the vegetables.

## Nutritional analysis

| *Per serving* | | *% energy* |
|---|---|---|
| Energy | 473 kcal | |
| Protein | 20 g | 17% |
| Fat | 12 g | 24% |
| Carbohydrate | 72 g | 59% |
| Fibre | 4.4 g | |

# Noodles with Salmon in Foil

This complete meal comes in a neat packet; just pop in the ingredients, put it in the oven and let all the flavours blend together.

*Makes 1 serving*

## Ingredients

75 g (3 oz) egg noodles, cooked according to directions on the packet
1 carrot, thinly sliced
2 spring onions, sliced
4 mushrooms
1 salmon steak (about 175 g/6 oz)
Fresh chopped parsley

## Method

(1) Place the noodles onto the centre of a piece of oiled foil approximately 50 x 30 cm (20 x 12 in).
(2) Lay the vegetables and salmon on top. Sprinkle with salt and parsley.
(3) Fold the foil over to enclose the salmon and seal the edges. Place on a baking tray.
(4) Bake at 180°C/350°F/gas mark 4 for 15 minutes.
(5) Turn onto a plate to serve.

## Nutritional analysis

| *Per serving* | | *% energy* |
|---|---|---|
| Energy | 681 kcal | |
| Protein | 47 g | 28% |
| Fat | 27 g | 35% |
| Carbohydrate | 68 g | 37% |
| Fibre | 4.7 g | |

# Stir Fry Indonesian Prawns in Peanut Sauce

*Makes 4 servings*

## Ingredients

225 g (8 oz) green beans,
cut in half cross-ways
450 g (1 lb) large peeled prawns
75 g (3 oz) chunky peanut butter
150 ml (¼ pt) unsweetened canned
coconut milk
1 tbsp soy sauce
2 tsps curry powder
350 g (12 oz) Chinese noodles,
cooked
A few spring onions, chopped
(optional)

## Method

(1) Place a wok over a high heat. Add the green beans and prawns and stir fry for 3 minutes.
(2) In a small bowl, whisk together the peanut butter, coconut milk, soy sauce, curry powder and 175 ml (6 fl oz) water.
(3) Pour over the beans and prawns. Add the spring onions, if applicable.
(4) Stir and cook for a few minutes until warmed through and thickened.
(5) Serve with the noodles.

*Variation*
◆ For a vegetarian version, substitute 450 g (1 lb) firm tofu, cut into cubes, for the prawns.

## Nutritional analysis

| *Per serving* | | *% energy* |
|---|---|---|
| Energy | 606 kcal | |
| Protein | 42 g | 28% |
| Fat | 18 g | 27% |
| Carbohydrate | 73 g | 45% |
| Fibre | 5 g | |

# Chicken and Broccoli Stir Fry

*Makes 4 servings*

## Ingredients

450 g (1 lb) boneless chicken,
skinned and cut into thin strips
1 tbsp oil
2 garlic cloves, chopped
1-in piece root ginger, chopped
450 g (1 lb) broccoli, cut into
small florets
1 red pepper, cut into strips
350 g (12 oz) rice or noodles

## Method

(1) Heat the oil in a wok or heavy-based pan over a high heat.
(2) Add the chicken strips, garlic and ginger and stir fry for 2 minutes.
(3) Mix in the broccoli and peppers and stir fry for about 5 minutes, until just tender.
(4) Cook the noodles or rice according to directions on the packet and serve with the chicken stir fry.

## Nutritional analysis

| *Per serving* | | *% energy* |
|---|---|---|
| Energy | 543 kcal | |
| Protein | 36 g | 26% |
| Fat | 11 g | 18% |
| Carbohydrate | 81 g | 56% |
| Fibre | 5 g | |

## Cous Cous

Cous cous is made from semolina flour which has been pre-cooked and rolled into tiny clumps. There are three methods of cooking it.

(1) Place 600 ml (1 pt) boiling water in a saucepan with a little salt and 350 g (12 oz) cous cous and simmer for 5 minutes.
(2) Cover 350 g (12 oz) cous cous with 600 ml (1 pt) boiling water, add a little salt and allow to stand for 15 minutes until all the water has been absorbed.
(3) Pour boiling water over the cous cous, allow to stand for a few minutes then transfer to a steamer and steam for 5–6 minutes.

## Vegetable Cous Cous

*Makes 4 servings*

### Ingredients

350 g (12 oz) cous cous
600 ml (1 pt) boiling water
1 tbsp oil
1 onion, chopped
2 tsps curry powder
450 g (1 lb) vegetables, e.g. carrots, courgettes, tomatoes, parsnips, green beans
1 tin (420 g) chick peas
1 vegetable stock cube dissolved in 150 ml (¼ pt) boiling water
50 g (2 oz) chopped dates/50 g (2 oz) blanched almonds (optional)

### Method

(1) Cover the cous cous with the boiling water and leave to stand for 15 minutes until all the liquid has been absorbed.
(2) Meanwhile, heat the oil in a pan and fry the onion for 5 minutes. Add the curry powder and cook for a further 2 minutes.
(3) Add the vegetables, chick peas and stock, cover and simmer for about 7–10 minutes, or until the vegetables are tender crisp (not soft).
(4) Fluff the cous cous with a fork and stir in the dates and almonds, if applicable.
(5) Serve topped with the vegetable mixture.

### Nutritional analysis

| *Per serving* | | *% energy* |
|---|---|---|
| Energy | 543 kcal | |
| Protein | 17 g | 12% |
| Fat | 7.1 g | 13% |
| Carbohydrate | 108 g | 75% |
| Fibre | 5.1 g | |

## Bulgar wheat

Bulgar wheat is made from whole wheat which has been cracked, steamed and redried. It requires little or no further cooking and is highly nutritious. You can prepare it in one of two ways.

1. Pour over boiling water (to cover by 2 cm) and leave for approximately 30 minutes to allow the wheat to absorb the water.
2. Boil in a saucepan for approximately 10 minutes.

## Bulgar Wheat Pilaff

*Makes 4 servings*

### Ingredients

1 tbsp olive oil
1 onion, chopped
1 red pepper, chopped
1 garlic clove, crushed
350 g (12 oz) bulgar wheat
900 ml (1½ pts) boiling water
Handful of fresh chopped herbs, e.g. parsley, mint
Lemon juice
Salt and freshly ground black pepper
100 g (4 oz) black olives/175 g (6 oz) diced feta cheese/100 g (4 oz) chopped apricots/ 100 g (4 oz) toasted cashews, pine nuts or almonds (all optional)

### Method

(1) Heat the olive oil in a pan and cook the onion and pepper for about 5 minutes. Add the garlic and cook for a further 3 minutes.
(2) Add the bulgar and boiling water, cover and simmer for 10 minutes until the wheat has absorbed the water and puffed up.
(3) Stir in the herbs, any optional ingredients and season with the lemon juice, salt and pepper.

### Nutritional analysis

| Per serving | | % energy |
|---|---|---|
| Energy | 353 kcal | |
| Protein | 9.1 g | 10% |
| Fat | 4.4 g | 11% |
| Carbohydrate | 71 g | 79% |
| Fibre | 0.9 g | |

## Millet

Millet is the seed of a hardy annual grass and is richer in protein and iron than other grains. It is fairly bland on its own but absorbs other flavours well. Use it as an alternative to rice in savoury dishes or in milk puddings.

## Millet Pilaff with Nuts and Raisins

*Makes 4 servings*

### Ingredients

1 tbsp oil
1 large onion, chopped
2 carrots, diced
1 garlic clove, crushed
350 g (12 oz) millet
900 ml (1½ pts) water
Salt and freshly ground
black pepper
50 g (2 oz) raisins
50 g (2 oz) toasted flaked almonds

### Method

(1) Heat the oil in a saucepan and cook the onion for 5 minutes. Add the carrots and garlic and cook for a further 5 minutes.
(2) Add the millet and water and season to taste with the salt and pepper. Bring to the boil, cover and simmer for 15–20 minutes, until the water has been absorbed.
(3) Stir in the raisins and almonds.

### Nutritional analysis

| Per serving | | % energy |
|---|---|---|
| Energy | 483 kcal | |
| Protein | 8.9 g | 7% |
| Fat | 13 g | 24% |
| Carbohydrate | 81 g | 69% |
| Fibre | 2.4 g | |

# 15

# Beans and lentils

Don't be put off by the rather cranky image attributed to beans and lentils; they can be used to make many delicious dishes to tempt even the most die-hard 'meat and two veg' person. Many of the following recipes have been inspired by Mexican and Asian cuisines, owing to the subtle spicy flavours and simplicity of cooking. Beans and lentils are among the most nutritious foods, rich in protein, fibre, B vitamins, iron, zinc and calcium. The recipes state tinned varieties to save time, but you may, of course, cook them from dried.

## Spicy Bean Enchiladas

*Makes 4 enchiladas*

### Ingredients

1 tbsp (15 ml) olive oil
1 onion, chopped
2 cloves of garlic, crushed
1 tin (420 g) pinto or red kidney beans (or use 175 g/6 oz dried beans, soaked, cooked and drained)
½ tin (200 g) chopped tomatoes
1 tbsp (15 g) taco seasoning mix or 150 g (5 oz) enchilada sauce
4 corn or wheat tortillas
225 g (8 oz) passata with herbs or garlic
50 g (2 oz) grated mature Cheddar cheese
Low fat plain yoghurt, sliced onions, shredded lettuce

### Method

(1) Heat the oil in a large frying pan. Sauté the onion and garlic for 5 minutes.
(2) Add the beans to the pan and mash roughly.
(3) Add the tomatoes, taco seasoning (or enchilada sauce) and continue to cook for a few minutes.
(4) Spread one quarter of the mixture over each tortilla. Roll up and place seam-side down in a baking dish sprayed with oil spray.
(5) Spoon the passata over the tortillas and sprinkle the cheese over the top.
(6) Cover with foil and bake at 180°C/350°F/gas mark 4 for 30 minutes. Alternatively, cover and microwave for 7 minutes.
(7) Serve with a spoonful of yoghurt, and sprinkle with onions and lettuce.

### Nutritional analysis

| *Per serving* | | *% energy* |
|---|---|---|
| Energy | 328 kcal | |
| Protein | 14 g | 17% |
| Fat | 9 g | 25% |
| Carbohydrate | 51 g | 58% |
| Fibre | 6.9 g | |

# Chicken Enchiladas

*Makes 4 enchiladas*

## Ingredients

150 g (5 oz) enchilada sauce
225 g (8 oz) tomato salsa
175 g (6 oz) cooked chicken, shredded
50 g (2 oz) canned green chillis, chopped (optional)
4 corn or wheat tortillas
225 g (8 oz) passata
50 g (2 oz) Cheddar cheese, grated
Low fat plain yoghurt, sliced onions, shredded lettuce

## Method

(1) In a saucepan, combine the enchilada sauce, salsa, chicken and chillis.
(2) Bring to the boil, stirring continuously, and simmer for a few minutes.
(3) Place one quarter of the chicken mixture on each tortilla and roll up. Place seam-side down in a baking dish sprayed with oil spray.
(4) Spoon the passata over the tortillas and sprinkle the cheese over the top.
(5) Cover with foil and bake at 180°C/350°F/gas mark 4 for 30 minutes. Alternatively, cover and microwave for 7 minutes.
(6) Serve with a spoonful of yoghurt, and sprinkle with onions and lettuce.

## Nutritional analysis

| Per serving | | % energy |
|---|---|---|
| Energy | 382 kcal | |
| Protein | 23 g | 24% |
| Fat | 10 g | 24% |
| Carbohydrate | 53 g | 52% |
| Fibre | 2.6 g | |

# Store-cupboard Bean Bake

Ideal as a midweek supper when you are pressed for time, this is one of the speediest dishes that can be assembled from ingredients in the store-cupboard. Use any variety of tinned beans in place of the red kidney beans if you wish.

*Makes 4 servings*

## Ingredients

1 onion, chopped
1 garlic clove, chopped
2 tsps oil or butter
1 tin (400 g) tomatoes with juice
2 tins (2 x 420 g) red kidney beans, drained
1 tsp mixed herbs
1 vegetable stock cube
40 g (1½ oz) grated Cheddar cheese

## Method

(1) Heat the oil in a large pan and sauté the onion and garlic over a high heat for 3–4 minutes until golden.
(2) Add the tomatoes (roughly broken up), beans, herbs and a crumbled stock cube. Stir well and bring to the boil. Simmer for a few minutes.
(3) Spoon into a baking dish and sprinkle with grated cheese.
(4) Melt the cheese under a hot grill or microwave for 2 minutes until the cheese is bubbling.

## Nutritional analysis

| Per serving | | % energy |
|---|---|---|
| Energy | 256 kcal | |
| Protein | 16 g | 25% |
| Fat | 6.6 g | 23% |
| Carbohydrate | 35 g | 52% |
| Fibre | 12 g | |

## Dahl

Lentils are a superb source of protein, iron, fibre and B vitamins. This is one of my favourite quick suppers!

*Makes 4 servings*

### Ingredients

2 tbsps oil
2 onions, chopped
3–4 garlic cloves, crushed
1 tsp ground cumin
2 tsps ground coriander
1 tsp turmeric
350 g (12 oz) red lentils
1.2 l (2 pts) water
Salt
Chopped fresh coriander, parsley, spring onion (optional)

### Method

(1) Heat the oil in a large pan and fry the onion for about 5 minutes. Add the garlic and spices and fry for a further minute.
(2) Add the lentils and water and bring to the boil. Cover and simmer for approximately 20 minutes. Alternatively, cook in a pressure cooker for 3 minutes then turn off the heat.
(3) Season with salt to taste and stir in the optional ingredients, if applicable.

### Nutritional analysis

| Per serving | | % energy |
|---|---|---|
| Energy | 338 kcal | |
| Protein | 21 g | 25% |
| Fat | 6.7 g | 18% |
| Carbohydrate | 52 g | 57% |
| Fibre | 4.7 g | |

## Bean and Tomato Casserole

This nutritious one-pot meal is simplicity itself. Use any other vegetables (e.g. onions, mushrooms) in place of the leeks if you prefer.

*Makes 4 servings*

### Ingredients

1 tbsp oil
2 leeks, sliced
1 tin (400 g) chopped tomatoes
2 tins (2 x 425 g) beans (any variety), drained
1 vegetable stock cube

### Method

(1) Heat the oil in a large saucepan. Add the leeks and cook for about 5 minutes until the leeks are soft.
(2) Add the remaining ingredients, stir and bring to the boil. Simmer for a further 10–15 minutes, or until the casserole has thickened.
(3) Accompany with warm pitta breads.

### Nutritional analysis

| Per serving | | % energy |
|---|---|---|
| Energy | 204 kcal | |
| Protein | 13 g | 25% |
| Fat | 4 g | 18% |
| Carbohydrate | 31 g | 57% |
| Fibre | 11 g | |

## Mexican Bean Bake

*Makes 4 servings*

### Ingredients

1 onion, chopped
2 cloves garlic, crushed
1 red and 1 green pepper, sliced
1 tsp each of basil and parsley
450 ml (1 pt) passata (sieved tomatoes)
1 vegetable stock cube
1 tin (420 g) red kidney beans, drained
1 tin (420 g) pinto beans, drained
100 g (4 oz) reduced fat mozzarella cheese, sliced

### Method

(1) In a large saucepan, place the onion, garlic, peppers, herbs, passata, stock cube and beans.
(2) Bring to the boil, stirring, and simmer for 10–15 minutes.
(3) Spoon the bean mixture into a baking dish then sprinkle over the cheese.
(4) Bake uncovered at 200°C/400°F/gas mark 6 for 15 minutes until the cheese is bubbling. Alternatively, microwave for 5 minutes.

### Nutritional analysis

| Per serving | | % energy |
|---|---|---|
| Energy | 290 kcal | |
| Protein | 24 g | 34% |
| Fat | 4.9 g | 15% |
| Carbohydrate | 40 g | 51% |
| Fibre | 13 g | |

## Tortilla Stack

*Makes 4 servings*

### Ingredients

2 tins (2 x 420 g) pinto beans, drained
1 tin (400 g) sweetcorn, drained
150 g (5 oz) enchilada sauce
8 wheat tortillas
50 g (2 oz) Cheddar cheese, grated
1 beef tomato, sliced onions, salsa (to serve)

### Method

(1) Place the beans, sweetcorn and enchilada sauce into a large saucepan. Cook and stir until heated through.
(2) Spray a large baking tray with oil spray.
(3) Place two tortillas side by side on the tray. Spoon one eighth of the bean mixture onto each tortilla. Sprinkle with about 2 tsps of the cheese.
(4) Place another tortilla on top and repeat the layers, finishing with beans and cheese.
(5) Loosely cover with foil and bake at 180°C/350°F/gas mark 4.

### Nutritional analysis

| Per serving | | % energy |
|---|---|---|
| Energy | 474 kcal | |
| Protein | 24 g | 20% |
| Fat | 9.3 g | 18% |
| Carbohydrate | 79 g | 62% |
| Fibre | 14 g | |

## One-minute Burrito

*Makes 1 serving*

### Ingredients

2 wheat tortillas
½ tin (210 g) re-fried beans
2 tbsps low fat fromage frais
1 tbsp tomato salsa
Shredded lettuce, sliced tomato

### Method

(1) Spoon the beans, fromage frais and salsa onto the tortillas.
(2) Top with shredded lettuce and tomato then fold over or roll up.
(3) Warm through in a microwave for 1 minute.

### Nutritional analysis

| Per serving | | % energy |
|---|---|---|
| Energy | 554 kcal | |
| Protein | 25 g | 18% |
| Fat | 3.4 g | 6% |
| Carbohydrate | 104 g | 76% |
| Fibre | 2.8 g | |

## Spicy Bean Lasagne

*Makes 4 servings*

### Ingredients

1 onion, chopped
2 tsps olive oil
1 tsp each cumin and coriander
2 tins (2 x 420 g) borlotti beans (or other variety of your choice), drained
1 tin (400 g) chopped tomatoes with peppers
12 sheets lasagne (not pre-cook variety)
350 g (12 oz) cottage cheese
40 g (1½ oz) reduced fat mozzarella, grated

### Method

(1) For the spicy beans, heat the oil in a pan and sauté the onions and spices for 5 minutes.
(2) Add the beans and tomatoes, bring to the boil and cook for a few more minutes.
(3) Spray a baking dish with oil spray or coat lightly with a little oil.
(4) Place 3 sheets of lasagne in the bottom of the dish and cover with one quarter of the beans and one quarter of the cottage cheese. Repeat the layers, finishing with the beans and cottage cheese.
(5) Sprinkle with the mozzarella and bake at 180°C/350°F/gas mark 4 for 30 minutes. Alternatively, microwave for 8 minutes, turning the dish twice.

### Nutritional analysis

| Per serving | | % energy |
|---|---|---|
| Energy | 626 kcal | |
| Protein | 39 g | 25% |
| Fat | 9.4 g | 14% |
| Carbohydrate | 103 g | 61% |
| Fibre | 15 g | |

## Mixed Bean Chilli

*Makes 4 servings*

**Ingredients**

1 tbsp (15 ml) oil
1 large onion, chopped
2–3 garlic cloves, crushed
Pinch of chilli powder, according to your taste
1 tbsp each of tomato purée and paprika
1 tin (420 g) chopped tomatoes
1 tin (420 g) red kidney beans, drained
1 tin (420 g) cannelini beans, drained
500 g (1 lb) mixed vegetables, e.g. carrots, peppers, courgettes

**Method**

(1) Heat the oil in a large pan. Add the onion, garlic and chilli and sauté for 5 minutes.
(2) Add the tomato purée and paprika and cook for 2 minutes.
(3) Add the tinned tomatoes, beans and vegetables. Stir and bring to the boil. Simmer for 20 minutes, until the vegetables are tender.
(4) Serve with cooked rice, tortillas or crusty bread.

**Nutritional analysis**

| Per serving | | % energy |
|---|---|---|
| Energy | 263 kcal | |
| Protein | 14 g | 22% |
| Fat | 4.3 g | 15% |
| Carbohydrate | 45 g | 63% |
| Fibre | 14 g | |

## Spicy Chick Peas with Tomatoes

*Makes 4 servings*

**Ingredients**

1 tbsp oil
1 onion, chopped
2 garlic cloves, crushed
1 tin (400 g) chopped tomatoes
1½ tsps curry paste (or according to taste)
2 tins (2 x 420 g) chick peas, drained
150 ml (¼ pt) thick yoghurt
Fresh coriander and mint, if available

**Method**

(1) Heat the oil in a large pan. Add the onion and garlic and fry for 5 minutes.
(2) Add the tomatoes, curry paste and chick peas. Bring to the boil then simmer for 10 minutes.
(3) Stir in the yoghurt and the chopped fresh herbs, if available, just before serving. Do not allow to boil.

**Nutritional analysis**

| Per serving | | % energy |
|---|---|---|
| Energy | 268 kcal | |
| Protein | 16 g | 23% |
| Fat | 8.3 g | 28% |
| Carbohydrate | 35 g | 49% |
| Fibre | 8.1 g | |

## Fish and Bean Cassoulet

*Makes 4 servings*

### Ingredients

750 g (1½ lb) haddock steaks
1 l (1¾ pts) stock or water
1 bay leaf
1 tbsp oil
1 onion, chopped
2 celery sticks, chopped
2 carrots, chopped
4 tbsps white wine or water
2 tins (2 x 420 g) haricot beans,
drained
1 tsp mixed herbs
4 tomatoes, chopped
4 tbsps fresh breadcrumbs
2 tbsps fresh chopped parsley

### Method

(1) Cook the fish in the stock or water with the bay leaf for about 10–15 minutes. Drain, reserving a pint of the liquid.
(2) Flake the fish, removing any bones.
(3) Heat the oil in a pan and fry the vegetables for about 5 minutes.
(4) Pour in the reserved fish liquid, wine or extra water, beans and herbs and cook for about 10 minutes, until the liquid has been reduced.
(5) Add the cooked fish and tomatoes. Check the seasoning and transfer into a shallow baking dish.
(6) Mix the breadcrumbs and parsley together and sprinkle on the top.
(7) Bake at 190°C/375°F/gas mark 5 for 30–35 minutes until the top is crisp and golden.

### Nutritional analysis

| *Per serving* | | *% energy* |
|---|---|---|
| Energy | 415 kcal | |
| Protein | 50 g | 48% |
| Fat | 5.5 g | 12% |
| Carbohydrate | 45 g | 40% |
| Fibre | 14 g | |

# Mixed Vegetable and Lentil Curry

Lentils add protein, fibre and iron to the curry. Vary the vegetables according to what you have available.

*Makes 4 servings*

### Ingredients

225 g (8 oz) red lentils
750 ml (1¼ pts) water
2 tbsps oil
1 large onion, sliced
1 tsp each of cumin, coriander, turmeric and chilli powder (alternatively use 1 tbsp curry powder)
2 garlic cloves, crushed
900 g (2 lb) vegetables, e.g. cauliflower, courgettes, mushrooms, okra, carrots, tomatoes
Salt

### Method

(1) Place the lentils and the water in a pan and boil for 15 minutes.
(2) Heat the oil in a large pan and sauté the onion for 5 minutes.
(3) Add the spices and the garlic and continue cooking for 2 minutes.
(4) Add the vegetables and lentils, cover and simmer for 10 minutes, or until the vegetables are just tender.
(5) Season with the salt.

### Nutritional analysis

| *Per serving* | | *% energy* |
|---|---|---|
| Energy | 294 kcal | |
| Protein | 18 g | 25% |
| Fat | 7.5 g | 23% |
| Carbohydrate | 41 g | 52% |
| Fibre | 6.6 g | |

# Chilli Con Carne

This is a low fat version of the classic dish, and one which is useful for smuggling extra vegetables into your diet. You may use any type of lean minced meat such as turkey, beef or pork.

*Makes 4 servings*

## Ingredients

350 g (12 oz) lean minced turkey or beef
1 tbsp oil
1 onion, chopped
2 garlic cloves, crushed
1 green pepper, chopped
2 celery sticks, chopped
1 tbsp paprika
1 tsp chilli powder
1–2 tsps ground cumin
2 tbsps tomato purée
600 ml (1 pt) stock or water
2 tins (2 x 420 g) red kidney beans
350 g (12 oz) rice

## Method

(1) Dry fry the mince in a non-stick pan for approximately 5 minutes until browned. Drain any fat that separates from the meat. Set aside.
(2) Heat the oil in a large pan and sauté the onion, pepper, celery and garlic for 3 minutes. Add the spices and fry for a further minute.
(3) Add the tomato purée, stock or water, and the beans, cover and simmer for approximately 1 hour (or longer if you wish).
(4) Cook the rice in about twice its volume of water and serve with the chilli.

## Nutritional analysis

| *Per serving* | | *% energy* |
|---|---|---|
| Energy | 643 kcal | |
| Protein | 39 g | 24% |
| Fat | 9.1 g | 13% |
| Carbohydrate | 109 g | 63% |
| Fibre | 12 g | |

# Bean and Courgette Provençale with Garlic Bread

*Makes 4 servings*

## Ingredients

Provençale:
1 tbsp olive oil
2 onions, sliced
2 garlic cloves, crushed
450 g (1 lb) courgettes, sliced
2 tins (2 x 420 g) flageolet beans,
drained
1 tin (400 g) tomatoes
1 tsp dried oregano
1 vegetable stock cube dissolved in
150 ml (¼ pt) water

Garlic bread:
1 French stick
40 g (1½ oz) low fat spread
1 garlic clove, crushed

## Method

(1) Heat the oil in a large pan and sauté the onion for approximately 5 minutes until softened.
(2) Add the garlic and courgettes and cook for a further 5 minutes.
(3) Add the remaining ingredients. Cover and simmer for another 10 minutes.
(4) To make the garlic bread, slice the stick diagonally three-quarters of the way through. Mix together the low fat spread and garlic. Spread the mixture in each slit, wrap in foil and bake in a preheated oven at 220°C/425°F/gas mark 7 for 5–10 minutes.

## Nutritional analysis

| *Per serving* | | *% energy* |
|---|---|---|
| Energy | 480 kcal | |
| Protein | 23 g | 19% |
| Fat | 10 g | 19% |
| Carbohydrate | 79 g | 62% |
| Fibre | 14 g | |

# 16

# Pasta

Pasta is the perfect food for active people. It has a relatively low glycaemic index which means it produces a gradual, sustained rise in blood sugar levels. It is extremely high in carbohydrate, low in fat and the wholemeal version is a good source of fibre, B vitamins and iron. It is also very quick and easy to cook and can be combined with ready-made or home-made sauces to make a substantial healthy meal.

---

◆ *Top cooking tips* ◆

- ◆ Cook pasta in a large pan of fast-boiling water.
- ◆ Add a tablespoon of oil to stop the pasta from sticking and the water from boiling over
- ◆ Stir the pasta briefly before partly covering with a lid.
- ◆ Cooking time will depend on the shape and thickness of the pasta. Most varieties take between 8–10 minutes; very small pasta takes only 5 minutes. Test a piece by removing from the pan and biting it – it should feel tender yet fairly firm to the bite.
- ◆ Drain through a colander.
- ◆ Mix the hot pasta with a little oil or accompanying sauce.

---

# Athletes Hot Pasta with Vegetables

This basic pasta recipe takes less than 15 minutes to prepare. Simply add whatever fresh or frozen vegetables you have handy to the pasta pot and – hey presto! Ideal for quick nutritious suppers and attractive enough to serve to guests at dinner. Any leftovers are also good served cold as a salad.

*Makes 4 servings*

## Ingredients

350 g (12 oz) dried pasta of your choice
2 tbsps olive oil or pesto sauce
2 tbsps parmesan, grated
450 g (1 lb) vegetables of your choice (strips of red, green or yellow peppers, broccoli florets, mushrooms, peas, courgettes)

## Method

(1) Cook the pasta in plenty of boiling water according to the directions on the packet. Add the vegetables during the last 5 minutes of cooking. Drain.
(2) While hot, combine with the olive oil or pesto and parmesan cheese.
(3) Stir in the vegetables.

## Nutritional analysis

| *Per serving* | | *% energy* |
|---|---|---|
| Energy | 399 kcal | |
| Protein | 15 g | 15% |
| Fat | 9.5 g | 21% |
| Carbohydrate | 68 g | 64% |
| Fibre | 5.4 g | |

## Pasta with Sauce

Accompany any of the following sauces with your favourite pasta shapes. In general, thin pasta and pasta ribbons (e.g. spaghetti, linguine, tagliatelle) go best with the smoother sauces; pasta shapes (e.g. fussilli, rigatoni, penne, farfelle) go best with chunky sauces containing larger pieces of vegetables or meat. I think pasta sauces are best stirred through the pasta rather than spooned on top. This also avoids the need for added olive oil or butter in the pasta.

As a rough guide, allow approximately 75 g (3 oz) dried pasta per portion. For those with higher carbohydrate needs, 100–150 g (4–5 oz) would be more suitable. For fresh pasta, allow approximately 100 g (4 oz) per portion.

## Vegetarian Bolognese

*Makes 4 servings*

### Ingredients

1 tbsp olive oil
1 onion, chopped
2 carrots, finely chopped
1 large courgette, finely chopped
1 tin (400 g) chopped tomatoes
1 tin (420 g) brown or green lentils
(or 100 g (4 oz) dried lentils,
soaked and cooked)
1 tsp mixed herbs
1 tbsp parmesan, grated

### Method

(1) Heat the oil in a large frying pan. Add the vegetables, stirring often until softened (about 5 minutes).
(2) Add the tomatoes, lentils and herbs. Cook for a few minutes until the sauce thickens slightly.
(3) Stir in the cheese and heat through.

### Nutritional analysis

| Per serving (including 75 g/3 oz dried pasta) | | % energy |
|---|---|---|
| Energy | 467 kcal | |
| Protein | 21 g | 18% |
| Fat | 6.1 g | 12% |
| Carbohydrate | 87 g | 70% |
| Fibre | 7.9 g | |

## Turkey Bolognese

*Makes 4 servings*

### Ingredients

1 tsp olive oil
350 g (12 oz) turkey mince
1 onion, chopped
3 celery stalks, chopped
2 carrots, chopped
1 tin (400 g) chopped tomatoes
2 tbsps tomato purée
1 tsp mixed herbs
Salt and pepper

### Method

(1) In a large non-stick frying pan, heat the oil. Add the turkey mince and cook, stirring for about 4–5 minutes, until no longer pink.
(2) Add the vegetables. Cook for 3–5 minutes, until just tender.
(3) Stir in the chopped tomatoes, tomato purée, herbs and seasoning to taste. Heat through.

### Nutritional analysis

*Per serving (including 75 g/3 oz dried pasta)*

|  |  | % energy |
|---|---|---|
| Energy | 470 kcal | |
| Protein | 37 g | 32% |
| Fat | 5.3 | 10% |
| Carbohydrate | 73 g | 58% |
| Fibre | 4.7 g | |

## A–Z Vegetable Sauce

*Makes 4 servings*

### Ingredients

1 onion, chopped
2 garlic cloves, crushed
1 tin (400 g) chopped tomatoes
2 tbsps tomato purée
2 or more vegetables from the list below*
1 tbsp chopped fresh or 1 tsp dried basil
25 g (1 oz) parmesan, grated

### Method

(1) Place the onions, garlic and tomatoes in a large non-stick saucepan and boil for 3 minutes, or until the onion is soft.
(2) Add the tomato purée, prepared vegetables and basil. Cook for 4 minutes, or until the vegetables are tender but still firm.
(3) After combining the sauce with the pasta, sprinkle over the parmesan.

* 225 g (8 oz) asparagus, chopped into 4 cm lengths/2 courgettes, sliced/1 red, green or yellow pepper, chopped/225 g (8 oz) broccoli florets/150 g (5 oz) mange tout/1 small aubergine, finely chopped/100 g (4 oz) mushrooms, sliced/100 g (4oz) peas/100 g (4 oz) French beans, chopped into 4-cm lengths.

### Nutritional analysis

*Per serving (including 75 g/3 oz dried pasta)*

|  |  | % energy |
|---|---|---|
| Energy | 386 kcal | |
| Protein | 18 g | 10% |
| Fat | 4.6 g | 11% |
| Carbohydrate | 73 g | 70% |
| Fibre | 6.2 g | |

## Vegetarian Chilli Sauce

*Makes 4 servings*

### Ingredients

2 tsps oil
1 large onion, chopped
2 garlic cloves, crushed
1 small red chilli, deseeded and finely chopped (or ½ tsp dried chilli)
1 tin (420 g) red kidney beans, drained
450 ml (1 pt) passata (smooth sieved tomatoes)
2 celery stalks, finely chopped/
1 green pepper, finely chopped (optional)

### Method

(1) Heat the oil in a large non-stick pan. Add the onion, garlic and chilli (and the optional vegetables, if applicable) and cook for 3–4 minutes.
(2) Stir in the red kidney beans and passata, bring to the boil and simmer for a few minutes until the sauce has thickened.

### Nutritional analysis

*Per serving (including 75 g/3 oz dried pasta)*

| | | % energy |
|---|---|---|
| Energy | 428 kcal | |
| Protein | 18 g | 17% |
| Fat | 4.2 g | 9% |
| Carbohydrate | 85 g | 74% |
| Fibre | 9 g | |

## Tomato and Tuna

*Makes 4 servings*

### Ingredients

1 onion, chopped
1 garlic clove, crushed
1 tin (400 g) chopped tomatoes
1 tbsp tomato purée
100 g (4 oz) vegetables of choice (e.g. mushrooms, courgettes)
1 tin (200 g/7 oz) tuna in water or brine, drained and flaked
1 tsp dried basil

### Method

(1) Place the onion, garlic and tomatoes in a large non-stick frying pan and cook for 4–5 minutes, until the onion is soft.
(?) Stir in the tomato purée and vegetables and cook for 5 minutes.
(3) Add the tuna and basil and heat through.

### Nutritional analysis

*Per serving (including 75 g/3 oz dried pasta)*

| | | % energy |
|---|---|---|
| Energy | 369 kcal | |
| Protein | 22 g | 24% |
| Fat | 2.2 g | 5% |
| Carbohydrate | 70 g | 71% |
| Fibre | 3.9 g | |

## Quick Tuna and Sweetcorn Sauce

*Makes 4 servings*

### Ingredients

1 jar (400 g) ready-made pasta
sauce (any variety)
1 tin (225 g) sweetcorn, drained
1 tin (200 g) tuna in water or brine,
drained and flaked

### Method

(1) Place the pasta sauce, sweetcorn and tuna in a saucepan and cook for 3–4 minutes, until well heated through.

### Nutritional analysis

| Per serving (including 75 g/3 oz dried pasta) | | % energy |
|---|---|---|
| Energy | 480 kcal | |
| Protein | 26 g | 22% |
| Fat | 6.4 g | 12% |
| Carbohydrate | 84 g | 66% |
| Fibre | 4.5 g | |

## Tomato and Herb Sauce

*Makes 4 servings*

### Ingredients

2 tsps olive oil
1 onion, chopped
2 garlic cloves, crushed
1 red and 1 green pepper, chopped
1 tin (400 g) chopped tomatoes
1 tbsp each of fresh basil, fresh
parsley and fresh chives
(alternatively, use 1 tbsp dried
mixed herbs)

### Method

(1) Heat the oil in a large frying pan. Add the onion and garlic and cook for 3 minutes.
(2) Add the peppers and cook for 3–4 minutes, until softened.
(3) Add the tinned tomatoes and heat through or, time permitting, simmer for 5 minutes.
(4) Stir in the herbs just before serving.

### Nutritional analysis

| Per serving (including 75 g/3 oz dried pasta) | | % energy |
|---|---|---|
| Energy | 355 kcal | |
| Protein | 12 g | 14% |
| Fat | 3.9 g | 10% |
| Carbohydrate | 72 g | 76% |
| Fibre | 4.8 g | |

## Cheese Sauce (low fat version)

*Makes 4 servings*

### Ingredients

600 ml (1 pt) skimmed or semi-
skimmed milk
2 level tbsps cornflour
½ tsp Dijon mustard
75 g (3 oz) extra mature Cheddar
cheese, grated
Freshly ground black pepper

### Method

(1) Blend the cornflour with a little of the milk in
a jug. Gradually add the remainder of the milk,
stirring to ensure a smooth sauce.
(2) Pour into a saucepan and heat, stirring constantly until the sauce just reaches the boil and
has thickened.
(3) Remove from the heat, stir in the mustard,
cheese and freshly ground black pepper to taste.
Serve immediately to prevent a skin forming over
the surface.

### Nutritional analysis

| *Per serving (including 75 g/3 oz dried pasta)* | | *% energy* |
|---|---|---|
| Energy | 463 kcal | |
| Protein | 21 g | 18% |
| Fat | 9.1 g | 18% |
| Carbohydrate | 79 g | 64% |
| Fibre | 2.6 g | |

## Ham and Mushroom Sauce

*Makes 4 servings*

### Ingredients

1 tsp oil
4 slices (100 g) ham (preferably
reduced salt), chopped
225 g (8 oz) small mushrooms,
halved
2 tbsps cornflour
600 ml (1 pt) skimmed or semi-
skimmed milk
1 tsp dried oregano or basil
Freshly ground black pepper

### Method

(1) Heat the oil in a large frying pan. Cook the
ham and mushrooms for 4–5 minutes.
(2) Stir in the cornflour together with a little milk.
Gradually add the rest of the milk, stirring
continuously.
(3) Heat until the sauce just reaches boiling point.
Remove from the heat and stir in the herbs and
pepper.

### Nutritional analysis

| *Per serving (including 75 g/3 oz dried pasta)* | | *% energy* |
|---|---|---|
| Energy | 429 kcal | |
| Protein | 22 g | 21% |
| Fat | 4.7 g | 10% |
| Carbohydrate | 79 g | 69% |
| Fibre | 3.2 g | |

## Chicken and Mushroom Sauce

*Makes 4 servings*

### Ingredients

1 tbsp oil
1 onion, chopped
4 boneless chicken breasts (approx.
75 g/3 oz each), sliced into 1-cm
strips
100 g (4 oz) mushrooms, sliced
225 g (8 oz) fromage blanc or quark
Juice of ½ lemon
Freshly ground black pepper

### Method

(1) Heat the oil in a non-stick frying pan. Cook the onion for 3–4 minutes until softened.
(2) Add the chicken strips and cook for 3 minutes.
(3) Stir in the mushrooms followed by the romage blanc or quark, lemon juice and black pepper to taste. Cook for 2–3 minutes until well heated through.

### Nutritional analysis

| Per serving (including 75 g/3 oz dried pasta) | | % energy |
|---|---|---|
| Energy | 465 kcal | |
| Protein | 34 g | 29% |
| Fat | 7.3 g | 14% |
| Carbohydrate | 70 g | 57% |
| Fibre | 3.1 g | |

## Broccoli and Cheese Sauce

*Makes 4 servings*

### Ingredients

1 quantity cheese sauce (see above)
450 g (1 lb) broccoli
Freshly ground black pepper to
taste

### Method

(1) Prepare the cheese sauce.
(2) Divide the broccoli into small florets. Either steam or cook in a little fast-boiling water for 3–4 minutes until tender crisp.
(3) Drain immediately and combine with the cheese sauce. Add freshly ground black pepper to taste.

### Nutritional analysis

| Per serving (including 75 g/3 oz dried pasta) | | % energy |
|---|---|---|
| Energy | 502 kcal | |
| Protein | 25 g | 20% |
| Fat | 10 g | 19% |
| Carbohydrate | 82 g | 61% |
| Fibre | 6.5 g | |

## Basic Red Lentil Sauce

*Makes 4 servings*

### Ingredients

2 tsps oil
1 onion, chopped
2 garlic cloves, crushed
225 g (8 oz) red lentils
800 ml (1½ pints) water
2 vegetable stock cubes or 2 tbsps
vegetable stock concentrate
1 red, yellow or green pepper/2
courgettes/2 carrots/100 g (4 oz)
mushrooms/1 small aubergine
(all optional)

### Method

(1) Heat the oil in a large non-stick saucepan or pressure cooker. Cook the onion and garlic for 3–4 minutes.
(2) Add the lentils, water and stock cubes or concentrate.
(3) Bring to the boil, stirring to dissolve the stock. Simmer for 30 minutes or cook in the pressure cooker for 3 minutes then remove from the heat.
(4) Add optional vegetables of your choice and continue to cook until the vegetables are tender.

### Nutritional analysis

*Per serving (including 75 g/3 oz dried pasta)*

|  |  | % energy |
|---|---|---|
| Energy | 502 kcal | |
| Protein | 24 g | 19% |
| Fat | 4.3 g | 8% |
| Carbohydrate | 98 g | 73% |
| Fibre | 5.5 g | |

## Pasta One-pot Dishes

## Pasta and Lentil Pot

*Makes 4 servings*

### Ingredients

350 g (12 oz) fusilli
2 large carrots, thinly sliced
100 g (4 oz) frozen peas
1 tbsp olive oil
1 onion, chopped
1 clove garlic, crushed
1 can (400 g) lentil soup
15 g (½ oz) parmesan cheese,
grated

### Method

(1) Boil the fusilli in a large saucepan of water for about 5 minutes. Add the carrots and continue cooking for a further 3 minutes. Add the peas and cook for a further 2 minutes. Drain.
(2) Meanwhile, sauté the onion and garlic in the olive oil until soft. Add to the fusilli.
(3) Add the soup to the pasta pot and cook until hot, about 2 minutes. Stir in the parmesan cheese and serve.

### Nutritional analysis

*Per serving*

|  |  | % energy |
|---|---|---|
| Energy | 476 kcal | |
| Protein | 19 g | 16% |
| Fat | 10 g | 19% |
| Carbohydrate | 84 g | 65% |
| Fibre | 6.4 g | |

## Baked Macaroni Pie

*Makes 4 servings*

### Ingredients

1 tsp olive oil
1 large onion, sliced
225 g (8 oz) sliced vegetables of
your choice, e.g. mushrooms,
peppers, tomatoes, courgettes
2 tbsps low fat spread
2 tbsps cornflour
600 ml (1 pt) skimmed milk
50 g (2 oz) mature (strong)
Cheddar cheese
350 g (12 oz) macaroni

### Method

(1) In a non-stick pan, sauté the vegetables in the olive oil over a high heat until browned.
(2) Whisk together the low fat spread, cornflour and milk in a saucepan over a medium heat until thickened. Stir in the cheese.
(3) Boil the macaroni for 10 minutes. Drain.
(4) In a large pyrex baking dish, layer half the macaroni, vegetables and sauce and repeat, finishing with a layer of sauce.
(5) Bake in an oven at 180°C/350°F/gas mark 4 until hot and bubbly (about 20 minutes). Alternatively, cook in a microwave at full power for 7 minutes.

### Nutritional analysis

| Per serving | | % energy |
|---|---|---|
| Energy | 495 kcal | |
| Protein | 21 g | 17% |
| Fat | 10 g | 19% |
| Carbohydrate | 85 g | 64% |
| Fibre | 8.5 g | |

## Tuna and Pasta Bake

*Makes 4 servings*

### Ingredients

Pasta bake:
2 tsps olive oil
1 onion, sliced
3 sticks of celery, chopped
100 g (4 oz) mushrooms, sliced
350 g (12 oz) dry weight pasta
shells, cooked
3 tbsps fresh parsley, chopped
1 tin (200 g/7 oz) tuna in water,
drained

White sauce:
1 tbsp low fat spread
1 tbsp cornflour
450 ml (¾ pt) skimmed milk

### Method

(1) In a non-stick frying pan, sauté the vegetables in the olive oil.
(2) Prepare the white sauce by whisking all the sauce ingredients in a pan over a medium heat until thickened.
(3) Spoon layers of the vegetables, pasta, tuna and white sauce into a baking dish, sprinkling parsley between each layer and finishing with a layer of the sauce.
(4) Bake at 190°C/375°F/gas mark 5 for 20 minutes. Alternatively cook in the microwave for 6 minutes.

### Nutritional analysis

| Per serving | | % energy |
|---|---|---|
| Energy | 437 kcal | |
| Protein | 26 g | 24% |
| Fat | 5.6 g | 11% |
| Carbohydrate | 76 g | 65% |
| Fibre | 3.5 g | |

## Pasta with Spinach and Cheese

*Makes 4 servings*

### Ingredients

350 g (12 oz) dried ribbon pasta,
e.g. tagliatelle
1 tbsp oil
2 garlic cloves, crushed
450 g (1 lb) fresh or frozen spinach
½ tsp nutmeg
100 g (4 oz) fromage blanc or low
fat soft cheese
Salt and freshly ground
black pepper

### Method

(1) Cook the pasta in boiling water according to directions on the packet. Drain.
(2) Meanwhile, heat the oil in a frying pan and sauté the garlic for 2 minutes.
(3) Add the spinach and stir until the spinach is wilted, about 2 minutes
(4) Add the nutmeg and fromage blanc or low fat soft cheese. Combine well and heat through.
(5) Add the drained pasta and season to taste.

### Nutritional analysis

| Per serving | | % energy |
|---|---|---|
| Energy | 370 kcal | |
| Protein | 16 g | 17% |
| Fat | 5.3 g | 13% |
| Carbohydrate | 69 g | 70% |
| Fibre | 4.9 g | |

## Pasta with Beans

*Makes 4 servings*

### Ingredients

350 g (12 oz) pasta shapes
1 jar (400 g) ready made pasta
sauce
1 tin (420 g) beans*
2 tbsps parmesan, grated

### Method

(1) Cook the pasta in boiling water according to directions on the packet. Drain.
(2) Meanwhile, combine the pasta sauce and beans in a saucepan and heat through.
(3) Add the drained pasta. Serve topped with the parmesan.

* This recipe works well with chick peas, red kidney beans, or pinto beans.

### Nutritional analysis

| Per serving | | % energy |
|---|---|---|
| Energy | 493 kcal | |
| Protein | 22 g | 18% |
| Fat | 8.6 g | 16% |
| Carbohydrate | 87 g | 66% |
| Fibre | 6.8 g | |

## Pasta with Cheese and Walnuts

This may sound like an odd combination if you've never tried it before, but it is one which works surprisingly well. This is an adapted version of my mother's Hungarian recipe.

*Makes 4 servings*

### Ingredients

350 g (12 oz) tagliatelle or other ribbon pasta
50 g (2 oz) chopped or roughly crushed walnuts
225 g (8 oz) cottage cheese
2 tsps brown sugar

### Method

(1) Cook the pasta according to directions on the packet. Drain.
(2) Combine the walnuts, cottage cheese and sugar.
(3) Stir in the pasta and heat through (do not bring to the boil).

### Nutritional analysis

| *Per serving* | | *% energy* |
|---|---|---|
| Energy | 467 kcal | |
| Protein | 20 g | 18% |
| Fat | 4 g | 27% |
| Carbohydrate | 69 g | 55% |
| Fibre | 3.1 g | |

## Meat Lasagne (low fat version)

*Makes 4 servings*

### Ingredients

1 onion, chopped
2 courgettes, sliced
225 g (8 oz) extra lean beef mince (or turkey mince)
1 tin (400 g) chopped tomatoes
3 tbsps tomato purée
1 tsp basil or oregano
Salt and pepper to taste
12 sheets lasagne (not pre-cook variety)
350 g (12 oz) cottage cheese
75 g (3 oz) reduced fat mozzarella

### Method

(1) Heat a large non-stick frying pan. Cook the onion, courgette and mince, stirring frequently, for 5–6 minutes until the mince is no longer pink. Drain off any fat.
(2) Add the tomatoes, tomato purée, and herbs. Season with salt and pepper to taste.
(3) Place 4 sheets of lasagne at the bottom of an oiled baking dish. Spoon over one third of the meat mixture and one third of the cottage cheese.
(4) Repeat the layers, finishing with a layer of cottage cheese.
(5) Cover with very thin slices of mozzarella.
(6) Bake at 180°C/350°F/gas mark 4 for 30 minutes.

*Variation*
♦ Add vegetables, e.g. mushrooms, peppers, spinach, to the mince mixture instead of the courgettes.

### Nutritional analysis

| *Per serving* | | *% energy* |
|---|---|---|
| Energy | 548 kcal | |
| Protein | 44 g | 32% |
| Fat | 10 g | 17% |
| Carbohydrate | 75 g | 51% |
| Fibre | 4.5 g | |

# Bean Lasagne

*Makes 4 servings*

## Ingredients

1 tbsp oil
1 onion
225 g (8 oz) vegetables of your choice*
1 tbsp taco seasoning mix (or mild curry powder)
1 tin (400 g) red kidney beans, drained
400 g (14 oz) passata (smooth sieved tomatoes)
225 g (8 oz) low fat fromage frais
40 g (1½ oz) mature Cheddar cheese, grated
12 sheets lasagne (not pre-cook variety)

## Method

(1) Heat the oil in a large frying pan. Cook the onion for 3–4 minutes. Add the vegetables and continue cooking for 2–3 minutes.
(2) Stir in the taco seasoning or curry powder, beans and passata. Simmer for a few minutes until the sauce thickens slightly.
(3) Lay 4 sheets of lasagne at the bottom of an oiled baking dish. Cover with one third of the bean mixture. Continue with the layers, finishing with the bean mixture.
(4) Spoon over the fromage frais and sprinkle with the cheese.
(5) Bake at 180°C/350°F/gas mark 4 for 30 minutes.

* Broccoli florets, green beans, courgettes, peppers

## Nutritional analysis

| Per serving | | % energy |
|---|---|---|
| Energy | 530 kcal | |
| Protein | 27 g | 20% |
| Fat | 9.3 g | 16% |
| Carbohydrate | 91 g | 64% |
| Fibre | 11 g | |

# Chicken and Mushrooms with Pasta

*Makes 4 servings*

## Ingredients

4 chicken drumsticks or thighs, skinned
1 tbsp olive oil
1 onion, sliced
2 green or red peppers, sliced
225 g (8 oz) mushrooms, sliced
450 ml (16 fl oz) passata (smooth sieved tomatoes)
350 g (12 oz) small pasta shapes
300 ml (½ pt) stock or water

## Method

(1) Sauté the chicken drumsticks in the oil over a high heat until it is browned. Remove from the pan and set aside on a plate.
(2) Add the onions, peppers and mushrooms to the pan and cook for 5–10 minutes.
(3) Add the passata, chicken, pasta and stock or water. Bring to the boil and simmer until the pasta is tender and the chicken cooked through, about 10 minutes.
(4) Accompany with warm French bread.

## Nutritional analysis

| Per serving | | % energy |
|---|---|---|
| Energy | 470 kcal | |
| Protein | 31 g | 26% |
| Fat | 8.6 g | 17% |
| Carbohydrate | 72 g | 57% |
| Fibre | 5.4 g | |

## Pasta 'n' Peas

This is one of my favourite emergency meals if I'm pressed for time and the store cupboard is nearly empty. It takes 10 minutes to make and is a near-perfect nutritionally balanced meal.

*Makes 4 servings*

### Ingredients

350 g (12 oz) pasta shapes
225 g (8 oz) frozen peas
250 ml (9 fl oz) passata (smooth sieved tomatoes)
Salt and freshly ground black pepper
1 tsp dried oregano
1–2 tbsps grated parmesan

### Method

(1) Cook the pasta in boiling water for 7 minutes. Add the peas and continue cooking for a further 3 minutes. Drain.
(2) Stir in the passata, salt, pepper, oregano and parmesan. Heat through then serve.

### Nutritional analysis

| *Per serving* | | *% energy* |
|---|---|---|
| Energy | 359 kcal | |
| Protein | 15 g | 17% |
| Fat | 3 g | 7% |
| Carbohydrate | 72 g | 76% |
| Fibre | 5.8 g | |

# 17

# Bread

Home-made bread is surprisingly easy to make, and good exercise for the forearms and shoulders! The effort is truly worth it as it tastes entirely different from mass-produced sliced bread. Don't be put off by the length of time it takes to make – go and have a workout while the dough rises!

## Basic Brown Bread

*Makes 2 loaves (12 slices each)*

### Ingredients

225 g (8 oz) strong white flour
225 g (8 oz) strong wholemeal flour
1 sachet easy blend yeast
1½ tsps salt
350 ml (12 fl oz) warm water (or half water, half milk)
1 tbsp oil

### Method

(1) Mix together the flours, yeast and salt in a large bowl.
(2) Make a well in the centre and add the oil and half of the water (or milk). Stir with a wooden spoon, gradually adding more liquid until you have a pliable dough.
(3) Turn the dough out onto a floured surface. Knead, adding a little more flour if necessary, until you have a smooth, elastic, not-too-sticky dough. This should take 5–10 minutes.
(4) Place the dough in a clean lightly-oiled bowl, cover with a tea towel and leave in a warm place for approximately 1 hour, or until doubled in size.
(5) Punch down the dough and knead for a further 5 minutes.
(6) Shape into 2 loaves and place in lightly-oiled tins or on a baking sheet. Make 3 or 4 shallow cuts with a knife, cover with a tea towel, and leave for 30 minutes until almost doubled in size.
(7) Brush with milk and bake at 200°C/400°F/gas mark 6 for 40–50 minutes. They should sound hollow when tapped on the bottom.

*Variations*
◆ White Bread: replace the wholemeal flour with white. You will need a little less liquid.
◆ Bread Rolls: after the first rising, roll the dough into balls. Reduce the baking time to 30–35 minutes.
◆ Herb Bread: add 2 tsps dried mixed herbs to the flour mixture.
◆ Italian Bread: add 2 tbsps olive oil and 2 tsps dried oregano or rosemary to the mixture. Shape into 2 flat rounds and brush with a little olive oil instead of milk.
◆ Oatmeal Bread: replace 100 g (4 oz) of the wholemeal flour with 100 g (4 oz) oatmeal.

## Nutritional analysis

*Per serving (1 slice)*

| | | *% energy* |
|---|---|---|
| Energy | 65 kcal | |
| Protein | 2.3 g | 14% |
| Fat | 0.8 g | 11% |
| Carbohydrate | 13 g | 75% |
| Fibre | 1.1 g | |

## Soda Bread

This recipe uses baking powder instead of yeast to make the bread rise, and also requires no kneading so it really is a super-quick method of making your own nutritious bread. The texture is between that of a bread and a cake – it is light, crumbly and definitely moreish. It only keeps fresh for two days but chances are there won't be anything left after a day!

*Makes 1 loaf (12 slices)*

### Ingredients

100 g (4 oz) wholemeal flour
100 g (4 oz) white flour
1 tbsp baking powder
½ tsp salt
2 cartons (2 x 125 g) plain yoghurt
200 ml (7 fl oz) skimmed milk
1 level tbsp honey

### Method

(1) Mix together the flours, baking powder and salt in a bowl. Make a well in the centre.
(2) Mix together the yoghurt, milk and honey in a separate bowl.
(3) Pour this liquid mixture into the centre of the dry ingredients. Mix with a wooden spoon until thoroughly blended. The dough should be very soft, almost like a stiff cake batter. Add a little more milk or flour if necessary.
(4) With your floured hands, form into a round loaf (or your preferred shape) and place on a lightly-oiled baking tray. Cut a shallow cross on the top.
(5) Bake at 200°C/400°F/gas mark 6 for approximately 35 minutes. It should sound hollow when tapped on the bottom.

*Variations*
◆ Cheese Soda Bread: add 50 g (2 oz) grated mature cheese to the dry ingredients.
◆ Nutty Soda Bread: add 75 g (3 oz) chopped walnuts, pecans or almonds to the dry ingredients.
◆ Herb Soda Bread: add ½ tsp each of dried basil, tarragon, parsley and thyme to the dry ingredients.

## Nutritional analysis

*Per serving (1 slice)*

| | | *% energy* |
|---|---|---|
| Energy | 90 kcal | |
| Protein | 3.9 g | 18% |
| Fat | 0.6 g | 5% |
| Carbohydrate | 18 g | 77% |
| Fibre | 1.3 g | |

# Cornmeal Bread

This recipe also uses baking powder to raise the bread and produces a fantastically light, cake-like result. It is particularly good served with soups, stews, hot pots and any Mexican dish. Cornmeal has a higher fibre and vitamin content than white flour.

*Makes 1 loaf (16 slices)*

## Ingredients

100 g (4 oz) white or wholemeal flour
100 g (4 oz) yellow cornmeal
1 tbsp baking powder
¼ tsp salt
1 tbsp honey or sugar
1 egg
2 cartons (2 x 125 g) plain yoghurt or 250 ml buttermilk
50 g (2 oz) chopped canned green chillies/1 can (112 g) creamed sweetcorn/½ tsp chilli powder/ 50 g (2 oz) grated cheese (all optional)

## Method

(1) Mix together the flour, cornmeal, baking powder and salt in a bowl.
(2) Make a well in the centre.
(3) Mix together the honey or sugar, egg and yoghurt or buttermilk. Pour this into the well together with any optional ingredients.
(4) Mix together briefly with a wooden spoon (do not overmix). This should produce a soft cake-like batter.
(5) Spread into an oiled 20 cm (8 in) square baking dish. Bake at 190°C/375°F/gas mark 5 for 30–35 minutes.

## Nutritional analysis

| *Per serving (1 slice)* | | *% energy* |
|---|---|---|
| Energy | 73 kcal | |
| Protein | 2.6 g | 15% |
| Fat | 0.9 g | 11% |
| Carbohydrate | 14 g | 74% |
| Fibre | 0.4 g | |

## Raisin Bread

The perfect snack food for eating on the run, it is high in complex carbohydrate, low in fat and the raisins add subtle sweetness and extra fibre.

*Makes 1 loaf (16 slices)*

### Ingredients

225 g (8 oz) flour (half wholemeal, half white)
1 tbsp baking powder
½ tsp salt
3 tbsps oil
1 egg
250 ml (8 fl oz) skimmed milk
1 tbsp honey
100 g (4 oz) raisins

### Method

(1) Mix together the flour, baking powder and salt in a bowl. Make a well in the centre.
(2) Mix together the egg, milk and honey in a separate bowl.
(3) Pour this liquid mixture into the centre of the dry ingredients together with the raisins. Mix with a wooden spoon until thoroughly blended. The batter should be very soft, almost like a stiff cake batter.
(4) Spoon into an oiled 20 cm (8 in) round cake tin or small loaf tin.
(5) Bake at 190°C/375°F/gas mark 5 for 30–35 minutes until lightly browned on top. It should sound hollow when tapped on the bottom.

### Nutritional analysis

| Per serving (1 slice) | | % energy |
|---|---|---|
| Energy | 100 kcal | |
| Protein | 2.7 g | 11% |
| Fat | 2.8 g | 25% |
| Carbohydrate | 17 g | 64% |
| Fibre | 1 g | |

# Focaccia Bread

Focaccia is a large flat Italian bread. It is traditionally flavoured with olive oil, salt, garlic or herbs.

*Makes 2 focaccia (8 slices each)*

## Ingredients

450 g (1 lb) strong white flour
1 sachet easy blend yeast
1 tsp salt
325 ml (11 fl oz) warm water
3 tbsps olive oil
12 black olives/3–4 chopped cloves garlic/2 tbsps chopped fresh rosemary (all optional)

## Method

(1) Mix together the flour, yeast and salt in a large bowl.
(2) Make a well in the centre and add 1 tbsp of the oil and the water. Stir with a wooden spoon until you have a soft dough.
(3) Turn the dough out onto a floured surface. Knead, adding a little more flour if necessary, until you have a smooth dough. This should take 5–10 minutes.
(4) Place the dough in a clean lightly-oiled bowl, cover with a tea towel and leave in a warm place for approximately 1 hour, or until doubled in size.
(5) Punch down the dough, knead briefly, halve and roll into 2 round or oval shapes.
(6) Brush the surface with a little olive oil, cover with a tea towel, and leave for approximately 30 minutes.
(7) Using your fingertips, dimple the surface of the dough, pushing about half-way in. Brush with the remaining olive oil and scatter over the optional ingredients if applicable. Bake at 200°C/400°F/gas mark 6 for 25 minutes, or until golden.

## Nutritional analysis

*Per serving (1 slice)*

|  |  | % energy |
| --- | --- | --- |
| Energy | 114 kcal | |
| Protein | 3.2 g | 11% |
| Fat | 2.5 g | 19% |
| Carbohydrate | 21 g | 70% |
| Fibre | 0.9 g | |

## Herb Flatbread

The perfect bread for eating with Italian food, main course salads, grilled vegetables and grilled chicken dishes.

*Makes 1 loaf (8 slices)*

### Ingredients

225 g (8 oz) strong white flour
½ tsp salt
1 tbsp olive oil
½ sachet easy blend yeast
175 ml (6 fl oz) warm water or milk
2 tbsps fresh chopped herbs, e.g.
oregano, rosemary, thyme

### Method

(1) Mix together the flour, salt, olive oil and yeast in a large bowl.
(2) Make a well in the middle and slowly add the warm water or milk, mixing with a large wooden spoon until the dough comes together.
(3) Turn out onto a floured surface and knead until you have a smooth elastic dough.
(4) Place in an oiled bowl, cover and leave in a warm place for approximately 1 hour, until the dough is doubled in volume.
(5) Punch the dough down. Knead a few times while incorporating the herbs.
(6) Shape into a large flat round loaf, about 30 cm (12 in) in diameter. Brush with a little olive oil. Place on a baking tray, and leave to rise in a warm place for a further 20–30 minutes. Bake at 200°C/400°F/gas mark 6 for about 25 minutes until golden.

*Variations*
◆ Cheese and Onion Flatbread: substitute 1 small finely chopped onion for the herbs. Sprinkle a little Cheddar over the top just before baking.
◆ Sun-dried Tomato Flatbread: add 75 g (3 oz) chopped sun-dried tomatoes (drained) and sprinkle the top with parmesan just before baking.

### Nutritional analysis

| *Per serving (1 slice)* | | *% energy* |
|---|---|---|
| Energy | 109 kcal | |
| Protein | 3.3 g | 12% |
| Fat | 1.8 g | 15% |
| Carbohydrate | 21 g | 73% |
| Fibre | 0.9 g | |

## Oatmeal Bread

A terrific loaf that's perfect with a chunk of cheese or spread with honey at breakfast. Oats add extra fibre (soluble), B vitamins and protein.

*Makes 1 loaf (16 slices)*

### Ingredients

225 g (8 oz) strong white flour
100 g (4 oz) oats
1½ tsps salt
1 sachet yeast
2 tbsps sugar
4 tbsps margarine or butter
250 ml (8 fl oz) warm water

### Method

(1) Mix together the flour, oats, salt, yeast and sugar in a large bowl. Rub in the margarine or butter.
(2) Make a well in the middle and slowly add the warm water, mixing with a wooden spoon until the dough comes together.
(3) Turn out onto a floured surface and knead until you have a smooth elastic dough.
(4) Place in an oiled bowl, cover and leave in a warm place for approximately 1 hour, until the dough is doubled in volume.
(5) Punch the dough down. Knead for a few more minutes.
(6) Shape into an oval or round loaf. Place on a baking tray, leave to rise in a warm place for a further 30 minutes and brush with a little milk. Sprinkle with some extra oats and bake at 200°C/400°F/gas mark 6 for about 25 minutes until golden.

*Variations*
◆ Cinnamon Oatmeal Bread: add ½ tsp cinnamon to the flour mixture.
◆ Honey Nut Oatmeal Bread: substitute honey for the sugar. Incorporate 100 g (4 oz) chopped walnuts during the second kneading.

### Nutritional analysis

| *Per serving (1 slice)* | | *% energy* |
|---|---|---|
| Energy | 105 kcal | |
| Protein | 2.6 g | 10% |
| Fat | 3 g | 25% |
| Carbohydrate | 18 g | 65% |
| Fibre | 1 g | |

## Sunflower Bread

This bread has a wonderful nutty taste and a slightly crumbly texture. The sunflower seeds are rich in vitamin E, essential fatty acids and protein (substitute pumpkin seeds if you prefer).

*Makes 1 loaf (16 slices)*

### Ingredients

100 g (4 oz) strong wholemeal flour
175 g (6 oz) strong white flour
50 g (2 oz) oats
¾ tsp salt
1 sachet easy blend yeast
250 ml (8 fl oz) warm water
2 tbsps oil
2 tbsps honey
50 g (2 oz) sunflower seeds

### Method

(1) Mix together the flours, oats, salt, and yeast in a large bowl.
(2) Mix together the water, oil and honey. Make a well in the middle of the flour and slowly add the liquid until the dough comes together.
(3) Turn out onto a floured surface and knead until you have a smooth elastic dough.
(4) Place in an oiled bowl, cover and leave in a warm place for approximately 1 hour, until the dough is doubled in volume.
(5) Punch the dough down. Knead for a few more minutes, incorporating the sunflower seeds (reserve 1 tablespoonful).
(6) Place in a 2 lb loaf tin, leave to rise in a warm place for a further 30 minutes and brush with a little milk. Sprinkle with the reserved sunflower seeds. Bake at 200°C/400°F/gas mark 6 for 30–40 minutes until firm and golden.

### Nutritional analysis

*Per serving (1 slice)*

| | | *% energy* |
|---|---|---|
| Energy | 118 kcal | |
| Protein | 3.5 g | 12% |
| Fat | 3.8 g | 29% |
| Carbohydrate | 19 g | 59% |
| Fibre | 1.5 g | |

## Banana Bread

Spread with a little butter, this slightly sweet bread is the perfect refuelling snack.

*Makes 1 loaf (16 slices)*

### Ingredients

225 g (8 oz) strong white flour
100 g (4 oz) oats
1 tsp salt
1 sachet easy blend yeast
1 tbsp honey or sugar
2 tbsps oil
150 ml (5 fl oz) warm water
2 large bananas, mashed

### Method

(1) Mix together the flour, oats, salt, yeast and honey or sugar in a large bowl.
(2) Mix the oil and water. Make a well in the middle and slowly add the liquid and mashed bananas, mixing with a wooden spoon until the dough comes together.
(3) Turn out onto a flourèd surface and knead until you have a smooth elastic dough.
(4) Place in an oiled bowl, cover and leave in a warm place for approximately 1 hour, until the dough is doubled in volume.
(5) Punch the dough down. Knead for a few more minutes.
(6) Place in a 2 lb loaf tin, leave to rise in a warm place for a further 30 minutes and brush with a little milk. Bake at 200°C/400°F/gas mark 6 for 30–40 minutes until golden.

### Nutritional analysis

*Per serving (1 slice)*

| | | % energy |
|---|---|---|
| Energy | 109 kcal | |
| Protein | 2.8 g | 10% |
| Fat | 2.3 g | 19% |
| Carbohydrate | 21 g | 71% |
| Fibre | 1.1 g | |

## Blueberry Bread

This is one of my favourites: it's slightly sweet with a light cake-like texture. If you cannot use blueberries, substitute raisins.

*Makes 1 loaf (16 slices)*

### Ingredients

100 g (4 oz) cornmeal
225 g (8 oz) strong white flour
1½ tsps salt
1 sachet easy blend yeast
2 tbsps sugar
175 g (6 oz) cottage cheese
1½ tbsps butter or margarine
75 ml (3 fl oz) warm water
175 g (6 oz) fresh blueberries (or 75 g/3 oz dried)

### Method

(1) Mix together the cornmeal, flour, salt, yeast and sugar in a large bowl.
(2) Mix in the cottage cheese and butter or margarine using a fork. Make a well in the middle and slowly add the water until the dough comes together.
(3) Turn out onto a floured surface and knead until you have a smooth elastic dough.
(4) Place in an oiled bowl, cover and leave in a warm place for approximately 1 hour, until the dough is doubled in volume.
(5) Punch the dough down. Knead for a few more minutes, incorporating the blueberries.
(6) Place in a 2 lb loaf tin, leave to rise in a warm place for a further 30 minutes and brush with a little milk. Bake at 200°C/400°F/gas mark 6 for 30–40 minutes until firm and golden.

### Nutritional analysis

| *Per serving (1 slice)* | | *% energy* |
|---|---|---|
| Energy | 105 kcal | |
| Protein | 4 g | 15% |
| Fat | 1.7 g | 14% |
| Carbohydrate | 19 g | 71% |
| Fibre | 1 g | |

## Coconut Pineapple Bread

A wonderful fun bread; great for Sunday brunch or for an afternoon snack.

*Makes 1 loaf (16 slices)*

### Ingredients

225 g (8 oz) strong white flour
⅔ tsp salt
1 sachet easy blend yeast
2 tbsps sugar
2½ tbsps grated coconut (or desiccated)
2½ tbsps oil
2–3 tbsps milk
175 g (6 oz) fromage frais
175 g (6 oz) tinned crushed pineapple, drained

### Method

(1) Mix together the flour, salt, yeast, sugar and coconut in a large bowl.
(2) Add the oil, milk, fromage frais and pineapple and mix using a fork.
(3) Turn out onto a floured surface and knead until you have a smooth elastic dough.
(4) Place in an oiled bowl, cover and leave in a warm place for approximately 1 hour, until the dough is doubled in volume.
(5) Punch the dough down. Knead for a few more minutes.
(6) Place in a 2 lb loaf tin, leave to rise in a warm place for a further 30 minutes and brush with a little milk. Bake at 200°C/400°F/gas mark 6 for 30–40 minutes until firm and golden.

### Nutritional analysis

| *Per serving (1 loaf)* | | *% energy* |
|---|---|---|
| Energy | 92 kcal | |
| Protein | 2.6 g | 12% |
| Fat | 2.9 g | 28% |
| Carbohydrate | 15 g | 60% |
| Fibre | 0.7 g | |

## Orange Cinnamon Bread

Excellent for boosting your energy levels in the morning.

*Makes 1 loaf (12 slices)*

### Ingredients

225 g (8 oz) strong white flour
½ tsp salt
1 sachet easy blend yeast
1 tsp sugar
1½ tsps cinnamon
1 tsp grated orange peel
1½ tbsps butter or margarine
175 ml (6 floz) orange juice

### Method

(1) Mix together the flour, salt, yeast, sugar, cinnamon and orange peel in a large bowl. Rub in the butter or margarine.
(2) Slowly add the orange juice until the dough comes together.
(3) Turn out onto a floured surface and knead until you have a smooth elastic dough.
(4) Place in an oiled bowl, cover and leave in a warm place for approximately 1 hour, until the dough is doubled in volume.
(5) Punch the dough down. Knead for a few more minutes.
(6) Place in a 2 lb loaf tin, leave to rise in a warm place for a further 30 minutes and brush with a little milk. Bake at 200°C/400°F/gas mark 6 for 30–40 minutes, until firm and golden.

### Nutritional analysis

| *Per serving (1 slice)* | | *% energy* |
|---|---|---|
| Energy | 80 kcal | |
| Protein | 2.2 g | 11% |
| Fat | 1.3 g | 15% |
| Carbohydrate | 16 g | 74% |
| Fibre | 0.6 g | |

## Fruit Buns

Make a large batch of these buns for the freezer. They are an excellent and convenient snack for post-workout refuelling or even for breakfast on the run.

*Makes 12 servings*

### Ingredients

350 g (12 oz) strong white flour
½ tsp salt
1 sachet easy blend yeast
40 g (1½ oz) sugar
1 tsp cinnamon
175 ml (6 fl oz) milk
2 eggs
3 tbsps butter or margarine, melted
100 g (4 oz) raisins

### Method

(1) Mix together the flour, salt, yeast, sugar and cinnamon in a large bowl.
(2) Mix together the milk, eggs and melted butter or margarine in a separate bowl. Make a well in the flour and gradually add the liquid, stirring with a spoon until the dough comes together.
(3) Turn out onto a floured surface and knead until you have a smooth elastic dough.
(4) Place in an oiled bowl, cover and leave in a warm place for approximately 1 hour, until the dough is doubled in volume.
(5) Punch the dough down. Knead for a few more minutes, incorporating the raisins.
(6) Cut the dough into 12 equal pieces, shape each one into a ball and place on an oiled baking tray. Cover and leave to rise in a warm place for approximately 30 minutes or until doubled in volume. Brush with milk and bake at 190°C/375°F/gas mark 5 for 20–25 minutes.

### Nutritional analysis

| Per serving (1 bun) | | % energy |
|---|---|---|
| Energy | 179 kcal | |
| Protein | 5.3 g | 12% |
| Fat | 3.6 g | 18% |
| Carbohydrate | 33 g | 70% |
| Fibre | 1.1 g | |

# Potatoes

Potatoes are the perfect energy food for athletes. They are high in complex carbohydrate and extremely low in fat. A plain baked potato eaten 30 minutes before your workout will boost blood sugar levels, sustain your energy levels during exercise, and delay fatigue. Eaten within two hours after exercise, the carbohydrates will quickly refuel your glycogen stores and speed your recovery.

---

### ♦ Nutrition facts ♦

- Almost half of the fibre is found in the skin of potatoes, so once you peel them you lose a good deal of the fibre.
- Potatoes contain lots of potassium and hardly any sodium, which is good for keeping cramps at bay and your blood pressure in check.
- Potatoes are also a great source of vitamin C, thiamin (a B vitamin), magnesium, iron and folic acid.
- New potatoes and freshly dug main crop potatoes contain the most vitamin C, but this steadily falls with storage. Freshly dug potatoes contain 21 mg of vitamin C per 100 g but this drops to 9 mg after three months of storage and 7 mg after nine months.

---

## Vitamin C

- You'll lose hefty amounts of vitamin C during peeling, preparation and cooking. A lot of the vitamin C is found just below the skin so cook potatoes in their skins for maximum goodness – bake or boil them in jackets, and leave the skins on when roasting and making chips.
- If you must peel potatoes, do so very thinly and just before cooking. Plunge into fast boiling water and only boil for as long as necessary to make them just soft (do not overcook). Drain and serve straight away.

## The vitamin C content of potatoes

|  | Vitamin C mg/200 g portion |
|---|---|
| Boiled new potatoes | 32 |
| Boiled old potatoes | 12 |
| Baked old potatoes | 16 |
| Chips (home-made) | 18 |

(The recommended daily intake of vitamin C is 40 mg.)

## Are potatoes fattening?

It's an old myth that potatoes are fattening, stemming from the '60s and '70s when low carbohydrate, high protein diets were in vogue. Nutritionists have since discovered that carbohydrates are definitely not the culprit – it is fat that makes us fat.

Carbohydrate gives us energy and helps satisfy our appetite; it's what you add to your potatoes that counts. A large jacket potato (225 g/8 oz) averages 154 kcal and 0.2 g fat. This rises to 236 kcal (8.2 g fat) with a couple of spoonfuls of soured cream, and to 265 kcal (12.3 g fat) with a tablespoon of butter.

## Just jackets

A jacket potato is one of the simplest, most delicious and most satisfying foods. With crisp skin and floury, tender flesh it makes a great centrepiece for an energy-boosting meal. It is also highly nutritious, providing complex carbohydrates, B vitamins, vitamin C, iron and fibre.

### Ingredients

Large potatoes (for a main course allow a 300 g/11 oz potato per person; for a light meal allow a 225 g/8 oz potato per person)
Oil
Salt

### Method

(1) Wash the potatoes and pierce with a fork.
(2) For a crispy skin, smear lightly in a very little oil. Rub in a little salt.
(3) Bake on the oven shelf at 220°C/425°F/gas mark 7 for 1¼ hours, or until the flesh is very tender.
(4) Save time by baking several potatoes at a time. They will keep wrapped in the fridge for up to 3 days.

## Twenty low fat toppings for jacket potatoes

1. Baked beans.
2. Fromage frais.
3. Plain yoghurt, pinch of cayenne pepper.
4. Half fat crème fraîche.
5. Stir fried vegetables.
6. Chicken mixed with fromage frais and paprika.
7. Cottage cheese, diced red pepper, chives and sweetcorn.
8. Prawns with low calorie salad cream and a dash of tomato sauce.
9. Ratatouille (aubergines, courgettes, onions, peppers, tomatoes, garlic).
10. Lentil dahl and plain yoghurt.
11. Tuna with plain yoghurt and a dash of chilli sauce.
12. Chopped turkey, diced apple and cranberry sauce.
13. Grilled mushrooms, fromage frais and freshly ground black pepper.
14. Ready-made salsa (mild or hot!).
15. Half a 400 g tin chilli beans in chilli sauce topped with a spoonful of yoghurt.
16. 1 scrambled egg mixed with a chopped tomato.
17. Low fat or fat-free salad dressing.
18. Sweetcorn with mixed peppers topped with a spoonful of thick yoghurt.
19. Tuna in brine (drained) mixed with 1 tbsp low fat soft cheese or reduced fat mayonnaise.
20. Apple sauce.

## Tomato and Mushroom Topping

*Makes 1 serving*

### Ingredients

1 tsp oil
1 tbsp chopped onion
50 g (2 oz) button mushrooms
1 tomato, chopped
Pinch of dried basil
Freshly ground black pepper

### Method

(1) Sauté the onion and mushrooms in the oil over a high heat for 3–4 minutes.
(2) Add the tomato, herbs and pepper and heat through.

### Nutritional analysis

| Per serving (including 300 g/11 oz potato) | | % energy |
|---|---|---|
| Energy | 292 kcal | |
| Protein | 8.3 g | 11% |
| Fat | 5.2 g | 16% |
| Carbohydrate | 56 g | 73% |
| Fibre | 5.8 g | |

## Spicy Bean Topping

*Makes 1 serving*

### Ingredients

2 tbsps salsa (mild or hot)
100 g (4 oz) tinned red kidney beans or pinto beans
1 tbsp Greek yoghurt

### Method

(1) Combine the salsa and drained beans.
(2) Pile onto the potato and top with the Greek yoghurt.

### Nutritional analysis

| Per serving (including 300 g/11 oz potato) | | % energy |
|---|---|---|
| Energy | 401 kcal | |
| Protein | 16 g | 16% |
| Fat | 2.33 g | 6% |
| Carbohydrate | 82 g | 78% |
| Fibre | 12 g | |

## Spinach and Cheese Topping

*Makes 1 serving*

### Ingredients

100 g (4 oz) fresh or thawed frozen spinach
100 g (4 oz) low fat soft cheese or cottage cheese
Salt and freshly ground black pepper
Ground nutmeg
1 tbsp grated parmesan or mature Cheddar cheese (optional)

### Method

(1) Wash the fresh spinach, if applicable. Place the spinach in a saucepan without additional water over a low heat and cook for 2 minutes until wilted.
(2) Meanwhile, scoop out the flesh from the jacket potatoes.
(3) Drain any surplus liquid from the spinach. Combine with the soft cheese, salt, pepper and ground nutmeg.
(4) Pile the spinach mixture back into the potato shells. Sprinkle with parmesan cheese, if applicable and heat through in the oven or microwave.

### Nutritional analysis

| Per serving (including 300 g/11 oz potato) | | % energy |
|---|---|---|
| Energy | 379 kcal | |
| Protein | 27 g | 29% |
| Fat | 6.5 g | 15% |
| Carbohydrate | 56 g | 56% |
| Fibre | 0.1 g | |

## Mighty Mash I

*Makes 1 serving*

### Ingredients

300 g (11 oz) potato, peeled
100 ml (4 fl oz) skimmed milk
Salt and freshly ground black pepper
Dash of tabasco sauce

### Method

(1) Cut the potato into rough pieces and cook in a little fast boiling water for 10 minutes, or until soft. Drain.
(2) Mash together the potato, most of the milk and seasonings. Add a little extra milk for a softer consistency.

### Nutritional analysis

| Per serving | | % energy |
|---|---|---|
| Energy | 266 kcal | |
| Protein | 10 g | 16% |
| Fat | 0.7 g | 3% |
| Carbohydrate | 58 g | 81% |
| Fibre | 3.9 g | |

## Mighty Mash II

*Makes 1 serving*

### Ingredients

175 g (6 oz) potato, peeled
175 g (6 oz) swede, peeled
1 carrot/1 parsnip (optional)
4 tbsps skimmed milk
Salt and freshly ground
black pepper
Dash of tabasco

### Method

(1) Cut the potato and swede into rough pieces
and cook in a little fast boiling water for
10 minutes, or until soft. Drain.
(2) Mash together the potato, swede (and carrot or
parsnip, if applicable), milk and seasonings. Add
a little extra milk for a softer consistency.

### Nutritional analysis

| Per serving | | % energy |
|---|---|---|
| Energy | 193 kcal | |
| Protein | 6.9 g | 14% |
| Fat | 0.9 g | 4% |
| Carbohydrate | 42 g | 82% |
| Fibre | 5.6 g | |

## Chunky Oven Chips

These low fat chips are healthy and delicious; they retain all their vitamin C as no boiling
is required. Keep the skins on for extra fibre and vitamins.

*Makes 1 serving*

### Ingredients

1 large potato, scrubbed
1 tsp sunflower or olive oil
Salt/garlic powder/parmesan
cheese/chilli powder (all optional)

### Method

(1) Cut the potato lengthways, then cut each half
into 6 wedges.
(2) Place in a baking tin and baste in the oil until
each piece is coated.
(3) Bake at 200°C/400°F/gas mark 6 for 20–25
minutes until the potatoes are soft inside and
golden brown on the outside.
(4) Sprinkle on any one of the optional ingredients
5 minutes before the end of cooking.

### Nutritional analysis

| Per serving | | % energy |
|---|---|---|
| Energy | 205 kcal | |
| Protein | 4.7 g | 9% |
| Fat | 4.6 g | 20% |
| Carbohydrate | 39 g | 71% |
| Fibre | 2.9 g | |

## Athlete's Bubble and Squeak

Bursting with flavour and goodness, this recipe is a terrific way to use up any leftover vegetables. It is also an ideal method of disguising green vegetables for those who are not keen on them!

*Makes 1 serving*

### Ingredients

225 g (8 oz) potato
225 g (8 oz) green leafy vegetables,
e.g. cabbage, spinach, Brussels
sprouts, spring greens
3–4 tbsps skimmed milk
Salt and freshly ground
black pepper
Chopped parsley

### Method

(1) Peel and chop the potatoes and other vegetables.
(2) Boil in a little fast boiling water for 10 minutes, or until soft. Drain, reserving the liquid for soups, stock, etc.
(3) Mash with the milk and seasoning.
(4) Spoon into a small ovenproof dish, level the surface and grill until the top is crispy (optional).

### Nutritional analysis

| *Per serving* | | *% energy* |
|---|---|---|
| Energy | 249 kcal | |
| Protein | 11 g | 18% |
| Fat | 1.6 g | 6% |
| Carbohydrate | 50 g | 76% |
| Fibre | 9.9 g | |

## Potato Griddle Scones

Eat these as an accompaniment to a main meal or as a savoury snack. Delicious on their own or spread with a little butter, fromage frais or jam. They are rich in complex carbohydrate and practically fat free!

*Makes 8 scones*

### Ingredients

450 g (1lb) potatoes, boiled
4 tbsps skimmed milk
100 g (4 oz) plain white flour
Salt and freshly ground
black pepper

### Method

(1) Mash the potatoes with the milk until very smooth.
(2) Add the flour, salt and black pepper and mix together with your hands until it forms a soft dough.
(3) Roll out and cut into 8 circles using a scone cutter of approximately 7½ cm (3 in) diameter.
(4) Heat a non-stick frying pan or griddle and cook the scones until lightly browned on both sides.

### Nutritional analysis

| *Per serving (1 scone)* | | *% energy* |
|---|---|---|
| Energy | 98 kcal | |
| Protein | 2.9 g | 12% |
| Fat | 0.3 g | 5% |
| Carbohydrate | 22 g | 85% |
| Fibre | 1.2 g | |

## Potato Tacos

*Makes 1 serving*

### Ingredients

1 large (275 g/10 oz) baking potato
Half a tin (210 g) red kidney or
pinto beans
2 tbsps mild taco sauce (ready-
made)
25 g (1 oz) grated Cheddar cheese
2 tbsps plain low fat yoghurt
Shredded Iceberg lettuce
Finely chopped fresh tomato
1 canned chilli, sliced (optional)

### Method

(1) Scrub the potato and prick with a fork. Smear
with a little oil and salt – this gives a crispy jacket.
Bake in a hot oven (200°C/400°F/gas mark 6) for
1 hour.
(2) Drain the beans and heat in a pan with the
taco sauce.
(3) Split the cooked potato. Spoon on the beans
and sauce.
(4) Top with the grated cheese and yoghurt.
Scatter with the lettuce, tomato and chilli (if you
can take the heat!).

### Nutritional analysis

| *Per serving* | | *% energy* |
|---|---|---|
| Energy | 527 kcal | |
| Protein | 25 g | 19% |
| Fat | 11 g | 18% |
| Carbohydrate | 87 g | 63% |
| Fibre | 14 g | |

## Perfect Potato Pie

Prepare this dish in advance. It can cook while you go out for a run or have a bath –
don't worry if you leave it for longer than 60 minutes as the cooking time isn't too
important.

*Makes 4 servings*

### Ingredients

1 kg (2.2 lb) potatoes
600 ml (1 pt) skimmed milk
50 g (2 oz) grated cheese
1 onion, thinly sliced
2 eggs
Salt and freshly ground
black pepper
Sliced leeks/broccoli florets/sliced
tomatoes (all optional)

### Method

(1) Peel and slice the potatoes. Arrange layers of
potato, cheese and onion (and any optional
vegetables) in a shallow baking dish, finishing
with the cheese.
(2) Beat the eggs with the milk, season and pour
over the potatoes.
(3) Cover with foil and bake at 200°C/400°F/gas
mark 6 for 45–60 minutes until the potatoes are
tender and the top golden brown.

### Nutritional analysis

| *Per serving* | | *% energy* |
|---|---|---|
| Energy | 348 kcal | |
| Protein | 18 g | 21% |
| Fat | 9.1 g | 23% |
| Carbohydrate | 52 g | 56% |
| Fibre | 3.5 g | |

## Garlic Roast Potatoes

*Makes 1 serving*

### Ingredients

1 large potato (approx. 300 g)
1 tsp oil
1 garlic clove, crushed

### Method

(1) Cut the potato into chunks (no need to peel).
(2) Place the oil and crushed garlic in a roasting tin and baste the potato chunks so they are evenly coated with oil.
(3) Bake in the oven at 200°C/400°F/gas mark 6 for 45 minutes or until golden brown.

### Nutritional analysis

| Per serving | | % energy |
|---|---|---|
| Energy | 261 kcal | |
| Protein | 6.3 g | 10% |
| Fat | 4.6 g | 16% |
| Carbohydrate | 52 g | 74% |
| Fibre | 3.9 g | |

## Potato Kugel

A vegetable kugel is a basic Jewish dish; a shallow casserole pudding that is held together with beaten egg, has a crispy top and is cut into squares. This adaptation of the classic potato kugel is ideal for increasing your carbohydrate intake.

*Makes 4 servings*

### Ingredients

4 large potatoes (approx. 225 g/ 8 oz each)
2 onions, chopped
1 tbsp oil
Salt and freshly ground black pepper
4 eggs
300 ml (½ pint) fromage frais or plain yoghurt
50 g (2 oz) fresh breadcrumbs
225 g (8 oz) mushrooms/ courgettes/grated carrots (all optional)

### Method

(1) Scrub and coarsely grate the potatoes in a bowl.
(2) Sauté the onion in the oil for 4–5 minutes together with any of the optional ingredients. Add to the grated potato.
(3) Add the seasoning, eggs, fromage frais and breadcrumbs. Combine well.
(4) Spread evenly into an oiled 9 x 13 in baking tin. Dust the top with paprika.
(5) Bake at 190°C/375°F/gas mark 5 for 1 hour or until crisp on the top. Cut into squares and serve.

### Nutritional analysis

| Per serving | | % energy |
|---|---|---|
| Energy | 389 kcal | |
| Protein | 20 g | 21% |
| Fat | 10 g | 23% |
| Carbohydrate | 58 g | 56% |
| Fibre | 3.7 g | |

# Cod and Potato Pie

*Makes 4 servings*

## Ingredients

550 g (1¼ lb) potatoes, peeled
2 large leeks, thinly sliced
550 g (1¼ lb) cod fillets
600 ml (1 pt) skimmed milk
1 bay leaf
2 heaped tbsps plain flour
Salt and freshly ground
black pepper
Dijon mustard
50 g (2 oz) mature Cheddar cheese,
grated

## Method

(1) Chop and cook the potatoes in a little fast-boiling water for 10 minutes, or until soft. Drain and mash with a little milk.
(2) Meanwhile, place the cod and leeks in a saucepan with the remaining milk and bay leaf. Bring to the boil and simmer for 5 minutes.
(3) Strain the milk into a jug. Roughly flake the fish.
(4) Stir the flour into the milk, return to the pan and bring to the boil, stirring until the sauce has thickened. Season with salt, pepper and Dijon mustard.
(5) Combine the sauce with the leeks and fish. Place in a baking dish.
(6) Cover evenly with the mashed potatoes and scatter the cheese on top.
(7) Bake at 190°C/375°F/gas mark 5 for 20 minutes or until the top is golden brown.

## Nutritional analysis

| *Per serving* | | *% energy* |
|---|---|---|
| Energy | 367 kcal | |
| Protein | 38 g | 42% |
| Fat | 6.9 g | 3% |
| Carbohydrate | 40 g | 41% |
| Fibre | 3 g | |

# Vegetable Crumble

A perfect warming winter dish that makes a nutritionally complete meal. The seeds and nuts in the topping are excellent sources of essential fatty acids.

*Makes 4 servings*

## Ingredients

Filling:
1 kg (2.2 lb) mixed root vegetables, e.g. potato, carrot, turnip, parsnip, swede
25 g (1 oz) butter or margarine
25 g (1 oz) flour
300 ml (½ pint) skimmed or semi-skimmed milk
Vegetable extract
Salt and freshly ground black pepper
Fresh parsley

Crumble:
75 g (3 oz) wholemeal flour
25 g (1 oz) oats
25 g (1 oz) butter or margarine
1 tbsp sunflower seeds/flaked almonds/peanuts (all optional)

## Method

(1) Slice the vegetables thickly and cook in boiling water for 15 minutes, or until just tender. Drain, reserving 250 ml (8 fl oz) cooking liquid.
(2) Melt the butter or margarine in a pan, stir in the flour and cook for 1–2 minutes. Slowly add the milk and reserved water, stirring continuously.
(3) Add vegetable extract, salt, pepper and parsley to taste.
(4) Spoon the vegetables and sauce into a large casserole dish.
(5) To make the crumble, mix the oats and flour together. Rub in the butter or margarine then stir in the remaining ingredients.
(6) Sprinkle over the vegetables and bake at 200°C/400°F/gas mark 6 for 30 minutes.

## Nutritional analysis

| *Per serving* | | *% energy* |
|---|---|---|
| Energy | 340 kcal | |
| Protein | 9.6 g | 11% |
| Fat | 12.4 g | 33% |
| Carbohydrate | 51 g | 56% |
| Fibre | 8.6 g | |

## Vegetable Gratin with Potatoes

A good way of serving vegetables to those who do not like them plain. The gratin topping can be used with any variety of vegetables.

*Makes 4 servings*

### Ingredients

1 cauliflower, cut into florets
450 g (1 lb) broccoli, cut into florets
450 ml (¾ pt) skimmed milk
2 tbsps cornflour
1 tsp mustard
50 g (2 oz) mature Cheddar cheese
900 g (2 lb) potatoes
1 tbsp sesame seeds/walnuts
(optional)

### Method

(1) Cook the cauliflower and broccoli in boiling water for 5 minutes. Drain and reserve the liquid.
(2) Blend the cornflour with a little of the milk. Gradually add the remaining milk and transfer into a saucepan.
(3) Heat, stirring constantly, until the sauce thickens. Add the mustard, three quarters of the cheese and some of the reserved cooking liquid to give a coating consistency.
(4) Arrange the vegetables in a baking dish, pour over the sauce and sprinkle with the remaining cheese and optional seeds or nuts.
(5) Place under a hot grill until golden brown.
(6) Serve with cooked potatoes.

### Nutritional analysis

| Per serving | | % energy |
|---|---|---|
| Energy | 368 kcal | |
| Protein | 20 g | 22% |
| Fat | 7.9 g | 19% |
| Carbohydrate | 57 g | 59% |
| Fibre | 8.7 g | |

## Potato and Vegetable Curry

*Makes 4 servings*

### Ingredients

675 g (1½ lb) potatoes
1 onion, chopped
1 tbsp oil
450 g (1 lb) vegetables, e.g. peas, mushrooms, sweetcorn, mange tout, green beans
1 tbsp curry powder
1 tin (400 g) chopped tomatoes

### Method

(1) Cut the potatoes into small chunks. Sauté the potatoes and onion in the oil in a large frying pan for 4–5 minutes.
(2) Add the remaining ingredients, stir, bring to the boil and simmer for 15 minutes, or until the potatoes and vegetables (optional) are tender.

### Nutritional analysis

| Per serving | | % energy |
|---|---|---|
| Energy | 240 kcal | |
| Protein | 9 g | 15% |
| Fat | 4.5 g | 17% |
| Carbohydrate | 43 g | 68% |
| Fibre | 6.5 g | |

# Aubergine and Potato Curry

*Makes 4 servings*

## Ingredients

1 tbsp butter or oil
2 onions, chopped
1 aubergine, cut into cubes
1 tbsp curry powder
8 new potatoes, cut into halves
1 tbsp tomato purée
50 ml (2 fl oz) water
175 g (6 oz) frozen peas

## Method

(1) Heat the butter or oil in a large pan and cook the onions and aubergine until soft, about 6–8 minutes.
(2) Add the curry powder and potatoes and cook for 1 minute.
(3) Add the water, tomato purée and peas and cook until the potatoes are tender and the curry has thickened.
(4) Serve with plain yoghurt and chapattis or naan bread.

## Nutritional analysis

| Per serving | | % energy |
|---|---|---|
| Energy | 141 kcal | |
| Protein | 5.3 g | 15% |
| Fat | 3.7 g | 24% |
| Carbohydrate | 23 g | 61% |
| Fibre | 5 g | |

# Potato Salad

This is an excellent portable snack or lunch. Accompany with a protein food such as cooked chicken drumsticks, boiled eggs or cottage cheese, and some vegetable crudités for a nutritionally complete meal on the run.

*Makes 1 serving*

## Ingredients

225 g (8 oz) new or old potatoes, cut into small chunks (no need to peel)
1 tbsp each of fresh chopped mint and parsley (or use 1 tsp dried)
1 tbsp plain yoghurt
1 tbsp reduced calorie salad cream or mayonnaise
Freshly ground black pepper
Chopped spring onions/onions/cucumber/peppers (all optional)

## Method

(1) Boil the potatoes in a little fast-boiling water for 5–7 minutes until just tender. Drain.
(2) Combine the remaining ingredients together. Toss in the cooled potatoes and any of the optional ingredients.

## Nutritional analysis

| Per serving | | % energy |
|---|---|---|
| Energy | 211 kcal | |
| Protein | 5.4 g | 10% |
| Fat | 4.4 g | 19% |
| Carbohydrate | 40 g | 71% |
| Fibre | 2.8 g | |

# Potato Bake with Tomatoes

An excellent source of complex carbohydrates, vitamin C and fibre. The olive oil not only adds a delicious flavour but also valuable monounsaturates.

*Makes 4 servings*

### Ingredients

900 g (2 lb) potatoes
4 large tomatoes, sliced
Handful of fresh herbs, e.g. parsley, rosemary, basil
Salt and freshly ground black pepper
2 tbsps olive oil
One small glass of white wine (or water)
4 tbsps breadcrumbs (optional)

### Method

(1) Boil the potatoes in their skins for 5 minutes. Cool then slice thickly.
(2) Layer the potatoes and tomatoes in a baking dish. Sprinkle salt, black pepper and herbs between the layers.
(3) Pour the olive oil and wine over the vegetables. Sprinkle with the breadcrumbs, if applicable.
(4) Bake at 180°C/350°F/gas mark 4 for 20 minutes or until the potatoes are soft. Alternatively, microwave for 8 minutes.

### Nutritional analysis

| Per serving | | % energy |
| --- | --- | --- |
| Energy | 255 kcal | |
| Protein | 5.5 g | 9% |
| Fat | 6.3 g | 22% |
| Carbohydrate | 42 g | 61% |
| Fibre | 4 g | |

# Pie crusts and pastry substitutes

Traditional pastry is loaded with fat and has no place in an athlete's daily diet. Here are some ideas for low fat pie crusts which you can substitute for pastry when making pies and quiches, and safely include in your sports diet. Many do not require the traditional rolling out – you simply pat them into the baking tin with a spoon, fork or your fingers. Fill and bake in the usual way.

## Potato Pastry

### Ingredients

450 g (1 lb) potatoes, peeled and roughly chopped
100 g (4 oz) self raising flour
½ tsp baking powder
1 egg
Salt and freshly ground black pepper

### Method

(1) Boil the potatoes for 10 minutes until just tender. Drain and mash. Cool slightly.
(2) Mix the potato with the flour, baking powder, seasoning and enough egg to form a soft dough. Allow to cool completely.
(3) Roll out or press into the baking tin. Bake at 190°C/375°F/gas mark 5 for 30 minutes.

### Nutritional analysis

| *Per ¼ recipe* | | *% energy* |
|---|---|---|
| Energy | 209 kcal | |
| Protein | 7 g | 13% |
| Fat | 2.2 g | 10% |
| Carbohydrate | 43 g | 77% |
| Fibre | 2.4 g | |

# Mashed Potato Pie Crust

## Ingredients

450 g (1 lb) potatoes
2 tbsps butter or margarine
Salt and freshly ground
black pepper
1 small onion, finely chopped

## Method

(1) Scrub the potatoes, cut into chunks and boil them until just soft. Drain and mash.
(2) Combine with the butter, seasoning and onion.
(3) Press into the baking tin using a spoon or spatula. Bake at 190°C/375°F/gas mark 5 for 45 minutes.

## Nutritional analysis

| Per ¼ recipe | | % energy |
|---|---|---|
| Energy | 125 kcal | |
| Protein | 2.5 g | 8% |
| Fat | 4.3 g | 31% |
| Carbohydrate | 20 g | 61% |
| Fibre | 1.6 g | |

# Crunchy Pie Crust

## Ingredients

50 g (2 oz) fresh wholemeal breadcrumbs
25 g (1 oz) wholemeal flour
25 g (1 oz) wheatgerm
25 g (1 oz) oats
Pinch of salt and dried basil
40 g (1½ oz) melted butter/low fat spread

## Method

(1) Mix together all the dry ingredients.
(2) Drizzle in the melted butter and mix with a fork until the mixture is evenly coated. Add a little water if necessary.
(3) Press into the baking tin. Bake at 180°C/350°F/gas mark 4 for 10 minutes.

## Nutritional analysis

| Per ¼ recipe | | % energy |
|---|---|---|
| Energy | 193 kcal | |
| Protein | 5 g | 10% |
| Fat | 9.6 g | 45% |
| Carbohydrate | 23 g | 45% |
| Fibre | 1.3 g | |

# Vegetable Pie Crust

## Ingredients

1 large parsnip, grated
2 carrots, grated
100 g (4 oz) swede, grated
½ tsp salt
2 tbsps melted butter or margarine
40 g (1½ oz) wholemeal flour

## Method

(1) Combine all of the ingredients and mix well.
(2) Press into a lightly-oiled baking tin and form a pie crust with your fingers. Bake at 190°C/375°F/gas mark 5 for 40 minutes.

## Nutritional analysis

| *Per ¼ recipe* | | *% energy* |
|---|---|---|
| Energy | 112 kcal | |
| Protein | 2.4 g | 9% |
| Fat | 4.9 g | 39% |
| Carbohydrate | 16 g | 52% |
| Fibre | 4.1 g | |

# Breakfasts

It's been proven that a high carbohydrate, low fat breakfast improves your mood, concentration and your physical and mental performance. Breakfast-eaters are leaner than those who skip this important meal and have higher intakes of most vitamins and minerals. If you cannot face breakfast very early in the day, aim to eat within two hours of waking.

## Oatmeal Scotties

*Makes 12 small pancakes*

**Ingredients**

175 g (6 oz) fine oatmeal
100 g (4 oz) plain wholemeal flour
2 tsps baking powder
350 ml (12 fl oz) buttermilk or half yoghurt/half skimmed milk
2 egg whites

**Method**

(1) Combine the oatmeal, flour and baking powder in a bowl or liquidiser.
(2) Whisk together the buttermilk and egg whites. Add to the flour and blend until smooth.
(3) If you have time, let the batter stand for about 10 minutes.
(4) Heat a large non-stick frying pan or cast-iron griddle and smear with a little oil or oil spray.
(5) Drop spoonfuls of the batter into the pan to make small pancakes 10–12 cm (4–5 in) diameter. You should be able to cook 3–4 pancakes at once.
(6) Cook for approximately 2 minutes until the pancakes are golden brown underneath. Turn over and cook for 1 more minute.
(7) Keep warm on a plate while you make the other pancakes.

*Topping variations*
♦ Scrambled eggs mixed with chopped tomatoes.
♦ Mashed or sliced bananas.
♦ Apricot fruit spread and cottage cheese.
♦ Sautéed mushrooms mixed with half fat crème fraîche.

**Nutritional analysis**

| *Per serving (1 pancake)* | | *% energy* |
|---|---|---|
| Energy | 103 kcal | |
| Protein | 4.6 g | 18% |
| Fat | 1.6 g | 14% |
| Carbohydrate | 19 g | 68% |
| Fibre | 1.9 g | |

## Pineapple Bagel

*Makes 1 serving*

### Ingredients

1 bagel
2 tbsps (75 g/3 oz) cottage cheese
with pineapple

### Method

(1) Split the bagel in half. If you have time, toast the cut sides under a hot grill.
(2) Spread the cottage cheese on the bagel slices.

### Nutritional analysis

| *Per serving* | | *% energy* |
|---|---|---|
| Energy | 309 kcal | |
| Protein | 19 g | 24% |
| Fat | 6.8 g | 20% |
| Carbohydrate | 45 g | 56% |
| Fibre | 1.3 g | |

## Raisin Toast

### Ingredients

3 slices raisin or currant bread
2 tbsps (75 g/3 oz) cottage cheese
Cinnamon

### Method

(1) Toast the raisin bread.
(2) Spread the cottage cheese on the toast and sprinkle with cinnamon.

### Nutritional analysis

| *Per serving* | | *% energy* |
|---|---|---|
| Energy | 343 kcal | |
| Protein | 18 g | 21% |
| Fat | 10 g | 25% |
| Carbohydrate | 47 g | 54% |
| Fibre | 1.5 g | |

## Breakfast Muffins

These take only a few minutes to make and are excellent for a weekend breakfast treat.

*Makes 12 muffins*

### Ingredients

100 g (4 oz) white self raising flour
100 g (4 oz) wholemeal self raising flour
1 tbsp (15 ml) oil
40 g (1½ oz) soft brown sugar
1 egg
150 ml (5 fl oz) skimmed milk
50 g (2 oz) dried fruit

### Method

(1) Preheat the oven to 220°C/425°F/gas mark 7.
(2) Mix the flours together in a bowl.
(3) Add the oil, sugar, egg and milk. Mix well.
(4) Stir in the dried fruit.
(5) Spoon into a non-stick muffin tray and bake for approximately 15 minutes until golden brown.

### Nutritional analysis

*Per serving (1 muffin)*

| | | % energy |
|---|---|---|
| Energy | 109 kcal | |
| Protein | 3 g | 11% |
| Fat | 1.8 g | 15% |
| Carbohydrate | 22 g | 74% |
| Fibre | 1.4 g | |

## Dried Fruit Muesli

*Makes 10 servings*

### Ingredients

100 g (4 oz) dried fruit salad
350 g (12 oz) porridge oats
150 g (5 oz) wheat flakes or bran flakes
65 g (2½ oz) wheatgerm
50 g (2 oz) each of raisins, dates and figs

### Method

(1) Chop the dried fruit salad.
(2) Put all the ingredients in a bowl and mix well.
(3) Store in an airtight container.
(4) Serve with low fat milk or low fat milk mixed with bioyoghurt.

*Variations*
- Substitute ready-mixed dried orchard fruit (apples, pears) for the dried fruit mixture.
- Substitute ready-mixed dried tropical fruit or dried chopped mango, apricot and pineapple.

### Nutritional analysis

*Per serving*

| | | % energy |
|---|---|---|
| Energy | 284 kcal | |
| Protein | 8.8 g | 12% |
| Fat | 4.2 g | 13% |
| Carbohydrate | 56 g | 75% |
| Fibre | 7.2 g | |

# Breakfast Pancakes

*Makes 6 pancakes*

## Ingredients

Batter:
65 g (2½ oz) plain white flour
65 g (2½ oz) plain wholemeal flour
1 egg
300 ml (½ pint) skimmed milk
(A little vegetable oil or oil spray
for frying)

Filling:
1 orange, peeled and cut into
segments
1 ruby grapefruit, peeled and cut
into segments
1 banana, peeled and sliced
1–2 tbsps clear honey

## Method

(1) Place all the batter ingredients in a liquidiser
and blend until smooth.
(2) Alternatively mix the flours in a bowl. Make a
well in the centre. Beat the egg and milk and
gradually add to the flour, beating to make a
smooth batter.
(3) Place a non-stick frying pan over a high heat.
Spray with oil spray or add a few drops of oil.
(4) Pour in enough batter to coat the pan thinly
and cook for 1–2 minutes until golden brown on
the underside.
(5) Turn the pancake and cook the other side for
30–60 seconds.
(6) Turn out onto a plate, cover, and keep warm
while you make the other pancakes.
(7) To make the fillings, combine the chopped
fruit with the honey.
(8) Divide the fruit between the pancakes and fold
them in half. Serve topped with low fat yoghurt.

*Filling variations*
◆ 1 banana mixed with 1 sliced peach and 1 tbsp honey.
◆ 8 fresh chopped apricots mixed with a 100 g (4 oz) carton of very low fat apricot
   yoghurt.
◆ 100 g (4 oz) sliced strawberries mixed with 100 g (4 oz) very low fat fromage frais.
◆ 100 g (4 oz) frozen summer fruit (thawed).

## Nutritional analysis

| *Per serving (1 pancake)* | | *% energy* |
|---|---|---|
| Energy | 155 kcal | |
| Protein | 6.2 g | 16% |
| Fat | 1.6 g | 10% |
| Carbohydrate | 31 g | 74% |
| Fibre | 2.4 g | |

## Banana Waffles

*Makes 4 large waffles*

### Ingredients

225 ml (8 fl oz) semi-skimmed milk
1 egg
2 tsps oil
75 g (3 oz) self raising white or
wholemeal flour
1 tsp sugar
Pinch of cinnamon
2 bananas
(Equipment necessary – waffle
iron)

### Method

(1) Beat together the milk, egg and oil.
(2) Mix together the flour, sugar and cinnamon.
(3) Beat the liquid mixture into the flour mixture until smooth. Alternatively blend in a liquidiser.
(4) Heat the waffle iron and spray or lightly smear with oil.
(5) Spoon one quarter of the mixture into each waffle compartment. Cook for approximately 2 minutes until golden and beginning to separate from the waffle iron. Repeat with the remainder of the mixture.
(6) Top the waffles with sliced bananas.

*Topping variations*
◆ Maple syrup or honey and sliced strawberries.
◆ Cottage cheese mixed with chopped apricots.
◆ Blueberry fruit spread.

### Nutritional analysis

*Per serving (1 waffle)*

| | | *% energy* |
|---|---|---|
| Energy | 191 kcal | |
| Protein | 6.5 g | 14% |
| Fat | 5 g | 23% |
| Carbohydrate | 32 g | 63% |
| Fibre | 1.2 g | |

## Apple Sauce Muffins

### Ingredients

1 wholemeal English muffin
2 tbsps low fat soft cheese or
ricotta cheese
2 tbsps unsweetened apple sauce
(bought or home-made)
Cinnamon

### Method

(1) Split the muffin in half and toast lightly under a hot grill.
(2) Spread the muffin halves with the cheese and apple sauce.
(3) Sprinkle with cinnamon and pop under the grill to heat through.

### Nutritional analysis

| Per serving | | % energy |
|---|---|---|
| Energy | 276 kcal | |
| Protein | 11 g | 16% |
| Fat | 8.8 g | 28% |
| Carbohydrate | 41 g | 56% |
| Fibre | 2.6 g | |

## Basic Granola

*Makes 10 servings*

### Ingredients

450 g (1 lb) oats
50 g (2 oz) brown sugar or honey
1 tsp cinnamon (optional)
3 tbsps oil
4 tbsps water
1 tsp vanilla
100 g (4 oz) bran flakes or wheat flakes
100 g (4 oz) raisins, sultanas, chopped dates, chopped figs or dried apricots/100 g (4 oz) dried apple/75 g (3 oz) chopped toasted hazelnuts or flaked toasted almonds/50 g (2 oz) toasted sunflower seeds (all optional)

### Method

(1) Combine the oats, sugar (or honey), cinnamon, oil, water and vanilla in a large bowl.
(2) Spread thinly over two baking trays.
(3) Bake for 30–35 minutes at 150°C/300°F/gas mark 2, stirring halfway through to ensure an even toasting.
(4) Allow to cool, then stir in the bran or wheat flakes. Stir in the optional ingredients and store in an airtight container.

### Nutritional analysis

| Per serving | | % energy |
|---|---|---|
| Energy | 274 kcal | |
| Protein | 6.9 g | 10% |
| Fat | 7.5 g | 25% |
| Carbohydrate | 48 g | 65% |
| Fibre | 4.7 g | |

## Power Porridge

*Makes 1 large serving*

### Ingredients

50 g (2 oz) porridge oats
350 ml (12 fl oz) skimmed milk
25 g (1 oz) raisins, dates or figs
1 banana, sliced
2 tsps honey or maple syrup

### Method

(1) Mix the oats and milk together. Cook in a microwave for approximately 4 minutes, stirring halfway through, or in a saucepan for approximately 5 minutes, stirring continuously.
(2) Add the raisins, banana and extra milk if desired.
(3) Spoon the honey or maple syrup over the top.

### Nutritional analysis

| *Per serving* | | *% energy* |
|---|---|---|
| Energy | 562 kcal | |
| Protein | 21 g | 15% |
| Fat | 6 g | 10% |
| Carbohydrate | 113 g | 75% |
| Fibre | 5.7 g | |

## Breakfast Bars

*Makes 12 bars*

### Ingredients

100 g (4 oz) ready-to-eat apricots, chopped
100 g (4 oz) dates, chopped
1 egg
1 tbsp oil
100 ml (4 fl oz) plain yoghurt
50 g (2 oz) sugar
50 g (2 oz) self raising wholemeal flour
4 Weetabix, crumbled

### Method

(1) Combine the apricots, dates, egg, oil and yoghurt in a bowl. Mix well.
(2) Stir in the sugar, flour and Weetabix. Add a little milk if the mixture is too stiff.
(3) Spoon into a lightly-oiled non-stick 8-in square baking dish.
(4) Bake at 190°C/375°F/gas mark 5 for 20–25 minutes.
(5) Cool and cut into bars.

### Nutritional analysis

| *Per serving (1 bar)* | | *% energy* |
|---|---|---|
| Energy | 129 kcal | |
| Protein | 3.2 g | 10% |
| Fat | 1.9 g | 13% |
| Carbohydrate | 26 g | 77% |
| Fibre | 2 g | |

## Baked French Toast

*Makes 2 servings*

### Ingredients

4 thick slices white bread
3 eggs
300 ml (½ pint) skimmed milk
½ tsp (2½ ml) cinnamon

### Method

(1) Spray a 9-in square baking tray with oil spray or lightly smear with oil.
(2) Cut the bread slices in half diagonally and arrange them in layers on the tray.
(3) Whisk together the eggs, milk and cinnamon. Pour over the bread.
(4) Bake for 25–30 minutes at 180°C/350°F/gas mark 4. (This recipe may be made the night before and refrigerated until the morning.) Serve with apple sauce or chopped fresh fruit.

*Variations*
◆ You may use other types of bread, such as raisin bread, wholemeal bread or French bread.

### Nutritional analysis

| *Per serving* | | *% energy* |
|---|---|---|
| Energy | 352 kcal | |
| Protein | 23 g | 26% |
| Fat | 11 g | 28% |
| Carbohydrate | 43 g | 46% |
| Fibre | 1.1 g | |

### ◆ *Cereal Toppings* ◆

Top ready-made cereals with any of the following to add extra carbohydrate, fibre, vitamins and minerals.

◆ Dried fruit, e.g. raisins, pineapple, apple, dates, figs
◆ Sliced bananas
◆ Fresh fruit, e.g. strawberries, raspberries, peaches, oranges
◆ Plain or fruit yoghurt
◆ Nuts, sunflower or pumpkin seeds

## How popular breakfasts compare

| | |
|---|---|
| **Cooked breakfast**<br><br>2 rashers fried streaky bacon<br>2 fried eggs<br>1 grilled tomato<br>2 slices white toast with butter<br><br>**600 kcal; 44 g fat; 8.5 g sugars; 3 g fibre.** | **Continental breakfast**<br><br>2 croissants<br>20 g butter<br>20 g jam<br><br>**612 kcal; 37 g fat; 29 g sugars; 1.6 g fibre.** |
| **Toast and marmalade**<br><br>2 slices white toast<br>20 g butter<br>20 g marmalade<br><br>**395 kcal; 17 g fat; 30 g sugars; 1.1 g fibre.** | **Breakfast cereal**<br><br>1 bowl (50 g) bran flakes<br>125 ml semi-skimmed milk<br><br>**218 kcal; 3 g fat; 18 g sugars; 6.5 g fibre.**<br><br>2 Weetabix<br>125 ml semi-skimmed milk<br><br>**180 kcal; 3 g fat; 8 g sugars; 5 g fibre.** |

### ◆ Top tips for a healthy breakfast ◆

- ◆ Always include at least one portion of fruit with your breakfast, e.g. 1 banana, 1 apple, 1 orange, 100 g (4 oz) strawberries.
- ◆ Include at least one high carbohydrate food, e.g. breakfast cereal, porridge oats, toast, bread, English muffins, bagels, pancakes, waffles.
- ◆ If you aren't keen on high fibre cereals, mix your favourite low fibre cereal with a cereal providing at last 7 g fibre/100 g.
- ◆ Use semi-skimmed milk or skimmed milk instead of full fat milk.
- ◆ Avoid fried foods, e.g. bacon, sausages, and high fat foods, e.g. croissants, pastries.
- ◆ Add dried fruit, e.g. raisins, dates, prunes, instead of sugar to sweeten your cereal. You'll also get extra fibre and vitamins.

# The nutritional value of breakfast cereals

|  | Calories/ 100 g | Sugars/ 100 g | Fat/ 100 g | Fibre/ 100 g |
|---|---|---|---|---|
| **Mueslis** | | | | |
| Jordans Natural Country Muesli | 350 | 17.6 | 5.9 | 7.4 |
| Weetabix Alpen Swiss Recipe Muesli (original) | 365 | 28.1 | 6.9 | 7 |
| Weetabix No Added Sugar Muesli | 363 | 15 | 6.4 | 7 |
| Sainsbury's Swiss Style Muesli | 361 | 26.3 | 5.4 | 6.1 |
| Kelloggs Country Store Muesli | 360 | 19 | 5 | 7 |
| | | | | |
| **Crunchy oat cereals** | | | | |
| Jordans Country Crisp Cereal with Luxury Raisins | 426 | 30 | 15. 4 | 7 |
| Jordans Original Crunchy Raisin and Almond | 387 | 28.2 | 11 | 7 |
| Quaker Harvest Luxury Raisin Crunch | 447 | 31.5 | 16 | 4 |
| Tesco Chocolate and Banana Crunch | 461 | 29.1 | 19.6 | 6 |
| | | | | |
| **Bran-based cereals** | | | | |
| Kelloggs Bran Flakes | 320 | 24 | 2 | 13 |
| Kelloggs All Bran | 270 | 18 | 3.5 | 24 |
| Kelloggs Fruit n' Fibre | 350 | 21 | 6 | 7 |
| | | | | |
| **Corn-based cereals** | | | | |
| Kelloggs Cornflakes | 370 | 8 | 0.8 | 1 |
| Kelloggs Crunchy Nut Cornflakes | 390 | 34 | 3.5 | 1 |
| Kelloggs Frosties | 380 | 39 | 0.5 | 0.6 |
| | | | | |
| **Rice-based cereals** | | | | |
| Kelloggs Rice Crispies | 370 | 10 | 0.9 | 0.7 |
| Kelloggs Coco-pops | 380 | 39 | 0.8 | 1 |
| Kelloggs Banana Bubbles | 380 | 35 | 0.6 | 0.5 |
| Kelloggs Ricicles | 380 | 38 | 0.6 | 0.5 |
| Kelloggs Special K | 370 | 15 | 1 | 2.5 |
| | | | | |
| **Wheat-based cereals** | | | | |
| Nestle Shredded Wheat | 352 | 0.7 | 2.2 | 10 |
| Nestle Shredded Wheat Bitesize | 356 | 0.7 | 2.3 | 10.2 |
| Nestle Shreddies | 353 | 15.4 | 1.9 | 8.3 |
| Weetabix | 342 | 4.7 | 2.7 | 10.1 |
| Weetabix Weeta Flakes | 354 | 19.6 | 2.6 | 8.6 |
| Quaker Sugar Puffs | 387 | 49 | 1 | 3 |
| Quaker Puffed Wheat | 328 | 0.3 | 1.3 | 5.6 |
| Kelloggs Sustain | 360 | 18 | 3 | 6 |
| Heinz Weight Watchers Perfect Balance | 318 | 6 | 1.4 | 10.7 |

# One-minute meals and lunch on the go

The following recipes can all be assembled in one minute or less. They are ideal for nutritious snacks, lunch on the go, or even a quick supper when you haven't got time to cook.

## Quick Tacos

*Makes 2 tacos*

**Ingredients**

2 tbsps chunky Mexican salsa
Half a tin (210 g) pinto or red kidney beans
2 taco shells
Diced tomato, shredded lettuce, beansprouts
2 tbsps grated cheese

**Method**

(1) Combine the salsa and beans in a pan and heat through.
(2) Meanwhile heat the tacos in a hot oven for a few minutes.
(3) Spoon the salsa into the taco shells and serve topped with the tomatoes, lettuce, beansprouts and cheese.

**Nutritional analysis**

| *Per serving* | | *% energy* |
|---|---|---|
| Energy | 386 kcal | |
| Protein | 19 g | 20% |
| Fat | 8.5 g | 20% |
| Carbohydrate | 62 g | 60% |
| Fibre | 11.5 g | |

## Bagel Melt

### Ingredients

1 bagel
2 thin slices (40 g/1½ oz) Cheddar cheese

### Method

(1) Split the bagel in half.
(2) Lay the cheese slices on the cut sides and toast under a hot grill until melted.
(3) Sandwich the two halves back together.
(4) Alternatively, place the cheese between the bagel halves and microwave until melted.

*Variations*
◆ Peanut Bagel Melt: spread the split bagel with peanut butter before adding the cheese.
◆ Tomato Bagel Melt: place six slices of beef tomatoes over the cheese before toasting.
◆ Onion Bagel Melt: scatter thin slices of onion or shallot over the cheese before toasting.
◆ Salad Bagel Melt: add chopped lettuce, cucumber and tomato to the melted cheese before sandwiching together.

### Nutritional analysis

| *Per serving* | | *% energy* |
|---|---|---|
| Energy | 331 kcal | |
| Protein | 14 g | 17 % |
| Fat | 12 g | 33% |
| Carbohydrate | 44 g | 50% |
| Fibre | 1.3 g | |

## Banana Hot Dog

### Ingredients

1 long roll, preferably wholemeal, e.g. Hoagie
Butter/low fat spread
1 banana

### Method

(1) Split the roll in half and spread thinly with the butter or low fat spread.
(2) Place a whole banana inside.
(3) Eat cold or microwave for 10–20 seconds to warm through.

### Nutritional analysis

| *Per serving* | | *% energy* |
|---|---|---|
| Energy | 339 kcal | |
| Protein | 9.4 g | 11% |
| Fat | 6.8 g | 18% |
| Carbohydrate | 64 g | 71% |
| Fibre | 3.9 g | |

## Turkey Pockets

### Ingredients

1 large or 2 mini wholemeal pittas
1 tbsp (15 ml) low fat salad
dressing
2 slices (50 g/2 oz) turkey breast
Salad leaves

### Method

(1) Toast then split the pittas.
(2) Spread with salad dressing and layer turkey
and salad leaves.

### Nutritional analysis

| Per serving | | % energy |
|---|---|---|
| Energy | 290 kcal | |
| Protein | 21 g | 29% |
| Fat | 4.1 g | 13% |
| Carbohydrate | 45 g | 58% |
| Fibre | 3.9 g | |

## Tortilla Sandwich

### Ingredients

2 wheat tortillas
100 g (4 oz) chopped cooked
chicken or turkey
25 g (1 oz) low fat soft cheese or
fromage frais
1 sliced tomato

### Method

(1) Combine the chicken or turkey with the soft
low fat cheese.
(2) Place half of the chicken mixture and tomatoes
onto the centre of each tortilla.
(3) Fold in half or roll up pancake-style.
(4) Eat cold or microwave for 10–12 seconds until
warmed through.

### Nutritional analysis

| Per serving | | % energy |
|---|---|---|
| Energy | 535 kcal | |
| Protein | 47 g | 35% |
| Fat | 9.3 g | 16% |
| Carbohydrate | 70 g | 49% |
| Fibre | 3.5 g | |

# Vegetarian Tortilla Sandwich

## Ingredients

2 wheat tortillas
4 tbsps (100 g/4 oz) canned pinto
or red kidney beans
25 g (1 oz) grated cheese
1 sliced tomato
1 tbsp (15 ml) taco relish (optional)

## Method

(1) Place half of the beans, cheese, tomatoes and relish (if applicable) onto the centre of each tortilla.
(2) Fold in half or roll up pancake-style.
(3) Microwave until the cheese melts.

## Nutritional analysis

| Per serving | | % energy |
|---|---|---|
| Energy | 548 kcal | |
| Protein | 24 g | 17% |
| Fat | 11 g | 18% |
| Carbohydrate | 95 g | 65% |
| Fibre | 11 g | |

# Greek Filled Pitta

## Ingredients

1 large pitta
1 tbsp (15 ml) hummous
(preferably reduced fat variety)
25 g (1 oz) crumbled feta cheese
Baby spinach leaves

## Method

(1) Toast and split the pitta.
(2) Spread with the hummous and fill with the feta cheese and baby spinach.

## Nutritional analysis

| Per serving | | % energy |
|---|---|---|
| Energy | 332 kcal | |
| Protein | 15 g | 18% |
| Fat | 10 g | 28% |
| Carbohydrate | 48 g | 54% |
| Fibre | 5.9 g | |

## Curried Chicken Baguette

### Ingredients

1 small baguette (approx. 6–8 in)
1 tbsp (15 ml) low fat salad
dressing or mayonnaise
50 g (2 oz) chopped cooked chicken
¼ tsp curry powder
1 stick of celery, finely chopped

### Method

(1) Split the baguette.
(2) Combine the dressing, chicken, curry powder and celery. Fill the baguette.

### Nutritional analysis

| Per serving | | % energy |
|---|---|---|
| Energy | 399 kcal | |
| Protein | 28 g | 28% |
| Fat | 8.3 g | 18% |
| Carbohydrate | 57 g | 54% |
| Fibre | 1.8 g | |

## Quesadilla

### Ingredients

2 corn tortillas
40 g (1½ oz) Edam, Gouda or
reduced fat Cheddar cheese, grated
or sliced
1 tbsp ready-made tomato salsa or
mild taco sauce

### Method

(1) Place half the cheese and salsa on each tortilla.
(2) Roll up and heat in a microwave until the cheese is melted.

*Variations*
◆ Add chopped spring onions to the filling.
◆ Add a few slices of avocado to the filling.
◆ Add a handful of shredded white cabbage to the filling.
◆ Substitute 1 tbsp (15 ml) of fromage frais for the tomato salsa.

### Nutritional analysis

| Per serving | | % energy |
|---|---|---|
| Energy | 308 kcal | |
| Protein | 15 g | 19% |
| Fat | 11 g | 31% |
| Carbohydrate | 40 g | 50% |
| Fibre | 1.6 g | |

# Muffin Pizza

## Ingredients

1 wholemeal English muffin
1 tbsp passata (smooth sieved
tomatoes) or pasta sauce
25 g (1 oz) reduced fat mozzarella
or Edam, sliced
Pinch of dried basil or mixed herbs

## Method

(1) Split and toast the muffin. Spread passata or
sauce over each cut side.
(2) Place the cheese on top and sprinkle with the
herbs.
(3) Pop under a hot grill until the cheese has
melted.

*Variations*
♦ Add thinly sliced red, green or yellow peppers to the topping.
♦ Add sliced onions and mushrooms to the topping.

## Nutritional analysis

| Per serving | | % energy |
|---|---|---|
| Energy | 264 kcal | |
| Protein | 16 g | 24% |
| Fat | 7.6 g | 26% |
| Carbohydrate | 36 g | 50% |
| Fibre | 1.5 g | |

# Bean and Corn Quesadillas

These are the ultimate healthy grilled cheese sandwiches.

*Makes 4 quesadillas*

## Ingredients

1 tin (420 g) red kidney or pinto
beans, drained
4 tbsps salsa
8 flour tortillas
100 g (4 oz) Cheddar cheese, grated
1 tbsp vegetable oil

## Method

(1) Mash the beans roughly with the salsa until
well combined.
(2) Divide the filling between four tortillas.
Spread all over the surface, leaving a 2½ cm (1 in)
border.
(3) Sprinkle the cheese over the top. Lay a second
tortilla on top of the filling and press all the way
round.
(3) Brush a large frying pan with half the oil. Lay
the quesadillas in the pan one at a time. Cook for
1 minute. Turn and cook the other side until the
cheese is melted, adding the remaining oil if they
begin to stick.

## Nutritional analysis

| Per serving | | % energy |
|---|---|---|
| Energy | 532 kcal | |
| Protein | 22 g | 17% |
| Fat | 15 g | 26% |
| Carbohydrate | 82 g | 58% |
| Fibre | 8.2 g | |

# Healthy fast food

In this chapter, popular fast foods such as burgers and pizzas have been given a subtle makeover to substantially reduce their fat content and boost their nutritional value. Not only do they taste good but they really are fun to make!

## Spicy Chicken Fillet Burgers

*Makes 4 burgers*

### Ingredients

4 boneless chicken breast fillets
2 tsps oil
1 tsp each of cumin, coriander and paprika
Pinch of chilli powder
4 wholemeal baps
Lettuce, tomato and low calorie salad dressing

### Method

(1) Lightly rub the chicken fillets in the oil.
(2) Mix together the spices in a shallow dish. Add the chicken to the spice mixture and toss to coat.
(3) Cook the chicken in a non-stick pan over a high heat for about 3–4 minutes each side until tender and cooked through.
(4) Toast the cut side of the baps. Place a chicken fillet, lettuce, tomatoes and dressing in each bap.

### Nutritional analysis

| *Per serving (excluding salad garnish)* | | *% energy* |
|---|---|---|
| Energy | 285 kcal | |
| Protein | 25 g | 35% |
| Fat | 6.8 g | 21% |
| Carbohydrate | 34 g | 44% |
| Fibre | 4.1 g | |

## Grilled Chicken Burgers

*Makes 4 servings*

### Ingredients

350 g (12 oz) lean minced chicken
50 g (2 oz) fresh breadcrumbs
½ small onion, finely chopped
2 tbsps fresh (or 1 tbsp dried)
herbs, e.g. parsley, thyme
Salt and freshly ground pepper to
taste
4 tbsps low fat salad dressing
1 tsp mustard
4 baps
Tomato slices

### Method

(1) In a bowl, combine the chicken, breadcrumbs, onion, fresh herbs and seasoning. Mix until well blended. Shape into 4 equal patties approximately 1½ cm (½ in) thick.
(2) Heat a non-stick pan over a medium-high heat. Dry fry the burgers 5–6 minutes on each side until browned on the outside and no longer pink in the centre.
(3) Mix together the salad dressing and mustard.
(4) Place the burgers in baps with the tomato slices and sauce.

### Nutritional analysis

*Per serving (excluding salad garnish)*

|              |          | % energy |
|--------------|----------|----------|
| Energy       | 347 kcal |          |
| Protein      | 27 g     | 31%      |
| Fat          | 6.9 g    | 18%      |
| Carbohydrate | 47 g     | 51%      |
| Fibre        | 4.7 g    |          |

## Fish Burgers

*Makes 4 burgers*

### Ingredients

4 white fish fillets (approx. 75 g/
3 oz each)
2 tsps oil
4 wholemeal baps
Lettuce leaves, cucumber slices
1 tbsp reduced fat mayonnaise
2 tbsps plain yoghurt
1 tbsp chopped chives
Freshly ground black pepper

### Method

(1) Cook the fish fillets in the oil over a high heat for about 2–3 minutes each side, or until the fish flakes easily when tested with a fork.
(2) Toast the baps.
(3) Combine the mayonnaise, yoghurt and chives.
(4) Place a fish fillet, lettuce and cucumber on the bottom half of each bap. Place a spoonful of mayonnaise dressing on top of the fish, season to taste with pepper and replace the top of the bap.

### Nutritional analysis

*Per serving (excluding salad garnish)*

|              |          | % energy |
|--------------|----------|----------|
| Energy       | 297 kcal |          |
| Protein      | 25 g     | 33%      |
| Fat          | 7.2 g    | 22%      |
| Carbohydrate | 36 g     | 45%      |
| Fibre        | 4.1 g    |          |

## Lean Hamburgers

*Makes 4 burgers*

### Ingredients

350 g (12 oz) extra-lean minced
meat
3 tbsps water
½ small onion, chopped
2 tbsps parsley
Freshly ground black pepper
4 wholemeal baps
Shredded lettuce, sliced tomato,
grated carrot

### Method

(1) Place the minced meat, water, onion, parsley
and pepper in a bowl. Mix well to combine.
(2) Divide the mixture into 4 patties. Dry fry in a
hot non-stick pan or over a barbecue for
3–4 minutes each side.
(3) Place lettuce, tomato and carrots on the bottom
half of each bap, top with a burger and replace
the top of the bap.

### Nutritional analysis

| Per serving (excluding salad garnish) | | % energy |
|---|---|---|
| Energy | 281 kcal | |
| Protein | 24 g | 35% |
| Fat | 6.1 g | 19% |
| Carbohydrate | 35 g | 46% |
| Fibre | 4.4 g | |

## Spicy Lentil Burgers

*Makes 4 burgers*

### Ingredients

1 tbsp oil
1 onion, finely chopped
1 tbsp curry powder
175 g (6 oz) red lentils
600 ml (1 pt) vegetable stock
100 g (4 oz) fresh wholemeal
breadcrumbs
Salt and freshly ground black
pepper to taste
A little oil for brushing
4 wholemeal baps
Salad leaves
4 tbsps Greek yoghurt mixed with
a pinch of curry powder

### Method

(1) Heat the oil in a large pan and cook the onion
until softened. Stir in the curry powder and cook
for a further 3 minutes.
(2) Add the lentils and stock. Bring to the boil and
simmer for 20–25 minutes. Alternatively, cook in a
pressure cooker for 3 minutes and turn off the
heat.
(3) Allow to cool slightly and mix in the breadcrumbs. Shape into 4 burgers.
(4) Place on a lightly-oiled baking tray and brush
with a little oil.
(5) Bake for 7–10 minutes at 200°C/400°F/gas
mark 6 until golden and firm.
(6) Split the baps and place one burger inside
each, together with salad leaves and a tablespoon
of yoghurt sauce.

### Nutritional analysis

| Per serving (excluding salad garnish) | | % energy |
|---|---|---|
| Energy | 449 kcal | |
| Protein | 21 g | 18% |
| Fat | 6 g | 12% |
| Carbohydrate | 84 g | 70% |
| Fibre | 7.2 g | |

## Bean Burgers

You can use any type of beans for this recipe, as all are high in protein, fibre, iron and B vitamins.

*Makes 4 burgers*

### Ingredients

1 tin (420 g) beans, drained, e.g. black eye beans, red kidney beans, butter beans, cannelini beans
1 tbsp oil
1 onion, chopped
1 celery stick
2 garlic cloves, crushed
1 tbsp curry powder
2 tbsps tomato purée
25 g (1 oz) fresh breadcrumbs
Salt and pepper
4 wholemeal baps
Salad leaves, sliced tomato
4 tbsps plain yoghurt

### Method

(1) Purée the beans in a food processor.
(2) Heat the oil in a pan and fry the onion and celery until softened. Add the garlic and curry powder and cook for 1 minute.
(3) Mix together the beans with the fried vegetables and tomato purée, mash them well then season with salt and pepper.
(4) Shape into 4 burgers and coat with breadcrumbs.
(5) Brush a non-stick pan with a little oil and cook the burgers for approximately 3 minutes each side until golden.
(6) Split and toast the baps and sandwich around the beanburgers, salad leaves, tomato and a spoonful of yoghurt.

### Nutritional analysis

| Per serving (excluding salad garnish) | | % energy |
|---|---|---|
| Energy | 331 kcal | |
| Protein | 15 g | 19% |
| Fat | 5.6 g | 15% |
| Carbohydrate | 59 g | 66% |
| Fibre | 7.9 g | |

## Basic Pizza

*Makes 1 large pizza*

### Ingredients

Base:
225 g (8 oz) strong white flour
½ sachet easy blend yeast
½ tsp salt
175 ml (6 fl oz) warm water
1 tbsp olive oil

Topping:
See page 214.

### Method

(1) Mix the flour, yeast and salt in a large bowl.
(2) Make a well in the centre and add the oil and half the water. Stir with a wooden spoon, gradually adding more liquid until you have a pliable dough.
(3) Turn the dough out onto a floured surface and knead for about 5 minutes until you have a smooth and elastic dough.
(4) Place the dough in a clean, lightly-oiled bowl, cover with a tea towel and leave in a warm place for about 1 hour or until doubled in size (go and have a workout!).
(5) Knock down the dough and knead briefly before rolling out on a surface to the desired shape.
(6) Transfer to an oiled pizza dish and finish shaping by hand. The dough should be approximately 5 mm (¼ in) thick. For a thicker crust, let the dough rise for another 30 minutes. The pizza is now ready for topping and baking.
(7) Bake at 220°C/425°F/gas mark 7 for 15–20 minutes or until the topping is bubbling and the crust golden brown.

### Nutritional analysis

| *Per serving (¼ pizza)* | | *% energy* |
|---|---|---|
| Energy | 297 kcal | |
| Protein | 13 g | 17% |
| Fat | 8.1 g | 25% |
| Carbohydrate | 46 g | 58% |
| Fibre | 2.6 g | |

# Quick Pizza

*Makes 1 large pizza*

## Ingredients

Base:
225 g (8 oz) self raising white flour
1 tsp baking powder
½ tsp salt
40 g (1½ oz) butter or margarine
150 ml (5 fl oz) skimmed milk

Topping:
See page 214.

## Method

(1) Mix the flour, baking powder and salt in a bowl.
(2) Rub in the butter or margarine until the mixture resembles breadcrumbs.
(3) Add the milk, quickly mixing with a fork until the mixture comes together.
(4) Roll or press the dough into a circle approx. 25 cm (10 in) in diameter and transfer onto a baking tray or pizza pan.
(5) The base is now ready for topping. Bake at 220°C/425°F/gas mark 7 for 15 minutes.

*Variations*
If you don't have time to make your own pizza base, use any of the following:
◆ ready-made chilled or frozen pizza base
◆ foccacia bread, halved horizontally
◆ ciabatta loaf, halved horizontally
◆ wholemeal or white pitta bread
◆ English muffins, toasted and split horizontally
◆ French bread, halved horizontally

## Nutritional analysis

| *Per serving (¼ pizza)* | | *% energy* |
|---|---|---|
| Energy | 352 kcal | |
| Protein | 13 g | 15% |
| Fat | 13 g | 34% |
| Carbohydrate | 48 g | 51% |
| Fibre | 2.6 g | |

# Basic Tomato and Cheese Topping

## Ingredients

300 ml (½ pt) passata (smooth
sieved tomatoes) or chopped
tinned tomatoes or ready-made
pasta sauce
1 tbsp tomato purée
2 tbsps fresh chopped herbs or
1 tbsp dried herbs
Half an onion, very thinly sliced
100 g (4 oz) mozzarella

## Method

(1) Mix together the passata, chopped tomatoes or
sauce, tomato purée and herbs.
(2) Spread on top of the pizza base. Scatter over
the onions, the grated cheese and any additional
toppings from the list below.
(3) Bake at 220°C/425°F/gas mark 7 for 15–20
minutes until the cheese is bubbling and golden
brown.

*Variations*
- Sliced raw vegetables, e.g. tomatoes, mushrooms, peppers, courgettes, asparagus, leeks.
- Well-drained, cooked spinach.
- Lightly cooked, small broccoli florets.
- Sweetcorn.
- Olives and sun dried tomatoes.
- Toasted sunflower seeds or pine nuts.
- Thinly sliced tinned artichoke hearts.
- Flaked tinned tuna.
- Colourful cheeses, e.g. Red Leicester or Double Gloucester.
- Strong flavoured cheeses, e.g. parmesan, blue-veined cheese, extra mature Cheddar cheese or feta cheese.
- Pesto sauce.

## Calzone

This is really a folded pizza pie and is great for wrapping and eating on the run as there are no messy toppings to worry about.

*Makes 1 calzone*

### Ingredients

Dough:
225 g (8 oz) strong white flour
½ sachet easy blend yeast
½ tsp salt
175 ml (6 fl oz) warm water
1 tbsp oil

Filling:
200 ml (7 fl oz) passata (smooth sieved tomatoes) or tinned chopped tomatoes
1 tbsp tomato purée
1 tbsp fresh or 1½ tsps dried mixed herbs
Your choice of vegetables, e.g. chopped onion, mushrooms, peppers, broccoli florets
75 g (3 oz) grated cheese of your choice

### Method

(1) Mix the flours, yeast and salt in a large bowl.
(2) Make a well in the centre and add the oil and half the water. Stir with a wooden spoon, gradually adding more liquid until you have a pliable dough.
(3) Turn the dough out onto a floured surface. Knead, adding a little more flour if necessary until you have a smooth, elastic, not-too-sticky dough. This should take 5–10 minutes.
(4) Place the dough in a clean lightly-oiled bowl, cover with a tea towel and leave in a warm place for approximately 1 hour, or until doubled in size.
(5) Punch down the dough and knead briefly.
(6) Roll out the dough into a large circle. Dampen the outside rim with a little water.
(7) Mix together the passata or chopped tomatoes, tomato purée and herbs. Spread over the circle leaving a 2 cm gap around the outside.
(8) Pile the vegetables and cheese on one half of the circle. Fold the circle in half and press the edges firmly together. Brush with milk.
(9) Place on a baking sheet and bake at 220°C/425°F/gas mark 7 for 15–20 minutes.

### Nutritional analysis

| Per serving (¼ calzone, excluding vegetables) | | % energy |
|---|---|---|
| Energy | 321 kcal | |
| Protein | 13 g | 16% |
| Fat | 11 g | 31% |
| Carbohydrate | 46 g | 53% |
| Fibre | 2.3 g | |

# Snack bars and cookies

Home-made snack bars and cookies are far cheaper than commercial varieties and, in most cases, lower in fat and higher in important nutrients. These recipes make use of highly nutritious ingredients such as oats and other cereals, dried fruit and nuts. They also make ideal snacks for eating on the run.

## Muesli Bars

*Makes 12 bars*

**Ingredients**

175 g (6 oz) oats
75 g (3 oz) muesli
150 g (5 oz) dried fruit mixture, e.g. raisins, dates, apricots, figs, apple, pineapple
3 heaped tbsps honey
2 egg whites
175 ml (6 fl oz) apple juice

**Method**

(1) Combine the oats, muesli and dried fruit in a bowl.
(2) Warm the honey in a small saucepan until it is runny. Add to the bowl.
(3) Stir in the remaining ingredients.
(4) Press the mixture into a lightly-oiled 18 x 28 cm (7 x 11 in) baking tin. Bake at 180°C/ 350°F/gas mark 4 for 20–25 minutes until golden. When cool, cut into bars.

**Nutritional analysis**

| *Per serving (1 bar)* | | *% energy* |
|---|---|---|
| Energy | 141 kcal | |
| Protein | 3.4 g | 10% |
| Fat | 1.9 g | 12% |
| Carbohydrate | 30 g | 78% |
| Fibre | 1.9 g | |

## Oaty Fruit Bars

An ideal post-workout snack, these bars are practically fat-free and are a great source of iron, vitamin A (beta-carotene) and carbohydrates.

*Makes 16 bars*

### Ingredients

175 g (6 oz) porridge oats
175 g (6 oz) plain white or wholemeal flour
175 g (6 oz) Demerara sugar
1 tsp mixed spice
225 g (8 oz) prunes puréed with 6 tbsps water
1 egg white
100 g (4 oz) no-soak dried apricots
100 g (4 oz) sultanas
225 ml (8 fl oz) orange juice

### Method

(1) Place the oats, flour, sugar, spice, prune purée and egg white in a large bowl. Combine with a fork or with your hands until you have a rough crumbly mixture.
(2) Cook the apricots, sultanas and orange juice in a saucepan for 5 minutes, or until the liquid has been absorbed.
(3) Mix the fruit with the oat mixture.
(4) Spoon into a 26 x 17 cm (10 x 7 in) baking tin. Bake at 180°C/350°F/gas mark 4 for 35–40 minutes, until firm and crisp on the surface. When cool, cut into bars.

### Nutritional analysis

| *Per serving (1 bar)* | | *% energy* |
|---|---|---|
| Energy | 186 kcal | |
| Protein | 3.6 g | 8% |
| Fat | 1.3 g | 6% |
| Carbohydrate | 43 g | 86% |
| Fibre | 2.7 g | |

## Date and Walnut Bars

*Makes 12 bars*

### Ingredients

225 g (8 oz) wholemeal self raising flour
1 tsp cinnamon
2 tbsps oil
75 g (3 oz) brown sugar
1 large egg
200 ml (7 fl oz) skimmed milk
175 g (6 oz) chopped dates
50 g (2 oz) chopped walnuts

### Method

(1) Place the first six ingredients in a bowl and mix together.
(2) Stir in the dates and walnuts.
(3) Spoon the mixture into a lightly-oiled shallow 18 x 28 cm (7 x 11 in) baking tin.
(4) Bake at 180°C/350°F/gas mark 4 for 20–25 minutes, until golden brown. When cool, cut into bars.

### Nutritional analysis

| *Per serving (1 bar)* | | *% energy* |
|---|---|---|
| Energy | 189 kcal | |
| Protein | 4.8 g | 10% |
| Fat | 6.3 g | 30% |
| Carbohydrate | 30 g | 60% |
| Fibre | 2.5 g | |

## Fruit and Nut Bars

*Makes 12 bars*

### Ingredients

50 g (2 oz) margarine or butter
3 heaped tbsps honey
2 x 125 g cartons plain yoghurt
225 g (8 oz) low fat soft cheese or cottage cheese
4 egg whites
50 g (2 oz) chopped nuts, e.g. almond, walnuts, brazils
75 g (3 oz) sultanas
225 g (8 oz) wholemeal self raising flour
50 ml (2 fl oz) skimmed milk
25 g (1 oz) sunflower or pumpkin seeds/40 g (1½ oz) desiccated coconut/50 g (2 oz) dried apricots/50 g (2 oz) chopped figs (all optional)

### Method

(1) Combine the margarine or butter, honey, yoghurt and soft cheese.
(2) Beat in the eggs.
(3) Stir in the remaining ingredients. Add extra milk if the mixture seems dry.
(4) Spoon the mixture into a lightly-oiled 18 x 28 cm (7 x 11 in) baking tin.
(5) Bake at 160°C/325°F/gas mark 3 for 35–40 minutes, until firm and golden brown. When cool, cut into bars.

### Nutritional analysis

| *Per serving (1 bar)* | | *% energy* |
|---|---|---|
| Energy | 152 kcal | |
| Protein | 6.3 g | 17% |
| Fat | 6.2 g | 36% |
| Carbohydrate | 19 g | 47% |
| Fibre | 1.7 g | |

## Apricot Bars

*Makes 8 bars*

### Ingredients

100 g (4 oz) ready to eat dried apricots
6 tbsps orange juice
100 g (4 oz) self raising white flour
50 g (2 oz) sugar
2 eggs
100 g (4 oz) sultanas

### Method

(1) Blend the apricots and juice together in a food processor until smooth.
(2) Mix together the flour and sugar in a bowl.
(3) Add the apricot purée, eggs and sultanas. Mix together.
(4) Spoon the mixture into a 7-in square cake tin. Bake at 180°C/350°F/gas mark 4 for 30–35 minutes, until golden brown. When cool, cut into bars.

### Nutritional analysis

| *Per serving (1 bar)* | | *% energy* |
|---|---|---|
| Energy | 155 kcal | |
| Protein | 3.9 g | 10% |
| Fat | 1.9 g | 11% |
| Carbohydrate | 33 g | 79% |
| Fibre | 1.1 g | |

# Raisin Scones

The secret to making light scones is to mix the dough very quickly and handle it as little as possible. These scones make a nutritious, low fat, sweet snack, great for refuelling after a workout.

*Makes 10 bars*

## Ingredients

100 g (4 oz) wholemeal self raising flour
100g (4 oz) self raising white flour
1 tsp baking powder
¼ tsp salt
½ tsp cinnamon
50 g (2 oz) butter
40 g (1½ oz) sugar
50 g (2 oz) raisins
175 ml (6 fl oz) skimmed milk

## Method

(1) In a large bowl, mix together the flours, baking powder, salt and cinnamon.
(2) Roughly chop the butter and rub into the flour mixture with your fingertips until it resembles breadcrumbs. Alternatively, mix in a food processor.
(3) Stir in the sugar and raisins.
(4) Add the milk gradually, mixing quickly with a fork until it forms a soft dough. Do not over mix.
(5) Press the dough to a thickness of about 1½ cm (½ in) on a floured surface. Cut into approximately 10 rounds using a scone cutter.
(6) Transfer onto a lightly-oiled baking tray, brush with milk, and bake at 200°C/400°F/gas mark 6 for 10 minutes, or until lightly browned on top.

*Variations*
- Apricot Scones: replace the raisins with 50 g (2 oz) chopped, dried, ready to eat apricots. Omit the cinnamon.
- Cheese Scones: omit the sugar, cinnamon and raisins. Add 50 g (2 oz) grated Cheddar cheese.
- Walnut Scones: replace the raisins with 50 g (2 oz) chopped walnuts.

## Nutritional analysis

| *Per serving (1 scone)* | | *% energy* |
|---|---|---|
| Energy | 162 kcal | |
| Protein | 3.4 g | 9% |
| Fat | 5.4 g | 29% |
| Carbohydrate | 27 g | 62% |
| Fibre | 1.6 g | |

## Fruit Cookies

Low fat cookies, packed with fibre, iron and protein.

*Makes 20 bars*

### Ingredients

225 g (8 oz) wholemeal self raising
flour
40 g (1½ oz) brown sugar
75 g (3 oz) dried fruit
2 tbsps oil
3 egg whites
4–5 tbsps skimmed milk

### Method

(1) Combine the flour, sugar and fruit in a bowl.
(2) Stir in the oil, egg whites and milk and lightly
mix together until you have a stiff dough.
(3) Place spoonfuls of the mixture onto a lightly-
oiled baking tray.
(4) Bake at 180°C/350°F/gas mark 4 for 12–15
minutes, until golden brown.

*Variations*
◆ Fruit & Nut Cookies: stir in 50 g (2 oz) chopped walnuts or almonds.
◆ Peanut Cookies: replace the dried fruit with 2 tbsps peanut butter.
◆ Muesli Cookies: substitute 75 g (3 oz) of the flour with the same weight of muesli.
◆ Sunflower Cookies: replace the dried fruit with 50 g (2 oz) sunflower seeds.

### Nutritional analysis

| *Per serving (1 cookie)* | | *% energy* |
|---|---|---|
| Energy | 67 kcal | |
| Protein | 2 g | 12% |
| Fat | 1.4 g | 18% |
| Carbohydrate | 12 g | 70% |
| Fibre | 1.1 g | |

## Oatmeal Cookies

*Makes 20 cookies*

### Ingredients

4 tbsps margarine or butter
75 g (3 oz) brown sugar
2 eggs
1 tsp vanilla essence
150 g (5 oz) porridge oats
75 g (3 oz) white flour
¼ tsp baking powder
¼ tsp cinnamon
50 g (2 oz) raisins

### Method

(1) Mix together the margarine or butter and
sugar until light and fluffy.
(2) Beat in the eggs and vanilla.
(3) Add the remaining ingredients and mix until
just combined. You should have a fairly stiff
mixture.
(4) Place spoonfuls onto a lightly-oiled baking
sheet.
(5) Bake at 180°C/350°F/gas mark 4 for 10
minutes, or until golden brown.

*Variations*
- Coconut Oatmeal Cookies: replace the raisins with the same weight of desiccated coconut.
- Pecan Oatmeal Cookies: replace the raisins with the same weight of chopped pecan nuts.

## Nutritional analysis

| *Per serving (1 cookie)* | | *% energy* |
|---|---|---|
| Energy | 91 kcal | |
| Protein | 2.1 g | 9% |
| Fat | 3 g | 30% |
| Carbohydrate | 15 g | 61% |
| Fibre | 0.7 g | |

## Apple Sauce Cookies

**Makes 20 bars**

### Ingredients

50 g (2 oz) butter or margarine
100 g (4 oz) brown sugar
1 large egg
250 ml (8 fl oz) apple sauce
175 g (6 oz) self raising white flour
½ tsp cinnamon
¼ tsp nutmeg
50 g (2 oz) currants
40 g (1½ oz) chopped walnuts
(optional)

### Method

(1) Mix together the butter or margarine and brown sugar in a large bowl.
(2) Add the egg and apple sauce and mix together until smooth.
(3) Add the flour, cinnamon and nutmeg and mix well.
(4) Stir in the currants and walnuts.
(5) Place heaped teaspoons of the mixture onto a lightly-oiled baking tray.
(6) Bake at 190°C/375°F/gas mark 5 for 8–10 minutes, until firm to the touch.

## Nutritional analysis

| *Per serving (1 cookie)* | | *% energy* |
|---|---|---|
| Energy | 92 kcal | |
| Protein | 1.3 g | 6% |
| Fat | 2.9 g | 28% |
| Carbohydrate | 16 g | 66% |
| Fibre | 0.5 g | |

# Puddings and desserts

Puddings and desserts can make a substantial contribution to the nutritional value of your meal. They are a superb way of getting extra fruit, extra milk or extra yoghurt into your daily diet. The following recipes contain significantly less fat than traditional puddings so you can confidently include them in your eating plans.

## Rum and Raisin Cheesecake

*Makes 8 large slices*

### Ingredients

Base:
25 g (1 oz) butter
1 tbsp golden syrup (or honey)
100 g (4 oz) ginger biscuits, crushed

Filling:
75 g (3 oz) raisins
3 tbsps dark rum
450 g (1 lb) cottage cheese or quark
75 g (3 oz) soft light brown sugar
2 eggs
1½ tbsps cornflour

### Method

(1) To make the base, melt together the butter and syrup. Stir in the biscuit crumbs then press into the base of a 20 cm (8 in) springform or cheesecake tin.
(2) Soak the raisins in the rum, ideally for half an hour (or as long as you can).
(3) Blend the remaining ingredients in a liquidiser or food processor until smooth. Alternatively, sieve the cottage cheese and beat the ingredients together in a bowl.
(4) Stir in the raisins and rum.
(5) Pour the filling into the tin.
(6) Bake at 180°C/350°F/gas mark 4 for 45 minutes. Turn off the oven and slightly open the door. Leave the cheesecake to cool in the oven until it reaches room temperature. Place the cheesecake in the fridge.

### Nutritional analysis

| *Per serving (1 slice)* | | *% energy* |
|---|---|---|
| Energy | 272 kcal | |
| Protein | 11 g | 16% |
| Fat | 8.8 g | 29% |
| Carbohydrate | 37 g | 50% |
| Fibre | 0.4 g | |

# Baked Lemon Cheesecake (basic recipe)

This is my favourite dessert and one I shall never tire of making or eating. This low fat version of the baked cheesecake takes only minutes to prepare and can be infinitely varied according to the fresh or tinned fruit you have available. The great news is that it is low in fat and a good source of protein, calcium and vitamins. (It is well worth investing in a cheesecake tin if you don't already have one.)

*Makes 8 large slices*

## Ingredients

Base:
100 g (4 oz) digestive biscuits, crushed into crumbs
25 g (1 oz) butter
1 heaped tbsp honey

Filling:
450 g (1 lb) cottage cheese (or quark)
75 g (3 oz) sugar
2 eggs
Grated rind and juice of 1 lemon
150 ml (¼ pint) low fat plain yoghurt
1 tbsp cornflour
100 g (4 oz) sultanas

## Method

(1) To make the base, melt the butter and honey together then stir in the biscuit crumbs. Press into the base of a 20 cm (8 in) springform or cheesecake tin.
(2) To make the filling, blend all the ingredients except the sultanas in a liquidiser or food processor until smooth. Alternatively, sieve the cottage cheese then beat the ingredients together in a mixing bowl.
(3) Stir in the sultanas and pour into the tin.
(4) Bake at 180°C/350°F/gas mark 4 for 45 minutes. Turn off the oven and slightly open the door. Leave the cheesecake to cool in the oven until it reaches room temperature. Place the cheesecake in the fridge; the flavour actually improves if it has been refrigerated overnight.

*Variations*
- Apricot: add 100 g (4 oz) puréed cooked dried apricots to the mixture. Omit the lemon and sultanas.
- Apple Spice: add 1 large grated cooking apple and 1 tsp cinnamon to the mixture.
- Vanilla: substitute 1 tsp vanilla extract for the lemon.
- Banana: add 2 mashed ripe bananas to the mixture. Omit the sultanas.
- Pineapple: add 1 tin (200 g) of pineapple (finely chopped) to the mixture. Omit the lemon and sultanas.
- Mango: add 1 tin (400 g) mango (well grained, and mashed) to the mixture. Omit the lemon and sultanas.
- Raspberry: add 225 g (8 oz) fresh or frozen raspberries and omit lemon and sultanas.
- Blackcurrant: add 4 tbsps blackcurrant conserve or jam.
- Date and Walnut: stir in 75 g (3 oz) chopped dates and 50 g (2 oz) chopped walnuts. Omit lemon and sultanas.
- Spicy Apple: add 2 grated apples and 1 tsp cinnamon. Omit the sultanas.
- Peanut and Raisin: add 2 heaped tbsps crunchy peanut butter and 50 g (2 oz) raisins.
- Strawberry: add 4 tbsps strawberry pure fruit spread to the filling and top with 100 g (4 oz) fresh sliced strawberries.
- Chocolate: add 100 g (4 oz) melted milk or plain chocolate.

## Nutritional analysis

| *Per serving (1 slice)* | | *% energy* |
|---|---|---|
| Energy | 293 kcal | |
| Protein | 12 g | 16% |
| Fat | 9.9 g | 30% |
| Carbohydrate | 42 g | 54% |
| Fibre | 0.7 g | |

## Chocolate Cookie Cheesecake

Heavenly, indulgent but, surprisingly, much healthier than it sounds!

### Ingredients

Base:
25 g (1 oz) butter
1 tbsp golden syrup or honey
100 g (4 oz) chocolate bourbon
biscuits, crushed

Filling:
450 g (1 lb) cottage cheese
75 g (3 oz) sugar
2 eggs
150 ml (¼ pint) thick plain yoghurt
100 g (4 oz) chocolate bourbon
biscuits, coarsely broken into small
pieces
3 tbsps half fat crème fraîche
Chocolate curls or flakes

### Method

(1) To make the base, melt the butter and syrup or honey. Stir in the biscuits and press into the base of a 20 cm (8 in) springform or cheesecake tin.
(2) To make the filling, place the cottage cheese, sugar, eggs and yoghurt in a food processor or liquidiser and blend until smooth.
(3) Pour half of this filling into the tin.
(4) Top with the broken biscuits.
(5) Cover with the remaining filling mixture.
(6) Bake at 180°C/350°F/gas mark 4 for 45 minutes. Turn off the oven and slightly open the door. Leave the cheesecake to cool in the oven until it reaches room temperature. Spread the half fat crème fraîche over the cheesecake and sprinkle with the chocolate curls or flake. Place the cheesecake in the fridge.

### Nutritional analysis

| Per serving (1 slice) | | % energy |
|---|---|---|
| Energy | 313 kcal | |
| Protein | 13 g | 17% |
| Fat | 13 g | 37% |
| Carbohydrate | 39 g | 46% |
| Fibre | 0 g | |

## Crunchy Apple Crumble

This dessert will help restock your glycogen stores. The oats and apples both have a low glycaemic index so you'll get a sustained energy release. It is also a delicious way of adding lots of fruit to your diet.

*Makes 4 servings*

### Ingredients

700 g (1½ lb) eating apples, sliced
50 g (2 oz) raisins
½ tsp cinnamon
50 g (2 oz) plain flour
50 g (2 oz) low fat spread
50 g (2 oz) porridge oats
40 g (1½ oz) brown sugar
25 g (1 oz) toasted almonds,
chopped (alternatively use
walnuts/pecans/hazelnuts)

### Method

(1) Place the apples, raisins and cinnamon in a deep baking dish. Combine well and add 3–4 tbsps water.
(2) For the topping, combine the flour and low fat spread in a food processor (or rub in by hand).
(3) Stir in the remaining ingredients. Sprinkle over the apples.
(4) Bake at 190°C/375°C/gas mark 5 for 20–25 minutes.

## Variations

Substitute 700 g (1½ lb) of prepared fruit for the apples. Try the following:
◆ chopped rhubarb and 40 g (1½ oz) sugar
◆ fresh or tinned apricots
◆ pears and raspberries
◆ fresh or frozen summer fruits, e.g. blackcurrants, raspberries, strawberries
◆ pears and bananas
◆ blackberries and apples.

## Nutritional analysis

| Per serving | | % energy |
|---|---|---|
| Energy | 312 kcal | |
| Protein | 5.6 g | 7% |
| Fat | 5.2 g | 15% |
| Carbohydrate | 65 g | 78% |
| Fibre | 5.4 g | |

## Fruit Rice Pudding

This super quick, high carbohydrate pudding is an excellent way of refuelling after exercise, and of sneaking extra fresh fruit into your diet.

### Makes 2 servings

**Ingredients**

1 tin (400 g) low fat rice pudding
225 g (8 oz) colourful fruit, e.g. raspberries, blackberries, blueberries
150 ml (5 fl oz) low fat fruit yoghurt, e.g. raspberry

**Method**

(1) Combine the rice pudding, fruit and yoghurt in a dish.
(2) Spoon into individual bowls.

## Variations
◆ You may use any of the following fresh or tinned fruits in place of the berries: peach, apricot, pineapple, mango and a complementary flavoured yoghurt.

## Nutritional analysis

| Per serving | | % energy |
|---|---|---|
| Energy | 282 kcal | |
| Protein | 13 g | 18% |
| Fat | 1.3 g | 4% |
| Carbohydrate | 59 g | 78% |
| Fibre | 3 g | |

## Hot Winter Fruit Salad

*Makes 4 servings*

### Ingredients

100 g (4 oz) dried fruit salad
mixture
250 ml (8 fl oz) orange juice
1 ruby grapefruit, segmented
1 orange, segmented
1 pear, chopped

### Method

(1) Place the dried fruit and orange juice into a
pan and bring to the boil. Simmer for 5 minutes.
(2) Add the remaining fruit.
(3) Serve with low fat yoghurt.

### Nutritional analysis

| *Per serving* | | *% energy* |
|---|---|---|
| Energy | 121 kcal | |
| Protein | 2.2 g | 7% |
| Fat | 0.3 g | 2% |
| Carbohydrate | 29 g | 91% |
| Fibre | 3.6 g | |

## Cool Summer Fruit Salad

*Makes 4 servings*

### Ingredients

100 g (4 oz) strawberries
100 g (4 oz) grapes
4 kiwi fruit, sliced
4 apricots, chopped
150 ml (5 fl oz) tropical fruit juice

### Method

(1) Combine the prepared fruit and fruit juice in a
bowl.
(2) Spoon into individual bowls and serve with
very low fat fromage frais.

### Nutritional analysis

| *Per serving* | | *% energy* |
|---|---|---|
| Energy | 167 kcal | |
| Protein | 3.1 g | 8% |
| Fat | 0.6 g | 3% |
| Carbohydrate | 40 g | 89% |
| Fibre | 5.4 g | |

## Banana Bread Pudding

*Makes 4 servings*

### Ingredients

10 slices wholemeal bread
2 bananas, sliced
50 g (2 oz) sugar
3 eggs
900 ml (1½ pints) skimmed milk
Cinnamon

### Method

(1) Trim the crusts from the bread and cut into quarters diagonally.
(2) Arrange one third of the bread triangles in a lightly greased baking dish.
(3) Arrange one sliced banana on top and then repeat the layers with the remaining bread and banana, finishing with the bread.
(4) Combine the sugar, eggs, and milk. Pour over the bread then sprinkle with cinnamon.
(5) If you have time, allow to stand for 30 minutes.
(6) Bake at 180°C/350°F/gas mark 4 for 40 minutes, or until the pudding is set and golden brown on top.

### Nutritional analysis

| Per serving | | % energy |
|---|---|---|
| Energy | 437 kcal | |
| Protein | 22 g | 20% |
| Fat | 7.5 g | 16% |
| Carbohydrate | 75 g | 64% |
| Fibre | 5.6 g | |

## Low Fat Ice Cream

This is really a cheat's ice cream as it is simplicity itself to make. The whisking incorporates a lot of air so all you need to do is put it in the freezer and wait – there is no stirring and refreezing. It is considerably lower in fat than standard ice cream, and is rich in protein, calcium and vitamin A. Adding extra fruit boosts the vitamin and fibre content.

*Makes 4 large servings*

### Ingredients

250 ml (8 fl oz) evaporated milk, chilled in the fridge
50 g (2 oz) castor sugar
2 tsps vanilla essence

### Method

(1) Pour the chilled milk into a bowl and whisk with an electric mixer for approximately 4 minutes, until thick and foamy and roughly tripled in volume.
(2) Whisk in the sugar and vanilla until incorporated.
(3) Pour the mixture into a shallow container and place in the freezer until frozen.

*Variations*
- Mango: purée the flesh of one large ripe mango and stir into the whisked milk. Omit the vanilla.
- Apricot: stir in 175 g (6 oz) puréed, soaked dried apricots and omit the vanilla.
- Raspberry: stir in 175 g (6 oz) mashed fresh or frozen raspberries and omit the vanilla.
- Blackcurrant or Blueberry: stir in 3 heaped tbsps blackcurrant or blueberry pure fruit spread. You may reduce the sugar by half.
- Hazelnut: stir in 50 g (2 oz) chopped toasted hazelnuts.
- Amaretto: stir in 1–2 tbsps amaretto (almond liqueur) and 50 g (2 oz) flaked toasted almonds. Omit the vanilla.

## Nutritional analysis

| *Per serving* | | *% energy* |
|---|---|---|
| Energy | 153 kcal | |
| Protein | 5.2 g | 14% |
| Fat | 5.9 g | 34% |
| Carbohydrate | 21 g | 52% |
| Fibre | 0 g | |

## Apricot and Date Bread Pudding

This low fat adaptation of the classic pudding has a higher content of fibre, vitamin A and potassium.

*Makes 4 servings*

### Ingredients

8 slices wholemeal bread, crusts trimmed
50 g (2 oz) dates, chopped
50 g (2 oz) dried ready-to-eat apricots
2 eggs
2 tbsps honey
750 ml (1½ pts) skimmed or semi-skimmed milk
Pinch of cinnamon

### Method

(1) Cut each slice of bread into diagonal quarters. Arrange one third of the triangles in a lightly-oiled 20 cm (8 in) square baking dish.
(2) Sprinkle with half of the dates and apricots.
(3) Place another layer of bread triangles on top. Sprinkle with the remaining dates and apricots and finish with a layer of the remaining bread.
(4) Beat together the eggs, honey and milk. Pour over the pudding and sprinkle with the cinnamon.
(5) Place the dish in a larger baking pan containing enough water to reach halfway up the sides of the dish. Bake at 180°C/350°F/gas mark 4 for 40 minutes, or until the pudding is just set and golden brown on top.

## Nutritional analysis

| *Per serving* | | *% energy* |
|---|---|---|
| Energy | 354 kcal | |
| Protein | 17 g | 20% |
| Fat | 5.4 g | 14% |
| Carbohydrate | 63 g | 66% |
| Fibre | 5.8 g | |

## Fruit Pancakes

*Makes 4 servings*

### Ingredients

Batter:
50 g (2 oz) plain white flour
50 g (2 oz) plain wholemeal flour
2 eggs
300 ml (½ pt) skimmed milk
A little vegetable oil or oil spray for frying

Filling:
225 g (8 oz) sliced fruit (see below)
200 g (7 oz) low fat vanilla fromage frais

### Method

(1) Place all of the batter ingredients in a liquidiser and blend until smooth.
(2) Alternatively mix the flours in a bowl. Make a well in the centre. Beat the egg and milk and gradually add to the flour, beating to make a smooth batter.
(3) Place a non-stick frying pan over a high heat. Spray with oil spray or add a few drops of oil.
(4) Pour in enough batter to coat the pan thinly and cook for 1–2 minutes until golden brown on the underside.
(5) Turn the pancake and cook the other side for 30–60 seconds until golden brown.
(5) Turn out onto a plate, cover and keep warm while you make the other pancakes.
(6) To make the filling, combine the sliced fruit with the fromage frais.
(7) Place spoonfuls of the fruit mixture over one half of each pancake then fold the pancakes into triangles.

*Fruit suggestions:* fresh strawberries, sliced mango, tinned pineapple, fresh or tinned apricots, sliced banana, mixed berry fruits, tinned cherries, sliced nectarines.

### Nutritional analysis

| Per serving | | % energy |
|---|---|---|
| Energy | 209 kcal | |
| Protein | 14 g | 26% |
| Fat | 4 g | 17% |
| Carbohydrate | 32 g | 57% |
| Fibre | 2.4 g | |

# Low Fat Tiramisu

Both the fat and calorie content of this healthy pudding are a fraction of the classic Italian version. You can substitute fruit juice for the alcohol if you prefer.

*Makes 4 servings*

## Ingredients

12 sponge fingers
100 ml (3½ fl oz ) strong black coffee
1 tsp vanilla essence
1 tbsp Amaretto
1 tbsp brandy
450 g (1 lb) soft fruit, e.g. raspberries, blackberries, strawberries, tinned black cherries
225 g (8 oz) plain low fat fromage frais
225 g (8 oz) quark or ricotta cheese
2½ tbsps icing sugar, sifted
1 tbsp cocoa or chocolate powder

## Method

(1) Line the bottom of a shallow baking dish with the sponge fingers.
(2) Mix together the coffee, vanilla, Amaretto and brandy. Slowly sprinkle this mixture over the sponge fingers so that they evenly soak up all the liquid.
(3) Place the fruit over the sponge fingers.
(4) Combine the fromage frais, quark, and 2 tbsps of the icing sugar. Spread over the sponge fingers.
(5) Combine the cocoa and the remaining icing sugar. Sift evenly over the surface of the pudding. Chill.

## Nutritional analysis

| Per serving | | % energy |
|---|---|---|
| Energy | 244 kcal | |
| Protein | 18 g | 29% |
| Fat | 3.1 g | 11% |
| Carbohydrate | 34 g | 60% |
| Fibre | 3.5 g | |

# Baked Bananas

One of the easiest desserts to make. It is high in carbohydrates, low in fat, and rich in potassium and magnesium. Topped with a little Greek yoghurt it is good enough to serve at dinner parties as well as for the family.

*Makes 4 servings*

### Ingredients

4 large bananas
4 tbsps water
2 tbsps honey or maple syrup
½ tsp mixed spice
2 tbsps dark rum/50 g (2 oz) raisins/50 g (2 oz) chocolate buttons/1 tbsp lemon juice (all optional)

### Method

(1) Chop the bananas into 2½-cm (1-in) chunks.
(2) Place in a baking dish and combine with the remaining ingredients.
(3) Bake at 200°C/400°F/gas mark 6 for 15 minutes, or microwave for 3 minutes.

### Nutritional analysis

| Per serving | | % energy |
| --- | --- | --- |
| Energy | 124 kcal | |
| Protein | 1.2 g | 4% |
| Fat | 0.3 g | 2% |
| Carbohydrate | 31 g | 94% |
| Fibre | 1.1 g | |

# Fruit Clafouti

This French fruit custard is equally good eaten hot or cold. It is low in fat and is a good source of protein, vitamins and calcium.

*Makes 4 servings*

### Ingredients

50 g (2 oz) plain white flour
50 g (2 oz) sugar
2 eggs
350 ml (12 fl oz) skimmed milk
450 g (1 lb) fruit, e.g. plums, tinned black cherries, raspberries, apples, tinned peaches
Pinch of nutmeg

### Method

(1) Blend the flour, sugar, eggs and milk in a liquidiser. Alternatively, beat together by hand until smooth.
(2) Place the fruit in the bottom of a shallow baking dish.
(3) Pour in the batter and sprinkle the top with nutmeg.
(4) Bake at 200°C/400°F/gas mark 6 for 40–45 minutes, until the custard is firm.

### Nutritional analysis

| Per serving | | % energy |
| --- | --- | --- |
| Energy | 221 kcal | |
| Protein | 8.6 g | 16% |
| Fat | 3.6 g | 15% |
| Carbohydrate | 41 g | 69% |
| Fibre | 2.1 g | |

## Yoghurt and Fruit Pudding

*Makes 1 serving*

### Ingredients

1 carton (125 g or 150 g) low fat or
virtually fat free fruit yoghurt
100 g (4 oz) fruit mixture, e.g.
strawberries, blueberries,
raspberries, peaches, bananas
1 tbsp toasted flaked
almonds/chopped hazelnuts
(optional)

### Method

(1) Spoon half of the yoghurt into a sundae glass
(or small dish).
(2) Top with half of the fruit followed by another
layer of yoghurt.
(3) Top with the remaining fruit and nuts
(optional).

### Nutritional analysis

| *Per serving* | | *% energy* |
|---|---|---|
| Energy | 169 kcal | |
| Protein | 7.1 g | 17% |
| Fat | 1.1 g | 6% |
| Carbohydrate | 34 g | 77% |
| Fibre | 1.4 g | |

## Oatmeal and Raisin Scotch Pancakes

A fantastic pudding which aids refuelling through slow release complex carbohydrates,
protein and soluble fibre. These pancakes also double up as a nutritious snack that you
can pop into your kit bag.

*Makes 8 pancakes*

### Ingredients

2 large eggs
225 g (8 oz) cottage cheese
1 tbsp margarine or low fat spread
100 g (4 oz) oatmeal or porridge
oats
75g (3 oz) raisins or currants

### Method

(1) Place the eggs, cottage cheese, margarine and
oatmeal in a liquidiser and blend until smooth.
Alternatively, beat together by hand in a bowl.
(2) Add the raisins or currants and stir in
carefully.
(3) Lightly brush a non-stick frying pan with oil.
Drop tablespoons of the batter onto the hot pan.
When bubbles appear on the surface, flip over
and cook for one more minute.
(4) Serve with fresh fruit, puréed fruit or pure
fruit spread.

### Nutritional analysis

| *Per serving (1 pancake)* | | *% energy* |
|---|---|---|
| Energy | 146 kcal | |
| Protein | 8 g | 22% |
| Fat | 4.6 g | 28% |
| Carbohydrate | 19 g | 50% |
| Fibre | 1.3 g | |

# Cottage Cheese Pancakes with Blueberry Sauce

Blueberries are rich in vitamin C and fibre. You may substitute them with other similar fruits, e.g. blackberries, blackcurrants or raspberries.

*Makes 4 servings (8 pancakes)*

## Ingredients

Sauce:
225 g (8 oz) fresh or frozen blueberries
1 heaped tsp cornflour
2 tbsps honey

Pancakes:
225 g (8 oz) cottage cheese
175 g (6 oz) flour
3 eggs
175 ml (6 fl oz) semi-skimmed milk
1 tbsp sugar

## Method

(1) Place the blueberries with 1 tbsp water in a saucepan and simmer for a few minutes until they burst.
(2) Mix together the cornflour, honey and 3 tbsps water in a cup and add to the blueberries. Bring to the boil, stirring to thicken. Leave to cool.
(3) In a bowl, combine the pancake ingredients.
(4) Lightly brush or spray a thick-based frying pan with oil. Over a medium heat, drop spoonfuls of the pancake batter onto the hot pan. Cook for approximately 2 minutes, or until lightly browned on the underside. Flip and cook on the other side until lightly browned, about 1 minute.
(5) Pile the pancakes onto a plate and spoon the blueberry sauce over the top.

## Nutritional analysis

| Per serving | | % energy |
| --- | --- | --- |
| Energy | 357 kcal | |
| Protein | 20 g | 22% |
| Fat | 8.4 g | 21% |
| Carbohydrate | 54 g | 57% |
| Fibre | 3.1 g | |

# Muffins

Muffins are basically mini-cakes, which makes them ideal as a portable healthy snack – all of the following recipes are low in fat. They are very easy to make, although it is worth investing in a non-stick deep muffin (bun) tin. Muffins will keep for up to three days or, alternatively, freeze and defrost as you need them. A word of warning: once you start making your own muffins you'll be hooked!

## Raisin Muffins

The perfect refuelling snack that no athlete should be without! You may use all wholemeal flour if you prefer but I find that a half and half mixture of white and wholemeal flour gives the lightest result.

*Makes 12 muffins*

**Ingredients**

100 g (4 oz) white self raising flour
100 g (4 oz) wholemeal self raising flour
Pinch of salt
40 g (1½ oz) soft brown sugar
1 tbsp oil
1 egg
200 ml (7 fl oz) skimmed milk
75 g (3 oz) raisins

**Method**

(1) Preheat the oven to 220°C/425°F/gas mark 7.
(2) Mix the flours and salt together in a bowl.
(3) Add the oil, sugar, egg and milk. Mix well.
(4) Stir in the raisins.
(5) Spoon into a non-stick muffin tray and bake for approximately 15 minutes until golden brown.

*Variations*
- Carrot and Nut: add 2 grated carrots and 50 g (2 oz) chopped walnuts or pecans. Omit the raisins.
- Blueberry: stir in 150 g (5 oz) fresh or 75 g (3 oz) dried blueberries instead of the raisins.
- Cherry: replace the raisins with 75 g (3 oz) halved glace cherries.

**Nutritional analysis**

| *Per serving (1 muffin)* | | *% energy* |
|---|---|---|
| Energy | 120 kcal | |
| Protein | 3.6 g | 12% |
| Fat | 1.9 g | 14% |
| Carbohydrate | 24 g | 74% |
| Fibre | 1.4 g | |

## Orange Muffins

Good for breakfast on the run, they are rich in carbohydrate and fibre, and low in fat.

*Makes 16 muffins*

### Ingredients

2 eggs
75 g (3 oz) sugar
3 tbsps oil
200 ml (7 fl oz) skimmed milk
Grated rind and juice of 2 oranges
150 g (5 oz) self raising white flour
100 g (4 oz) wholemeal flour
½ tsp salt

### Method

(1) Combine the eggs, sugar, oil, milk and rind and juice of the oranges in a bowl.
(2) Combine the flours and salt in a bowl then fold into the wet mixture.
(3) Spoon into lightly-oiled muffin tins and bake at 200°C/400°F/gas mark 6 for 20 minutes.

### Nutritional analysis

| *Per serving (1 muffin)* | | *% energy* |
|---|---|---|
| Energy | 112 kcal | |
| Protein | 3.2 g | 12% |
| Fat | 3.2 g | 25% |
| Carbohydrate | 19 g | 63% |
| Fibre | 1.0 g | |

## Chocolate Chip Muffins

*Makes 12 muffins*

### Ingredients

225 g (8 oz) self raising flour (half white/half wholemeal)
1 tsp baking powder
75 g (3 oz) sugar
40 g (1½ oz) cocoa, sieved
½ tsp salt
3 egg whites
3 tbsps oil
1 tsp vanilla essence
300 ml (½ pint) skimmed milk
50 g (2 oz) chocolate chips

### Method

(1) Mix together the flour, baking powder, sugar, cocoa and salt in a large bowl.
(2) Add the egg whites, oil, vanilla and milk and fold together. Add a little extra milk if necessary to produce a very soft mixture.
(3) Fold the chocolate into the mixture.
(4) Bake at 200°C/400°F/gas mark 6 for 20 minutes.

### Nutritional analysis

| *Per serving (1 muffin)* | | *% energy* |
|---|---|---|
| Energy | 159 kcal | |
| Protein | 4.4 g | 11% |
| Fat | 5.2 g | 29% |
| Carbohydrate | 25 g | 60% |
| Fibre | 1.7 g | |

# Oatmeal Muffins

Oats provide slow release complex carbohydrate thanks to their soluble fibre content. These muffins are the perfect refuelling food for active people. Add whatever fresh or dried fruit you have handy for extra vitamins and fibre.

*Makes 12 muffins*

## Ingredients

175 g (6 oz) self raising flour (all white, or half wholemeal/ half white)
100 g (4 oz) oats
100 g (4 oz) brown sugar
2 tsps baking powder
½ tsp salt
4 tbsps oil
1 tsp vanilla essence
1 large egg
225 ml (8 fl oz) skimmed milk or buttermilk
100 g (4 oz) fresh fruit or dried fruit (see variations)

## Method

(1) In a large bowl, mix together the flour, oats, sugar, baking powder and salt.
(2) Combine the oil, vanilla, egg and milk in a separate bowl then stir into the flour mixture.
(3) Fold the fruit into the mixture.
(4) Spoon the mixture into lightly-oiled muffin tins, filling them two-thirds full.
(5) Bake at 190°C/375°F/gas mark 5 for about 20 minutes until firm to the touch and light brown.

*Variations*
◆ Oatmeal Apple: add 100 g (4 oz) grated apples.
◆ Oatmeal Pineapple: add 100–175 g (4–6 oz) tinned chopped pineapple.
◆ Oatmeal Fig: add 75–100 g (3–4 oz) chopped dried figs.
◆ Oatmeal Blueberry: add 100 g (4 oz) fresh blueberries.
◆ Oatmeal Coconut: add 100 g (4 oz) shredded unsweetened coconut or desiccated coconut to the flour mixture.

## Nutritional analysis

| *Per serving (1 muffin)* | | *% energy* |
|---|---|---|
| Energy | 188 kcal | |
| Protein | 4.3 g | 9% |
| Fat | 5.5 g | 26% |
| Carbohydrate | 32 g | 65% |
| Fibre | 1.4 g | |

## Banana Muffins

*Makes 12 muffins*

### Ingredients

2 large ripe bananas, mashed
75 g (3 oz) sugar
50 g (2 oz) butter
1 egg
100 ml (4 fl oz) skimmed milk
200 g (7 oz) self raising flour
Pinch of salt
½ tsp nutmeg
50 g (2 oz) chopped walnuts/50 g
(2 oz) raisins (optional)

### Method

(1) Mix together the bananas, sugar and butter.
(2) Beat in the egg and milk.
(3) Fold in the flour, salt and nutmeg. And walnuts or raisins if applicable.
(4) Spoon into a lightly-oiled muffin tin and bake at 190°C/375°F/gas mark 5 for 20 minutes.

### Nutritional analysis

| *Per serving (1 muffin)* | | *% energy* |
|---|---|---|
| Energy | 150 kcal | |
| Protein | 2.7 g | 7% |
| Fat | 4.9 g | 29% |
| Carbohydrate | 25 g | 64% |
| Fibre | 0.7 g | |

## Corn Muffins

Eat these savoury muffins for breakfast or for supper with a bowl of tomato soup. They are low in fat, and high in complex carbohydrate and fibre.

*Makes 12 muffins*

### Ingredients

175 g (6 oz) cornmeal
1 tbsp baking powder
1 tsp salt
2 eggs
2 tbsps oil
250 g (9 oz) tin of creamed corn
250 ml (9 fl oz) plain yoghurt

### Method

(1) Mix together the cornmeal, baking powder and salt in a large bowl.
(2) In a separate bowl, combine the remaining ingredients.
(3) Add the wet mixture to the cornmeal mixture and combine well.
(4) Spoon into a lightly-oiled muffin tin.
(5) Bake at 200°C/400°F/gas mark 6 for 20 minutes until risen and golden.

### Nutritional analysis

| *Per serving (1 muffin)* | | *% energy* |
|---|---|---|
| Energy | 122 kcal | |
| Protein | 4.3 g | 14% |
| Fat | 3.8 g | 28% |
| Carbohydrate | 18 g | 58% |
| Fibre | 0.6 g | |

# Cakes

This is a collection of my favourite low fat cake recipes, developed over several years and tested by many willing volunteers! Most make use of added fresh and dried fruit which obviously boosts the nutritional value as well as reducing the fat content. In fact, the following recipes are healthy enough to be regarded as everyday snacks instead of occasional treats.

## Banana Cake

Bursting with vitamins, this high carbohydrate, fat-free snack could be a staple part of every athlete's diet.

*Makes 12 slices*

### Ingredients

2 large ripe bananas
225 ml (8 fl oz) orange juice
300 g (10 oz) self raising flour (half wholemeal/half white)
100 g (4 oz) brown sugar
Pinch of salt
½ tsp each of mixed spice and cinnamon
2 egg whites
1 tbsp oil

### Method

(1) Mash the bananas with the orange juice.
(2) Mix together the flour, sugar, salt and spices in a bowl.
(3) Add the banana juice mixture together with the egg whites and oil. Combine together.
(4) Spoon into a lightly-oiled 2 lb loaf tin.
(5) Bake at 160°C/325°F/gas mark 3 for about 1 hour. Check the cake is cooked by inserting a skewer or knife into the centre. It should come out clean.

### Nutritional analysis

| *Per serving (1 slice)* | | *% energy* |
|---|---|---|
| Energy | 158 kcal | |
| Protein | 3.5 g | 9% |
| Fat | 1.4 g | 8% |
| Carbohydrate | 35 g | 83% |
| Fibre | 1.8 g | |

# Apple Cake

*Makes 12 slices*

## Ingredients

3 apples
300 g (10 oz) self raising flour (half wholemeal/half white)
100 g (4 oz) brown sugar
1 tsp cinnamon
2 egg whites
100 ml (4 fl oz) apple juice

## Method

(1) Grate the apples and place in a bowl with the remaining ingredients.
(2) Mix together well.
(3) Spoon into a lightly-oiled loaf tin and bake at 160°C/325°F/gas mark 3 for about 1–1¼ hours. Check the cake is cooked by inserting a skewer or knife into the centre. It should come out clean.

## Nutritional analysis

*Per serving (1 slice)*

| | | *% energy* |
|---|---|---|
| Energy | 98 kcal | |
| Protein | 3.3 g | 13% |
| Fat | 0.5 g | 4% |
| Carbohydrate | 22 g | 83% |
| Fibre | 2 g | |

# Carrot Cake

Traditional carrot cakes have a very high oil/fat and sugar content and are smothered in cream cheese. This low fat version is perfect for active people and tastes even better!

*Makes 16 slices*

## Ingredients

225 g (8 oz) self raising flour (half wholemeal/half white)
Pinch of salt
2 tsps mixed spice
100 g (4 oz) brown sugar
3 carrots, grated
2 apples, grated
100 g (4 oz) sultanas or raisins
2 tbsps oil
175 ml (6 fl oz) orange or apple juice
2 egg whites

## Method

(1) Mix together the flour, salt, spice and sugar in a bowl.
(2) Stir in the carrots, apples and sultanas.
(3) Add the oil, fruit juice and egg whites. Mix together well.
(4) Spoon into a loaf tin or a 20 cm (8 in) round cake tin and bake at 160°C/325°F/gas mark 3 for about 1½ hours. Check the cake is cooked by inserting a skewer or knife into the centre. It should come out clean.

## Nutritional analysis

*Per serving (1 slice)*

| | | *% energy* |
|---|---|---|
| Energy | 125 kcal | |
| Protein | 2.2 g | 7% |
| Fat | 1.7 g | 12% |
| Carbohydrate | 27 g | 81% |
| Fibre | 1.5 g | |

## Pumpkin Cake

Make this cake in the autumn when pumpkins are plentiful and cheap. This low fat cake is surprisingly moist and moreish, and pumpkin is a terrific source of beta-carotene, potassium and fibre.

*Makes 12 slices*

### Ingredients

225 g (8 oz) cooked mashed pumpkin
1 carton (125 g) low fat plain yoghurt
1 egg
100 g (4 oz) sugar
175 g (6 oz) self raising flour (or half wholemeal/half white)
1 tsp vanilla essence
75 g (3 oz) raisins

### Method

(1) In a large bowl, mix together the pumpkin, yoghurt and egg.
(2) Fold in the remaining ingredients.
(3) Spoon the mixture into a lightly-oiled shallow 18 x 28 cm (7 x 11 in) baking tin.
(4) Bake at 180°C/350°F/gas mark 4 for 35–40 minutes until firm and golden brown. Cut into slices.

### Nutritional analysis

*Per serving (1 slice)*

| | | % energy |
|---|---|---|
| Energy | 124 kcal | |
| Protein | 2.7 g | 9% |
| Fat | 0.9 g | 6% |
| Carbohydrate | 28 g | 85% |
| Fibre | 0.8 g | |

## Raisin Cake

*Makes 8 squares*

### Ingredients

75 g (3 oz) raisins
100 ml (4 fl oz) orange juice
50 g (2 oz) sugar
50g (2 oz) low fat spread, melted
1 tsp vanilla essence
1 egg and 1 egg white
100 g (4 oz) self raising flour (wholemeal or white)
½ tsp cinnamon

### Method

(1) Combine the raisins, orange juice, low fat spread, sugar and vanilla in a bowl.
(2) Add the egg and egg white. Mix well.
(3) Fold in the flour and cinnamon.
(4) Spoon the mixture into a baking tin.
(5) Bake at 180°C/350°F/gas mark 4 for about 15 minutes, until golden and firm to the touch. Cool and cut into squares.

### Nutritional analysis

*Per serving (1 square)*

| | | % energy |
|---|---|---|
| Energy | 154 kcal | |
| Protein | 4 g | 10% |
| Fat | 4.2 g | 25% |
| Carbohydrate | 25 g | 65% |
| Fibre | 1.6 g | |

## Fruit Cake

*Makes 16 slices*

### Ingredients

225 g (8 oz) self raising flour (half wholemeal/half white)
75 g (3 oz) brown sugar
1 tsp cinnamon
2 eggs
4 tbsps oil
1 tsp vanilla
225 g (8 oz) dried fruit mixture (any combination of raisins, sultanas, currants, apricots, dates, pineapple, mango, apple, peaches, figs, papaya)
1 apple, grated
75 ml (3 fl oz) skimmed milk
100 g (4 oz) chopped nuts of any variety/100 g (4 oz) grated courgettes/2 grated carrots/ 75 g (3 oz) glace cherries/grated lemon or orange rind (all optional)

### Method

(1) Mix together the flour, sugar, and cinnamon in a bowl.
(2) Make a well in the centre and add the eggs, oil, vanilla, fruit and milk and any extra optional ingredients. Combine together well.
(3) Spoon into a 23 cm (9 in) round or square baking tin and bake at 160°C/325°F/gas mark 3 for about 1¼–1½ hours. Check the cake is cooked by inserting a skewer or knife into the centre. It should come out clean.

### Nutritional analysis

| *Per serving (1 slice)* | | *% energy* |
|---|---|---|
| Energy | 145 kcal | |
| Protein | 2.9 g | 8% |
| Fat | 3.9 g | 24% |
| Carbohydrate | 26 g | 68% |
| Fibre | 1.2 g | |

# Chocolate and Banana Cake

*Makes 12 slices*

## Ingredients

2 ripe bananas, mashed
75 g (3 oz) brown sugar
3 tbsps oil
2 tsps vanilla essence
1 egg or 2 egg whites
1 carton (125 g) plain yoghurt
200 g (7 oz) self raising flour (half wholemeal/half white)
25 g (1 oz) cocoa powder, sieved
Pinch of salt
50 g (2 oz) raisins/75 g (3 oz) chopped dates/50 g (2 oz) walnuts (all optional)

## Method

(1) Combine the bananas, sugar, oil, vanilla, egg and yoghurt in a bowl.
(2) Stir in the remaining ingredients and mix until just blended.
(3) Transfer the mixture into a 23 cm (9 in) square lightly-oiled cake tin.
(4) Bake at 180°C/350°F/gas mark 4 for 25–30 minutes until it is firm and springy to the touch.

*Variations*
◆ Chocolate Orange: omit the bananas and add the grated rind and juice of 2 oranges.
◆ Double Chocolate Chip: omit 1 banana and add 50 g (2 oz) chocolate chips or broken chocolate pieces.

## Nutritional analysis

*Per serving (1 slice)*

| | | *% energy* |
|---|---|---|
| Energy | 136 kcal | |
| Protein | 3.4 g | 10% |
| Fat | 3.6 g | 24% |
| Carbohydrate | 24 g | 66% |
| Fibre | 1.4 g | |

# Chocolate Cocoa Cake

My all-time favourite recipe for chocolate cake – it tastes like sheer heaven yet is unbelievably low in fat!

*Makes 16 slices*

## Ingredients

350 g (12 oz) self raising flour (half wholemeal/half white)
6 tbsps cocoa, sieved
1 tsp salt
200 g (7 oz) brown sugar
1 tsp vanilla
4 tbsps oil
2 eggs
1 carton (125 g) plain yoghurt
300 ml (½ pt) skimmed milk

## Method

(1) Combine the flour, cocoa, salt and sugar together in a bowl.
(2) Add the remaining ingredients and mix well.
(3) Transfer into a lightly-oiled 18 x 28 cm (7 x 11 in) baking tin. Bake at 180°C/350°F/gas mark 4 for 25–30 minutes until golden. When cool, cut into slices.

*Variations*
- Chocolate Date Cake: add 75 g (3 oz) chopped dates to the mixture.
- Chocolate Chip Chocolate Cake: add 75 g (3 oz) chocolate chips to the mixture.
- Chocolate Raisin Cake: add 75 g (3 oz) raisins (or sultanas) to the mixture.

**Nutritional analysis**

| *Per serving (1 slice)* | | *% energy* |
|---|---|---|
| Energy | 166 kcal | |
| Protein | 4.1 g | 10% |
| Fat | 4 g | 22% |
| Carbohydrate | 30 g | 68% |
| Fibre | 1.8 g | |

## Low Fat Chocolate Brownies

Traditional brownies consist mainly of butter, chocolate and sugar – a high fat nightmare. This healthier version has the fat content substantially reduced and the chocolate replaced by cocoa and yoghurt.

### Makes 16 squares

**Ingredients**

75 g (3 oz) self raising white flour
40 g (1½ oz) cocoa powder
175 g (6 oz) castor sugar
100 g (4 fl oz) vanilla yoghurt
2 eggs
1 tsp vanilla essence
1½ tbsps oil

**Method**

(1) Sift the flour and cocoa into a bowl. Add the remaining ingredients and mix together.
(2) Spoon the mixture into a lightly-oiled 20 cm (8 in) square baking tin and bake at 180°C/350°F/ gas mark 4 for approximately 25 minutes, until springy to the touch.
(3) Cool and cut into squares.

**Nutritional analysis**

| *Per serving (1 brownie)* | | *% energy* |
|---|---|---|
| Energy | 95 kcal | |
| Protein | 2.2 g | 9% |
| Fat | 2.5 g | 23% |
| Carbohydrate | 17 g | 68% |
| Fibre | 0.5 g | |

## Chocolate Fudge Brownies

This low fat version of brownies uses puréed prunes to replace the fat; surprisingly you can't taste the prunes at all and they keep the brownies wonderfully moist. Prune purée also contains fibre, iron, vitamin A and potassium.

*Makes 16 squares*

### Ingredients

100 g (4 oz) plain chocolate
100 g (4 oz) prunes
3 tbsps water
3 egg whites
200 g (7 oz) light brown sugar
1 tsp salt
1 tsp vanilla essence
65 g (2½ oz) plain flour
25 g (1 oz) chopped walnuts
(optional)

### Method

(1) Melt the chocolate in a bowl placed over a saucepan of simmering water.
(2) Purée the prunes with the water in a liquidiser or food processor until roughly smooth.
(3) In a bowl, mix together the prune purée, egg whites, sugar, salt and vanilla essence.
(4) Add the melted chocolate and stir until smooth.
(5) Fold in the sieved flour.
(6) Spread the mixture into a lightly-oiled 15 cm (6 in) square tin. Sprinkle with the walnuts, if applicable.
(7) Bake at 180°C/350°F/gas mark 4 for 1 hour. When cool, cut into squares.

### Nutritional analysis

| *Per serving (1 brownie)* | | *% energy* |
|---|---|---|
| Energy | 118 kcal | |
| Protein | 1.5 g | 5% |
| Fat | 2.3 g | 17% |
| Carbohydrate | 24 g | 78% |
| Fibre | 0.8 g | |

# Index

aerobics   38, 47, 51, 95–7
alcohol   11
amino acids   60–1
anaemia   58
antioxidants   58
appetite   50

beans   139-48
beta carotene   32
body image   51–2
bodybuilding   38, 85–8
bread   163–75
breakfast cereals   201
breakfasts   192–201
bulgar wheat   137
bulking up 36–44
    eating plans   39–44

cakes   238–44
calcium   34, 58, 62
calories   45–7
    expenditure   47
carbohydrate   14–21
    counter   16–17
    digestion   19–21
    exercise   20
    high fibre   46
    loading   98–9
    recovery   18
catabolism   38
cereals   5–6
combat sports   83–5
competition   98–106
cookies   216–21
cous cous   136
creatine   86

dairy products   7
dehydration   73–5
desserts   222–33
diet
    demi-vegetarian   59
    pescatarian   59
    vegan   57–8
    vegetarian   58
drinking   73–7, 100

energy drinks   76
exercise 50–1

fast carbs   20
fast food   69, 208–15
fat free mass   47
fats   10, 22–9
    food content   26
    hidden   25
fatty acids
    essential   24
    linoleic   22
    linolenic   22
    monounsaturated   23, 25
    omega-3   25
    omega-6   24
    polyunsaturated   23–4
    saturated   23–4
    trans   24
fatty foods   12–13
fish   8–9
folic acid   33
food diary   45, 50
fruit   2–3

glucose polymers   76
glycaemic index   20–1

HDL cholesterol   24–5
heat stress   73
high fat food   27
hypoglycaemia   19
hypotonic   76–7

iodine   62
iron   34, 58, 62
isotonic   75–7

LDL cholesterol   24–5, 58
lifestyle   48
long distance
    cycling   88–90
    running   38, 78–80
low fat food   22, 26, 29, 49–50

magnesium   34
meat   8–9
medium fat food   27
milk   7
millet   138
minerals   30–5
muffins   234–7

oils   10
one-minute meals   202–7

pantothenic acid   33
pasta   149–62
pastry   189–91
plate model   1–2
post-competition   101–2
potassium   34
potatoes   176–88
pre-competition   98–100
    eating plans   102–6
protein   38, 59–60, 62
    complementation   59–60
puddings 222–33

resting metabolic rate   46–7
rice   125–38
    cooking   125

salad dressings   121–3
salads   115–24
sandwiches   68
selenium   34
set point   48
slow carbs   20
snack bars   216–21
snacks   71–2
sodium   34
soups   108–15
sports drink   75, 77
sprinting   38, 80–3
store-cupboard   70
strength training   38, 51
sugar   12–13
supplements
    mineral   30–1
    multi-vitamin   30–1
swimming   38, 93–5

team sports 90–2
training diet   1
travelling   72

urine   100

vegetables   2–4
    starchy   5–6
vegetarianism   57–66
    eating plans   62–6
    menu planner   61
    nutrients   62
vitamins   30–5
    vitamin A   32
    vitamin B   32
    vitamin $B_2$   32
    vitamin $B_3$   32
    vitamin $B_6$   32
    vitamin $B_{12}$   33, 62
    vitamin C   33, 176
    vitamin D   33
    vitamin E   33

weight loss   45–56
    eating plans   53–6
weight training   38, 85–8

zinc   34, 62

# Index of Recipes

A–Z Vegetable Sauce   152
A–Z Vegetable Soup   110
Apple Cake   239
Apple Sauce Cookies   221
Apple Sauce Muffins   197
Apricot and Date Bread Pudding   228
Apricot Bars   218
Athlete's Bubble and Squeak   181
Athlete's Cold Pasta Salad   115
Athlete's Hot Pasta with Vegetables   150
Aubergine and Potato Curry   187

Bagel Melt   203
Baked Bananas   231
Baked Bean and Vegetable Soup   114
Baked French Toast   199
Baked Lemon Cheesecake   223
Baked Macaroni Pie   158
Banana Bread   171
Banana Bread Pudding   227
Banana Cake   238
Banana Hot Dog   203
Banana Muffins   237
Banana Waffles   196
Basic Brown Bread   163
Basic Cheese and Tomato Topping   214
Basic Granola   197
Basic Pizza   212
Basic Red Lentil Sauce   157
Bean and Corn Quesadillas   207
Bean and Courgette Provençale
  with Garlic Bread   148
Bean and Tomato Casserole   141
Bean and Tuna Salad   119
Bean Burgers   211
Bean Feast   119
Bean Lasagne   161
Beans 'n' Rice   131
Blueberry Bread   172
Breakfast Bars   198
Breakfast Muffins   194
Breakfast Pancakes   195
Broccoli and Bean Soup   111
Broccoli and Cheese Sauce   156
Brown Rice and Bean Salad   118
Bulgar Wheat Pilaff   137

Calzone   215
Carrot Cake   239
Cauliflower Cheese Soup   113
Cheese Sauce   155
Chicken and Broccoli Stir Fry   135
Chicken and Mushroom Sauce   156
Chicken and Mushroom Soup   114
Chicken and Mushrooms
  with Pasta   161
Chicken and Pepper Risotto   127
Chicken Enchiladas   140
Chicken Paella   126
Chilli Con Carne   147
Chinese Fried Rice   128

Chocolate and Banana Cake   242
Chocolate Chip Muffins   235
Chocolate Cocoa Cake   242
Chocolate Cookie Cheesecake   224
Chocolate Fudge Brownies   244
Chunky Oven Chips   180
Coconut Pineapple Bread   173
Cod and Potato Pie   184
Cool Summer Fruit Salad   226
Corn Chowder   112
Corn Muffins   237
Cornmeal Bread   165
Cottage Cheese Pancakes
  with Blueberry Sauce   233
Cream of Tomato Soup   109
Crunchy Apple Crumble   224
Crunchy Pie Crust   190
Cucumber and Lime Dressing   123
Curried Chicken and Rice   130
Curried Chicken Baguette   206

Dahl   141
Date and Walnut Bars   217
Dried Fruit Muesli   194

Fish and Bean Cassoulet   145
Fish Burgers   209
Focaccia Bread   167
Fruit and Nut Bars   218
Fruit Buns   175
Fruit Cake   241
Fruit Clafouti   231
Fruit Cookies   220
Fruit Pancakes   229
Fruit Rice Pudding   225

Garlic and Herb Dressing   121
Garlic Roast Potatoes   183
Greek Filled Pitta   205
Grilled Chicken Burgers   209

Ham and Mushroom Sauce   155
Hawaiian Rice   128
Herb Flatbread   168
Hot Winter Fruit Salad   226

Italian Dressing   122

Lean Hamburgers   210
Lentil and Vegetable Soup   112
Low Fat Chocolate Brownies   243
Low Fat Ice Cream   227
Low Fat Tiramisu   230

Mashed Potato Pie Crust   190
Meat Lasagne   160
Mexican Bean Bake   142
Mexican Rice   132
Mighty Mash I   179
Mighty Mash II   180
Millet Pilaff with Nuts and Raisins   138

Minestrone Soup   110
Mixed Bean Chilli   144
Mixed Vegetable and Lentil Curry   146
Muesli Bars   216
Muffin Pizza   207

New Potato Salad   117
Noodles with Salmon in Foil   134

Oatmeal and Raisin Scotch Pancakes   232
Oatmeal Bread   169
Oatmeal Cookies   220
Oatmeal Muffins   236
Oatmeal Scotties   192
Oaty Fruit Bars   217
One-minute Burrito   143
Orange Cinnamon Bread   174
Orange Muffins   235
Oriental Chicken Noodle Salad   120

Pasta and Bean Soup   113
Pasta and Lentil Pot   157
Pasta 'n' Peas   162
Pasta with Beans   159
Pasta with Cheese and Walnuts   160
Pasta with Spinach and Cheese   159
Pea and Potato Soup   111
Perfect Potato Pie   182
Pineapple Bagel   193
Pork and Vegetable Stir Fry   129
Potato and Leek Soup   109
Potato and Vegetable Curry   186
Potato Bake with Tomatoes   188
Potato Griddle Scones   181
Potato Kugel   183
Potato Pastry   189
Potato Salad   187
Potato Tacos   182
Power Porridge   198
Pumpkin Cake   240

Quesadilla   206
Quick Pizza   213
Quick Supper Salad   116
Quick Tacos   202
Quick Tuna and Sweetcorn Sauce   154
Quick Vegetable Curry   133

Raisin Bread   166
Raisin Cake   240
Raisin Muffins   234
Raisin Scones   219
Raisin Toast   193
Rice and Sweetcorn Salad   116
Rice with Haddock and Peas   131
Rum and Raisin Cheesecake   222

Soda Bread   164
Spicy Bean Enchiladas   139
Spicy Bean Lasagne   143
Spicy Bean Topping   178
Spicy Bulgar Wheat Salad   117
Spicy Chick Peas with Tomatoes   144
Spicy Chicken Fillet Burgers   208
Spicy Dressing   123
Spicy Lentil Burgers   210
Spicy Rice   127
Spinach and Cheese Topping   179
Stir Fried Rice with Vegetables   130
Stir Fry Indonesian Prawns   135
Store-cupboard Bean Bake   140
Sunflower Bread   170

Tangy Yoghurt Dressing   122
Thai Chicken and Rice   129
Thai-Style Green Fish Curry   133
Three Grain Salad   118
Tofu and Mushroom Stir Fry   134
Tomato and Herb Sauce   154
Tomato and Mushroom Topping   178
Tomato and Tuna   153
Tortilla Sandwich   204
Tortilla Stack   142
Tuna and Pasta Bake   158
Turkey Bolognese   152
Turkey Pockets   204

Vegetable Cous Cous   136
Vegetable Crumble   185
Vegetable Gratin with Potatoes   186
Vegetable Paella   126
Vegetable Pie Crust   191
Vegetable Salads   124
Vegetarian Bolognese   151
Vegetarian Chilli Sauce   153
Vegetarian Tortilla Sandwich   205

Yoghurt and Fruit Pudding   232